We, the Lonely People

RALPH KEYES

We, the Lonely People

Searching For Community

HARPER & ROW, PUBLISHERS
New York · Evanston · San Francisco · London

In addition to the credits that appear in the text, the author wishes to acknowledge permission to reprint from the following:
"Suburb in the Sky" by Ken Sobol. Reprinted by permission of The Village Voice. Copyrighted by The Village Voice, Inc., 1971.
Columns by Abigail Van Buren and Art Buchwald respectively. Permission granted by the authors.

 For information address Harper & Row, Publishers, Inc., 10 East 53rd Street, New York, N.Y. 10022. Published simultaneously in Canada by Fitzhenry & Whiteside Limited, Toronto.

FIRST EDITION

Designed by C. Linda Dingler

Library of Congress Cataloging in Publication Data
Keyes, Ralph.
We, the lonely people.
Includes bibliographical references.
1. United States—Social life and customs—1945– I. Title. [DNLM: 1. Interpersonal relations. 2. Psychology, Social. 3. Social isolation. HM 251 K44w 1973]
E169.02.K49 1973 917.3'03'92 72-78077
ISBN 0-06-064552-0

To my parents, with whom this book began.

am·biv′a·lence: (ăm·bĭv′a·lĕns), noun. Simultaneous attraction toward and repulsion from an object, person, or action.

CONTENTS

Part II: Seeking Community

Part III: Building Community

Acknowledgments

Though finally rewarding, writing a book is painful and frustrating along the way—something like giving birth to a baby, I'm told. Without the support, patience and help of many friends, this book could easily have miscarried. Among these friends are Bill and Anne Stillwell, Phil and Cathy Elsbree, George and Beer Sargent, Charley O'Leary, John K. Wood, Bruce and Betty Meador, Dick Farson, Bob Sherrill, Sam Keen, Bill McGaw, Bill Moyers, Bob Egan, Gay Swenson, Ray Wilkie, Bill Coulson and Selma Joiner. When I was clutching toward the end of the first draft and sent out a call for typing help, Bill Stillwell, George Sargent and Bob Sherrill each took a chapter, Joanne Justyn took more, and Sue Wells rescued me by giving up several days and evenings to type chapter after chapter for "just friendship." Thanks.

Meyer and Reba Gordon, my parents-in-law supported me all the way, and Reba has the distinction of being the only person besides my editors to read two drafts of the book, giving me good feedback in the process.

Elizabeth Hall gave me shrewd editorial comment at times when I needed it, and the book is better for her help. George Harris also gave me good advice along the way, as did my agent Elizabeth

Otis. (To her a longer thanks for years of patience.) My editors, Clayton Carlson and especially Davis Yeuell, have given me on-going support and help in making this a better book. (No one, of course, except me, gets responsibility for whatever is wrong with the final product.)

Too many people to mention have kindly responded to my letters, phone calls and ideas sent for comment but I would like to particularly thank Jud Jerome, Rosabeth Moss Kanter, Bennet Berger, Bob Smith, Bob Frankel, Bill and Jane Canby, Bob Green, James Dixon, Van Richards, Roy Fairfield, Frank Potter, Alan Gartner, Hugh Gardner, Donald Muhich, David Hamilton, Barbara and Fuller Torrey, Peter Robinson, George Mansfield, Jean Ann Fossett and George Hillery for helpful comments.

I'm afraid to start detailing the ways Muriel, my wife, helped in bringing this book about, and kept me sane in the process. Advice, support, consolation, typing and finally becoming my best editor covers just a fraction of the ways Muriel helped the book, and me. Without her, this book would not have happened, and I might be writing the inside story of Bellevue rather than optimistic comments on marriage and community.

Muriel made the difference.

Preface

This book is its own paradox.

Writing it took me out of community. I wanted to write it more than I wanted to be with others.

That is the problem we face in restoring a sense of community to our lives. We love so the things which cut us off from each other.

Part I

Losing Community

1.

Losing Touch

Kids have taken over the shopping centers.

Especially on weekends you see them, arrogant occupiers, an army marching up and down the mall, mugging at each other and stabbing their cigarettes at passersby.

While working for *Newsday*, I went to Long Island's Walt Whitman Shopping Center to expose this latest chapter in modern materialism.

The first day in, I hung around and asked kids why they spent so much time there. They seemed genuinely puzzled, and usually could only mumble things like, "Well, you know, its warm . . . and I have friends here."

That didn't seem reason enough, so I stopped asking the question and on the second day just hung around and kept my eyes open. A lot of the faces were becoming familiar, on bodies walking up and down the mall, and sometimes congregating around the bird cages.

The third day in, I forgot my jacket, although it was mid-February. But it didn't matter because the mall's heated. It snowed that day, but the mall's covered. The whoosh of warm air, the potted plants and chirping birds all pleased my senses as I pushed open the glass doors. And when I hit the mall, a chorus of young voices called out, "Hey, Ralph." "What's happening, man?" "Hey, it's the *Newsday* freak."

I was recognized! Known! My name, my face, something about me! After an anonymous year and a half on Long Island I had finally found a place where people knew me. Where I could be sure of finding familiar faces. The Walt Whitman Shopping Center!

And in that instant I understood why kids hang around shopping centers. Because it's warm, and you have friends inside.

The experience got me wondering: How many such places are left in urban/suburban America? Places where you're known?

CARETAKERS

Stewart Udall must have wondered, the time they nabbed him outside a big Washington drugstore with unpaid-for cigars in his pocket. The former Interior Secretary is probably more absent-minded than kleptomaniacal, as his abductors soon realized, but no one seemed to have the authority to let Mr. Udall go. He was booked and fingerprinted before being released on $250 bail. Udall attributed the whole affair to "a dehumanized store protection system . . . that made everyone automatons and left no room for human communication." Days later, the drugstore finally dropped charges and a judge dismissed the case. "Maybe I ought to patronize small stores where people know you," was Udall's parting thought.[1]

But where? Where are they, these points of human contact, these places to be known?

Social scientists say that society has long been served by intimate forms of commerce, the small corner store whose proprietors got to know their customers, and cared about them. "Gatekeepers," they call such ministers passing as merchants, or "caretakers" and "indigenous therapists."

Most of us have known such a person.

For Sara Jane Johnson it's been her butcher in Pullman, Washington. She says they built trust over a decade's time. Sara Jane is married to a Washington State University professor, and when State students went out on strike, her butcher was the only townsperson with whom Sara Jane felt safe to discuss the issue.

Dave Jacobs, proprietor of a neighborhood grocery in Berkeley was special to Elizabeth Hall while she was at the University of California in the late 1940s. Six feet tall with warm blue eyes and a shock of white hair, Jacobs would choose produce for customers personally and advise them against bad purchases. For penniless students he would go down the bill knocking a penny or two off each item. Once he loaned Elizabeth and her husband $40 to get their car out of the garage. Even with no purchase to make, they would stop in Jacob's little store every day just to say Hi or to discuss some problem. Elizabeth can't remember any advice she ever got from him, but it was good just having someone to listen. She named her first son David, after Dave Jacobs.

Just two decades ago, sociologist Gregory Stone[2] surveyed the reasons Chicago housewives gave for shopping at particular stores, and was surprised to find "affection for the help" ranking just below good prices. "People in small stores greet you cordially when you come in," explained one woman.

Said others: "They're more personal. They get to know your name. They take more of an interest in you as a human being."

"They get so they know you."

"In the big store no one knows you. . . . Maybe it's because I feel at home in the smaller store. When you're in there, you feel more wanted."

Stone was surprised to find how important his subjects considered such feelings. He said that the involvement of housewives with small store owners in Chicago neighborhoods seemed almost intimate, and was a major balance for them to the anonymity of city life.

I've never lived anywhere long enough to get so involved with a merchant-friend, and may have been born too late. A barber

I've never lived anywhere long enough to get so involved with a merchant-friend, and may have been born too late. A barber did ask me once if I wanted "the same as last time." That gave me a lift.

Any neighborhood bartender will tell you that once you've learned how to pour with either hand, the key to success is learning your customers' names and what they drink.

A tavern owner I met said he'd not only listen to lonely drinkers, but try to introduce them to each other. After a while his place had quite a "family" to feel to it, and when he sold out after eight years, eighty regulars gave him a going-away party.

"It sounds like a simple statement," says psychiatrist Donald Muhich, "but not everybody realizes that people don't go to bars to drink—they can do that at home and for less money. People go to bars as a social function. Bars can be one of the invisible caretakers of a community, a place where people go to solve problems, meet friends, contract business, kick around ideas, deal with one another. A kind of leaderless group therapy. . . ."[3]

Muhich, who headed community mental health programs in Minnesota and Los Angeles, has for the past decade surveyed what he calls "the invisible caretakers" of our society, who supplement visible ones like clergymen and doctors.

Beauty parlors are the feminine counterpart to bars, and hairdressers important caretakers. Their very "laying on of hands" seems to build a trust with customers, and Muhich has found that women confide to their beautician things they will tell no one else.

John Steinbeck once called beauty parlor employees the most influential members of a community. "When women go to the hairdresser," he explained, "something happens to them. They feel safe, they relax. And they don't have to keep up any pretense. The hairdresser knows what their skin is like under the makeup, he knows their age, their face-liftings. This being so, women tell a hairdresser things they wouldn't dare confess to a priest, and they are more open about matters they'd try to conceal from a doctor."[4]

> My hairdresser covers up the grey
> And I paint on a put-on smile to go out every day
> I've kept the hurt concealed, the real me never shows
> Only me and my hairdresser know.[5]

THE CRUMBLING NETWORK

Dave Jacobs died a few years ago, and someone sent Elizabeth Hall his obituary from the Berkeley *Gazette*. Elizabeth lives in Rancho Santa Fe now, and makes a decent income writing and editing. She shops at Safeway.

Sara Jane Johnson recently returned to Pullman after a few years' absence to find the meats wrapped in plastic and her butcher hidden behind a screen. There was a button newly installed which she could use to ring for him, but Sara Jane's finger has yet to touch that button. She determinedly knocks on the side door whenever she wants to see her butcher, her friend. But Sara Jane says their relationship is no longer the same. She knows it's a losing battle, that the war is already lost.

The network is crumbling.

The local bar is on its way to extinction, a victim of television, pop-tops, and decaying neighborhoods. Two-thirds of the liquor bought in this country today is for home consumption, compared to 10 percent after World War II. It's not that we're drinking any less. We just don't seem to need the company.[6]

Those bars which hang on can now buy National Cash Register's "Electra-Bar"—an electronic bartender capable of mixing thirty-six kinds of drinks more precisely than human hands.[7]

The latest thing in beauty shop hardware is in-dryer cassettes which combine music and talk with commercials.[8] These are being marketed by a firm headed by actress Jeanne Moreau, who points out that women are especially vulnerable to a sales pitc while under the hairdryer.

The beauty parlor of the future may be in the Northridg section of Los Angeles. There, at Bullock's Beauty Salon, eac customer has a TV before her seat, almost continuous show and demonstrations with earphones for listening to either, or t FM music.[9]

Hair styling is the trend in men's hair care and the old-tim barber shop-hangout may soon be a museum piece. Tomorrow' cutter of hair, says an official of the barbers' union, will be "to much of a professional to talk, except in giving advice to th customer on how to keep his hair in shape."[10]

My friend John Wood recently visited his hair stylist, wh had little to say while working over John's thinning, gray-brow locks. Later, however, the stylist did send John a two-page lette of diagnosis and advice. At the end of the letter, some boxes wer checked indicating alternatives John might like to consider, suc as a hairpiece.

Muriel, my wife, has recently learned how to administer m semiannual haircut, so I've bypassed the need for any professiona barber, talkative or otherwise.

Like Elizabeth Hall, we get our groceries at supermarkets, an Sav-On is our pharmacy. Sav-On is the huge super-drug up th street. I don't know any of the help up there, or they me, but the prices are good, and so is the selection.

In fact, even if we wanted to patronize one, I don't know c any independent druggist in the vicinity. (Their number ha dropped from 50,000 nationwide to 40,000 in the past decade.[11]

American Druggist says that with existing technology, we coul have a totally computerized drugstore in which transactions woul be conducted by IBM card, conversation with the druggist b videophone.[12]

I think concern about the decline of such human conta points is more than mere nostalgia. Each lost contact—druggis butcher, bartender, beautician or barber—may not mean muc by itself. But as one mounts on another, each of us feels a litt more alone. Who knows me? By name, by face, by history and quirk?

Does anyone know who I am around here?

LOSS OF COMMUNITY

At one time there was no such problem, when you were *known* within family, including the extended family of relatives. When family became tribe and tribes grew into villages, their members still knew each other to a large degree. Neighbors, friends, and family freely intermingled, were often one and the same. There wasn't much choice. One lived, worked, and died among a small number of faces. One was born into community and belonged automatically; the only alternative to belonging would be to leave.

An Englishman I know grew up in such a small village in Yorkshire. He says the most striking quality of the town, and the thing he misses most, was the feeling of being *known* there. He said it wasn't even a spoken thing. Nobody would say anything out loud about your beating your wife. But they knew, you knew they knew, they knew you knew they knew—and in that there was comfort.

There are problems with that kind of life, to be sure. Oppression and gossip. Rigidity. I wouldn't want it. My English friend had fled it. But at least it was an existence where people knew who you were. It was a community.

Today we talk about our "loss of community" in city and suburb. Often we discuss it intellectually while sipping scotch. Sometimes mystically, passing a joint. Or nostalgically over beer.

Loss of community. That seems to cover the feeling, the feeling unknown, but when we try to pin it down, the term is elusive. We talk of the neighborhood community, the academic community, the world community, or just *the* community.

When we try to be more specific about just what "community" means, we usually think first of a place, the place where we live. I think this is what Carnation Milk has in mind when they implore me on their carton to "help keep our community litter-free."

But when we consider where we find a "sense of community,"

it's rarely where we live. We use the word interchangeably, but it means two different things.

A *sense* of community is what we find among the people who know us, with whom we feel safe. That rarely includes the neighbors.

It wasn't always so. For most of history man found his sense of community where he lived, with the people among whom he was born and with whom he died. For some that remains true today. But most of us in city and suburb live one place, and find "community" in another. Or nowhere.

So many of us want back the more intimate sense of community, the one where the grocer knew our name and the butcher could comment on meat and life.

Business knows, and they're trying to sell that feeling back to us, some sense of community.

THE MARKET FOR INTIMACY

Howard Johnson's recently ran a "Howard Johnson's Loves You" campaign complete with birthday clubs, Monday chicken fries, and Wednesday fish fries. Their advertising director explained that the intent was "to try to make our 825 restaurants memorable as warm, friendly, family-type places."[12a]

My affair with Howard Johnson's didn't survive its cooking, so now Shakey's Pizza Parlor has rushed in asking "How Much Do We Love You," Answer: "Enough to give you $1.00 off on any family-size pizza." The dollar-off certificate reminds me that "AT SHAKEY'S WE LOVE YOU."[13]

"A good friend is now easy to come by," advertises Buick. It's their Opel 1900 Sport Coupé.[14]

Sears has "10 Ways We'll Prove We Care about You:

"1. We'll greet you with a smile.

"2. . . . ."[15]

My parents joined a credit card company, and soon afterward received in the mail a handsomely printed brochure which announced on the cover: "We have so many things in common these days that you ought to have a friend in court." They opened the brochure and on the next page read: "Therefore meet your friend at court." Above these words was the sketch of a man—Mr. P. Dudley.

According to his picture, P. Dudley is dark, strong, and a little stern. There are circles underneath his eyes, presumably put there by long, wearying hours spent helping customers in need. Dudley looks like a powerful friend to have in court. "Write him direct whenever you wish," invited the brochure.

My parents soon had a problem, being overcharged due to a misplaced decimal point. As the bill-collecting computer grew increasingly testy, they wrote their friend in court—Mr. P. Dudley. Dudley returned brief notes, assuring my parents that he'd taken care of the problem. But the computer wasn't listening.

When Mom started putting through phone calls to Mr. P. Dudley, he was always "out." He did keep answering her letters in a reassuring way. But his four responses had three different signatures.

My parents then turned the whole thing over to a lawyer who finally scared off the credit card company.

A New York real estate broker had a similar problem with the same company. (He kept getting billed for an imaginary airplane ticket.) So this broker called "his man" in their office. With a frustration level lower than my folks', after several fruitless exchanges the guy just turned his whole file over to Art Buchwald. Buchwald (calling the broker Dave Parsons and his man Fred Barkle) imagined this exchange between the two:

"Say, Fred, this is Dave Parsons. In spite of the fact that you said you would take care of the matter, I just received another bill about my plane ticket."

"I have no idea what you're talking about, Mr. Parsons."

"Oh, I'm sorry, I'd better fill you in," and then Parsons proceeded to tell Barkle the whole story again.

"Well, I'll be happy to look into the matter, Mr. Parsons."

"What happened when you looked into the matter before?" Parsons wanted to know.

"I never looked into the matter."

"I spoke to you two weeks ago about it."

"You never spoke to me. What day did you call?"

"Wednesday."

"Ah, that explains it. You spoke to the Mr. Fred Barkle who is on duty Wednesday. I'm the Fred Barkle who works on Friday."

"You mean there's more than one Fred Barkle in your organization?"

"There is no Fred Barkle in our organization. It's just a name we use so our customers have someone to call."

"If I called Fred Barkle on Friday again would I be able to get you?"

"It's very unlikely. The company switches us around every week so we don't get too friendly with the customers."

The broker wrote me that he later received a credit card bill which had computer-typed on it: MERRY CHRISTMAS YOUR ACCOUNT IS SERIOUSLY OVERDUE.[16]

None of it works, and won't work. The qualities which make a good mass marketer can't also produce a feeling of community. I find it a toss-up as to who loves me more, Shakey's or Howard Johnson's.

But business is hardly pernicious for trying. Their job is to be sensitive to markets, and there's obviously a market for intimacy. The market, however, is a package deal, part of a consumer's double message: give us all the advantages of a supermarket with all the familiarity of a corner store. Sixty-nine percent of two hundred Bostonians surveyed in 1970 agreed that "stores are so big these days that the customer gets lost in the shuffle."[17]

But 81 percent believe that "supermarkets are a great advance over the corner store."

We want both, and business tries to comply. It's an impossible task. If they're confused, it's because we're confused.

It's not that we don't want more community. We do. We crave community, we lust after it. "Community" is a national obsession. But we want other things more. I wanted to write this book more. Not getting involved with the neighbors is worth more to us than "community," and Keeping Up Appearances for friends, while preserving all the benefits of mass marketing.

It's this confusion, this ambivalence, which confounds our quest for community. We yearn for a simpler, more communal life; we sincerely want more sense of community. But not at the sacrifice of any advantages which mass society has brought us, even ones we presumably scorn.

It's a trade-off. We give up some hypothetical "community." In return we get tangible benefits: better prices and a bigger selection.

We didn't lose community. We bought it off. And rediscovering community isn't a matter of finding "the solution." We know how to do it. It's more a question of how much we're willing to trade-in.

I could find a Mom & Pop store if I really wanted one. But I don't. I prefer a supermarket's prices and selection. Also the anonymity, the fact that I'm *not* burdened by knowing the help.

THE POWER OF ANONYMITY

I spent the other day at San Diego State University doing research for this book. Near the college I picked up a hitchhiker, a State student. We talked about what it's like to attend such a huge multiversity. He called it "cruel," especially the mating part. He said you'd meet a girl and have just a few moments to make it, or lose the opportunity forever. Among 26,000 students, mostly commuters, it could be no other way.

I got to the university, parked a half-mile away, and started weaving to the library through streams of people. On some stairs leading up the campus was a note scribbled on lined yellow paper and taped to the bannister. It read: "Will the girl who said 'Hi' to me at *10:45* on *Monday* when she was coming down the steps be here *Friday* at the same time."

At the library, I had left some books sitting overnight in a carrel. The evening before I began to scribble a note saying to

hold them for a friend who's a professor at State. Then I worried that this might get him in trouble, so I started changing my note to read "Hold for Professor Papagoras" (a character in the comic strip "Apartment 3-G"). Then I thought, No, I'll just hold them for Professor Keyes. I began a new sign, then stopped. That was unethical. But then I remembered—I'm an Adjunct Professor of the Union Graduate School. I am Professor Keyes. So I scribbled "Please hold for Prof. Keyes," and left.

The next morning I returned to find all the books gone, "Please hold for" crossed out on my sign, and "see the circulation librarian concerning the books left in this carrel" written after 'Prof. Keyes.'"

I chewed on that for a while, first tempted to go straighten things out, then hesitant. In checking out the hesitancy, I realized that my first rule for manipulating bureaucracies is "DON'T GET KNOWN." Once you're recognized as a person in particular—especially if you don't belong—you're done for. The bureaucrats will never give you peace. But if they don't single you out for any reason, even if they know your name but can't assign it a face, you're safe. You can continue to function as if you belong.

So I didn't contact the Circulation Librarian. My anonymity was just too precious under the circumstances.

This is the kind of ambivalence which permeates our quest for community. To me, community—real community—is the place where I'm known, where I'm safe to be known, for better or worse, on many levels. But it's so powerful to be unknown, to be anonymous, even as it's lonely. Am I willing to trade in my freedom to come and go unobserved for some "sense of community"?

We may hate mass society and its institutions, hate the feeling of not being known anywhere—but it's power, a power we'd give up very reluctantly.

In *The Secular City*, Harvey Cox went so far as to say, "We need to develop a viable theology of anonymity. . . . Despite its pitfalls, the anonymous shape of urban life helps free man from the Law. For many people it is a glorious liberation, a deliverance from the saddling traditions and burdensome expectations of town life and an entry into the exciting new possibilities of choice which pervade the secular metropolis."[18]

The oppression of small towns is related directly to being *known*, watched over a life's time—for better or worse. The freedom of life in city or suburb grows directly from *not* being known by neighbors, friends, or even family. Anonymity is freedom. Anonymity is power.

The great reforms of the past few centuries have been based on making us less known to each other as they made us more free. Literacy did this, took us to books for wisdom rather than to each other. The civil service helped out, requiring that strangers be hired on merit, rather than relatives or friends. "Professionalism" contributed, by sanctifying detachment.

The jury system is a clear example of the reform-through-anonymity process. In their original form, in early medieval England, juries were composed of people known to the accused, friends and neighbors who presumably were acquainted with the defendant and his case. The great reform of latter-day England was to reverse this criterion, to make being *unknown* to the defendant the qualification for jury duty. This ensured a jury which was more detached, more objective and impartial, since not emotionally involved with the defendant.[19]

Thus do we become more free of each other as we also grow less known. We cherish this freedom and loathe it. We curse the loneliness of anonymity, yet crave its power. We want to stand revealed to each other, and do everything possible to avoid it.

That ambivalence makes the problem of community one without a "solution." Rather, it's a question of what we'd trade in on greater human contact. Better prices and a bigger selection? The power of anonymity? The right to keep to ourselves?

Even as we hate being unknown to each other, we crave anonymity. And rather than take paths which might lead us back together, we pursue the very things which keep us cut off from each other. There are three things we cherish in particular—mobility, privacy, and convenience—which are the very sources of our lack of community.

2.

The Trade-ins

Mobility: The Stewardess Syndrome

We moved around a lot as I grew up—Ohio, Pennsylvan
Puerto Rico, Illinois. The moves were interesting; they taught n
how to meet people and how to move on.

This rootlessness never struck me as any kind of issue un
several years ago when I met a white-goateed farmer in a sm
Illinois town upstate. The farmer was a guy whom lots of peop
in town said I might find interesting. "Crazy" was the wo
they used.

He may have been that. The fellow's little beard set him
from the rest of the town, as did his flashing eyes and libe
views on race (in 1966). We talked at length about the loneline
of being the town eccentric. I listened, heard, then asked wh
seemed to me the obvious question: "Why don't you leave?"

This fiery old eccentric fixed his eyes on mine, burned into n
skull for a few seconds, then gave his obvious answer: "Boy
did you ever hears of *roots*?"

Roots. No, the truth was I hadn't. Not that way, not fro
someone I respected. I had always thought rootedness an oppr
sion, a relic. It was the anonymity of city or suburb which w
liberating, and the means to keep moving.

Which only makes me a good American. Moving on is the national pasttime, "a fresh start," our basic right.

When a woman wrote Abby wondering if she should give up lifelong friends, home, and relatives nearby to move to another state where her husband had a better job opportunity, Abby replied: "Are you kidding? I would go with him and never look back. And I have done it three times!"[1]

I followed you to Texas
I followed you to Utah
    We didn't find it there
    So we moved on

I followed you to Alabam'
Things looked good in Birmingham
    We didn't find it there
    So we moved on

I had your child in Memphis
You heard of work in Nashville
    We didn't find it there
    So we moved on

To a small farm in Nebraska
To a gold mine in Alaska
    We didn't find it there
    So we moved on

And now we've left Alaska
Because there was no gold mine

I know you're tired of following
My elusive dreams and schemes
On and on with fleeting wings
My elusive dreams[2]

"It is astonishing," wrote Scottish journalist Alexander McKay in 1849, "how readily . . . an American makes up his mind to try his fortunes elsewhere."[3] One historian says that "the M-factor" —movement, migration and mobility—is the shaping influence of our national character, America's "great postponement."[4]

Our national milling about is nothing new. The only thing new is acceleration of the pace. One in five Americans changes homes annually and nearly half do every five years. In 1960 the average professional held three jobs in a career. Today that figure has risen to 4.2 jobs and continues to rise.[5]

In nearly two decades of studying top corporation executives, industrial psychologist Eugene Jennings has found an increasingly close relationship between mobility and success, leading to what Jennings calls "mobicentricity." "To the mobility-centered person," he explains, "a new American phenomenon, movement is not so much a way to get someplace or a means to an end as it is an end in itself. The mobicentric man values motion and action not because they lead to change but because they are change, and change is his ultimate value."[6]

The migration is in no way limited to corporate mobicentrics. The young are our most footloose of all, 45 percent of those between twenty-two and twenty-four changing residence in 1969 alone.[7] "We do not ask for reasons to move," says one hitchhiker. "The motion is its own reward."[8]

Those studying communes have found a curious paradox. Experiments in communal living are top-heavy with the root-seeking children of nomadic corporation men. Yet these same utopian ventures are witness to a perpetual flow from one to the next, communards changing communes just as their fathers transferred between corporations. "Repeating the quintessentially American trait," writes an analyst of this movement, "when conditions of communal life become intolerable, the residents simply move elsewhere."[9]

"Community members were constantly on the go," recalls the scarred veteran on one northwestern commune, "down to San Francisco, back East, moving in and out of the community or from house to house within it. This mobility was guarded above all else. Martha [the commune leader], for example, held that her house would be a success if people living there could leave altogether without anyone feeling a sense of strain."[10]

With all this coming and going, we're becoming ingenious at anesthetizing the process. The Interstate Highway System makes movement so smooth as to seem like running in place.[11] Relocation services for executives promise to "take the time, tension and chance out of relocating."[12] With BankAmericard or Master-Charge, your credit is good the country around. The National Football League has even set up a clearing house for those wishing to trade season tickets when they move to a new city.[13]

Looking ahead, *Playboy* has toyed with the idea of a computerized relocation service with which you could dial a toll-free number from one city, book an apartment in the next, get on a plane, and be resettled the same day.[14]

Many welcome such developments, and see in our new nomadism a liberation from place to join our various other liberations. Futurist Alvin Toffler calls it "the overthrow of the tyranny of geography." In *Future Shock* he writes, "particularly among those I have characterized as 'the people of the future,' commuting, traveling and regularly relocating one's family have become second nature. . . . We are breeding a new race of nomads, and few suspect quite how massive, widespread and significant their migrations are."[15]

Although he bends over backward not to judge, there's little question that Toffler welcomes this new nomadism. He and most of those recording our accelerating mobility are thick in the middle of it themselves. Toffler researched his book by spending years jetting around among institutions, colleges, and people. Eugene Jennings, the student of mobicentricity, claims four addresses himself.[16] Buckminster Fuller, who welcomes the future with widely opened arms, boasted in 1968 of having traveled 3.5 million miles in his life, one hundred times the average distance traveled in a lifetime by people up to the time of his father.[17]

There's a critical difference between this new nomadism and the more primitive kind. Traditional nomads move *in* community. As a Gypsy or Bedouin shuttles from place to place, clansmen are

always along. For such a nomad to move physically isn't to mov
psychologically. They carry their community with them.

Our new nomads travel lighter. At most they take a mate
or family. Sociologist Warren Bennis, a confessed mobiocentric
says his wife calls herself their "portable roots."

The futurists are confident we'll adapt, evolve into "people o
the future" who slip in and out of relationships like underwear
Toffler talks of learning to handle the accelerated "through-put'
of people in our lives with new styles of friendship, ones whicl
have built-in self-destruct mechanisms.

"To remain human," advises Bennis, "we have to learn to de
velop intense and deep human relationships quickly, and learr
to let go. In other words, learning quickly how to love, to ge
love and to lose love."[18]

Annie Elsbree moved to San Diego from Illinois last year, whe
she was five. Sometimes Annie talks about her old friends bac
home and big tears well up in her eyes, then float down her cheeks
She says the old friends are "special." Her new friends here i
Southern California don't understand. They tell her one friend'
as good as another. When she tries to tell them how much sh
misses her friends in Illinois, they say she's being silly.

Katy Miller doesn't understand either. She's in her seventie
and we've got to know and trust each other in two years of living
next door. We talk over the fence, and once she made us som
kumquat jelly. The other day Katy stopped in for coffee.

Realtors have been driving slowly by our house recently and i
looks as though it may be sold. Probably they'll want to tear th
house down, and we'll have to move. When Katy heard that, sh
came over with tears in her eyes. "Darn," she said, "I don't want
you to move. Here you get to like people and then they have t
go and move." She sniffed in frustration but didn't know what t
do. Katy's old, she lives alone now, after spending most of he
life on Montana's frontier. It's hard for her to get close to people
and she doesn't know what to do when friends have to move.

I want to lash out at Toffler, and Bennis, and Jennings, and hi them hard for celebrating just those currents which are driving us away from each other, the trends of the future which are making Katy Miller and Annie Elsbree cry.

But I'm too conscious that my anger at them is also at myself for unreconstructed gypsyism. I like our house, and it's felt good to stay put there for two years. When I heard we may have to move, I was upset. But since I've been thinking about it, the idea doesn't feel so bad. A change of scene, new neighborhood, new stores, maybe a house with more windows. New neighbors.

Actually, I don't think the move will be too hard. But I know it will cost me, and I don't want to overlook that cost or pretend it doesn't exist.

"FRIENDSHIP"

Gilbert Bartell was initially perplexed by the casual use of the word "friend" among suburban "swingers" (or mate-swappers) about whom he was doing research in the late 1960s. Swingers would claim friendship with anyone with whom they were sharing sex. But they made a point of not getting emotionally involved with any of these "friends," and avoided even seeing them more than once or twice.

"We were perplexed," writes Bartell, an anthropologist, "by the inconsistency of looking for 'friends' and simultaneously rejecting the possibility of friendship developing."

"Then this seemingly inconsistent behavior began to fall into pattern. . . . In most other cultures one can readily distinguish acquaintances (people one only knows) from real friends (meaning long-time emotional intimacy). But we believe that suburban swingers (and most other suburbanites) do not really want to become emotionally involved *at all* with *any* friends, and that this phenomenon may be a defense against the absence of kinship bonds, a desire to be self-sufficient so no one will be hurt when one 'pulls up roots,' moves to another suburb, and must start building friendships all over again."[19]

The worst part of mobiocentricity may not be the moves themselves so much as the certainty that one will move again, and again, and again. Why get involved with people where you are, when you know you'll soon be leaving them? Why get close to anyone, when you know in advance that making friends, close friends, only means more pain at parting?

In its purest meaning, friendship assumes an absolute psychological intimacy. Even more than lovers, friends in this sense can become close, can know each other fully, without the distractions of sex, the peaks and valleys of romance. But such friendship, known perhaps only in antiquity, was based on many premises, particularly knowing only a small number of people and being rooted in one place.

Friendship today, especially for those of us on the move, means something completely different. I knew a college student in Miami who referred to any person he met a second time as a "close personal friend." At first I thought he was putting me on. Then I realized that friendship had an altogether different meaning for him. Intimacy wasn't included.

But there's a paradox in this approach to companionship. The less intimate our friendships become, the more we seek "friends"—any kind of friends—friends in bars, friends in clubs, friends at meetings or in bed. "Why do we need friends?" asks *The National Enquirer* in its article on "The Secret of Friendship." Answer: "So we won't be lonely."[20]

So we redub acquaintances "friends"; and the word changes meaning.

"Friendship patterns of the majority in the future," says a psychologist quoted by Toffler, "will provide for many satisfactions, while substituting many close relationships of shorter durability for the few long-term friendships formed in the past."[21]

Our inspiration for this trend comes from stewardesses. They've developed icy warmth to a high art. They smile you on the plane and smile you off, though regulations forbid getting too friendly with passengers.

A stewardess once wrote of her two and a half years with Pan

Am: "Like all of us who fly for Pan Am, I was constantly in a state of adjustment which has provided a fine education in adaptability but is double-edged, since it can result in repeatedly shallow experience. . . . I began seeing how mechanized my method of dealing with [passengers] had become. . . . what had originally been clever quips had now been used over and over until I had a computer full of remarks to fit almost any given situation (which slipped out with or without my attention to what was happening). . . . My depth was suffering and I could see it in little things, my mind always wandering, rarely being able to stay with anything for a long time, always looking for something new to entertain me."[22]

It all leads to a kind of "stewardess syndrome"—smiling warmly at strangers as you part after a few hours, or minutes, as if you had shared the intimacy of a lifetime.

I get this stewardess approach a lot in the counter-culture. When I meet someone bearded and barefoot like myself, or a girl in work-shirt and Levis, we're supposed to lock thumbs, whisper "brother" or "sister," and exchange the warmth of friendship for a few moments in passing. If there isn't time to get close, we may at least smoke some grass together, which is almost the same thing, or at least seems like it.

While constantly on the move, appearances become all. Without time to come to know each other we must depend on outer signals. Eventually it becomes hard to remember that there's an inner person not so easily exhibited, a person more important than any badge or secret handshake. The worst part of mobiocentricity is being doomed to travel about seeking one's identity in the eyes of near strangers.

GROWING UP GYPSY

For some years, I've been conducting a highly unscientific survey of "the transient personality" or the "nation of stewardesses," or something like that—the multitude of people who like myself have no real place to call home, the people who trip over their tongues when asked, "Where are you from?"

One woman I know grew up on Air Force bases around the world. She's a bright and cheerful person, easy and gracious to meet. But the woman pays a price. Marriage, for her, proved a whole new experience. It was the first time she felt free to make a mistake in a relationship, and know that the other person would stand by her, would love her anyway.

Gay Swenson, now thirty-five, lived in forty-two states before the seventh grade, says she learned young the "quick-entry techniques," the easy smiles, the cute patter, the cordial distance which takes the sting out of blending into an ever-changing cast of characters.

Gay is attractive, so this hasn't been hard for her. Other people, who were fat when young, or just plain, say moving around all the time has made them shy, and hesitant in making friends. One man I know says it wasn't many moves before he simply gave up trying.

George Sargent, twenty-nine—who moved seventeen times before age fifteen—says the main thing he learned was how to "make friends" quickly. "Now I know that I was also learning how to forget friends instantly. Of course, frequent movement has its advantages. On the positive side, one learns how to adjust to new situations and relationships. On the negative side, you learn that you can leave behind your mistakes, your enemies, and your angry teachers. You learn that you can start some thing which you don't have to finish, and so impressions and auspicious beginnings mean more than productive endings.

"I often wish that this aspect of my life had been different. I envy those who enjoyed a constant group of friends and teachers in their youth."[23]

The biggest irony is that when we move on in search of change, we also escape it. Mobility involves not only a going to, but a fleeing from. A dark truth lurking in the basement of mobiocentricity, the one we hate to bring up to light for examination, is the fear that staying too long in any one place might mean we'd be found out. Each new place holds the promise of social success, for a while at least, until that situation also starts to deteriorate and its time to move once again.

Lucy knows, and Charlie Brown.

Mobility is a major enemy of the community of intimate friendship. Except I'm not clear where it is cause and where effect: whether we're afraid to get close because we're always moving on, or whether we're always moving on because we're afraid to get close.

Mobility has also made a major contribution to the decline of neighborhood life, of our community of place. But in that it's had help, in particular from our love of privacy.

Privacy: Everyone A Howard Hughes

After a big mail strike, I did a feature for *Newsday* on Long Islanders' reaction to it. I found that the more crowded the neighborhood, the more involved people seemed to be with their mailman. They usually knew the mail carrier by name, and had discussed the strike with him at length.

But in secluded upper-middle areas people rarely talked with their mailman at all and usually didn't know who he was because their mailbox was at the foot of the drive.

Our mailbox was at the foot of the drive that year. Making good salaries, Muriel and I rented a fancy house on Long Island's north shore. It was set back, had thick walls, a big yard, and lush hedges to hold the neighbors off. We were at last free from being spied upon.

I don't think I've ever spent a lonelier year. Nobody knew us, or seemed to care to. We knew no one.

Six months after leaving I finally learned who lived next door. We were forwarded a *Reader's Digest* promotional letter which, in an attempt to look intimate, mentioned our neighbor's names.

PEANUTS
featuring
"Good ol' Charlie Brown"
by SCHULZ
PSYCHIATRIC HELP 5¢
THE DOCTOR IS IN
SEE THAT PLANE UP THERE ?
IT'S FILLED WITH PEOPLE WHO ARE ALL GOING SOMEPLACE..THAT'S WHAT I'D LIKE TO DO.. GO OFF SOMEPLACE, AND START A NEW LIFE...
BUT MAYBE WHEN I GOT TO THIS NEW PLACE, THE NEW PEOPLE WOULD LIKE ME BETTER
ONLY UNTIL THEY GOT TO KNOW YOU, CHARLIE BROWN..THEN YOU'D BE RIGHT BACK WHERE YOU STARTED..
BUT MAYBE THESE NEW PEOPLE WOULD BE MORE UNDERSTANDING
PEOPLE ARE PEOPLE, CHARLIE BROWN...
Tm. Reg. U.S. Pat. Off.—All rights reserved © 1971 by United Feature Syndicate, Inc.
FORGET IT, CHARLIE BROWN
BUT..
NOPE!
UH..
FIVE CENTS, PLEASE
SIGH

It's nothing new that privacy and money go hand in hand. Since lords lived in manors, seclusion has been synonymous with wealth.

When Joan Didion interviewed a Greek shipping heiress in her New York suite on the second day of a city-stopping blizzard, the woman casually inquired whether it was snowing outside.[25]

Americans are not unique in the quest of seclusion, just richer. More and more of us can afford to move greater and greater distances away from each other—and we do.

Psychologist Chester Bennett says that he's concerned about the "privacy bandwagon" gathering steam in America. Privacy, says Bennett, is a relatively modern fetish, and not always what it seems.

"There is minimal concern over privacy when people know each other," he points out. "In the frontier community, or even in rural America a generation ago, few secrets were kept and no one seemed to care. There were tensions of course, in this kind of intimacy; but basically there was security in knowing one's neighbors—and in being known."[26]

Privacy as an ideal, even as a concept, is relatively modern. Marshall McLuhan says it took the invention of print to tear man from his tribes and plant the dream of isolation in his brain.[27] Historian Jacob Burckhardt says that prior to the Renaissance, Western man was barely aware of himself as an individual. Mostly he drew identity from membership in groups—family, tribe, church, guild.[28]

But since the Renaissance especially, Western man has sought increasing amounts of isolation, of distance from his neighbors. In America, with more land in which to seek elbow room, and with more money to buy it, the ideal of the unfettered individual, rugged, free and secluded, has reached its zenith. Howard Hughes is only the logical conclusion, an inspiration to us all.

Not all cultures value isolation so, nor have they the means to pursue it. Anthropologist Edward T. Hall points out that neither the Japanese, who live within paper walls, nor the Arabs, whose rooms are huge and few, have a word for "privacy."[29]

In much of the world, shelter is designed for group living with high visibility, courtyards, doors facing streets, and balconies. Town squares are provided for the promenade. Street cafés provide places to see and be seen, a setting in which to linger without guilt. The French make a habit of entertaining in restaurants, and spend outrageous amounts of time lingering in cafés, watching each other. Even the British, in many ways more private than Americans, still drink all but 4 percent of their beer in pubs.[30]

America, settled by footloose singles and nuclear families, has historically had a passion for the private home and little tradition of common space.

True, New England does have its greens, and the Southwest retains some Spanish town squares. But such space is exceptional and always subject to the bulldozer.

Street cafés have never caught on in this country, and the New York City Health Department once warned people that it was unhealthy to tarry too long at those which do exist.[31] In general we tend to be suspicious of gatherings without purpose.

We have, in the past, had more points of public contact than we do today—taverns, barbershops, soda fountains. Even homes until recently were built with front porches where residents could, just by stepping outside, announce themselves available for casual neighborhood visiting.

Canon James Hannay of Dublin, who visited this country on the eve of World War I, was struck by our front porches. "The passer-by, the casual wanderer along the road outside," wrote Canon Hannay, "sees the American family in its porch, can, if he cares to, note what each member of the family is doing. The American has no objection to this publicity. He is not doing anything of which he is the least ashamed. If other people can see him, he can see them in return. The arrangement gratifies his instinct for sociability."[32]

David Meador says his favorite memories of growing up in small-town Texas are of swinging on the front porch for an evening, waving and saying "Howdy" to passersby.

"Oh, how I loved it!" recalls another front-porch nostalgic.[33]

"It was our forum, our trysting place and air conditioning all rolled into one. It was a place to see and be seen, a bridge for the generation gap. . . . Perhaps the most important function of the porch was the feeling of togetherness it gave the neighborhood. . . . The nightly nod and the friendly wave of the hand brought a warm feeling of brotherhood, of things shared and comradeship."

Even in Southern California, such porch/community centers were common until World War II. Writer Richard Armour says that when he grew up in a small town there, virtually every house had a front porch.

But when it's time came, "First we had it screened in. Then, when my father could afford it, we had it glassed in. And then we put up curtains we could pull to shut out the outdoors completely. At that point it ceased being a porch. It became another room."[34]

Their next house was built without a front porch. And today, says Armour, the only houses left with porches are in the rundown part of town, which is slated for urban renewal anyway.

Eventually our fetish for privacy becomes self-feeding. "The initial drive towards privacy makes even more privacy inevitable," writes architecture critic John Pastier. "The city notes that most people have their own backyards, and concludes that public parks are superfluous. . . . Recreation then becomes divorced from the normal pattern of the city."[35]

Or, as we grow more affluent, we simply install at home the facilities we used to share as a community: swimming pools, sauna baths, gyms, tennis courts. As more and more people can afford these luxuries, the home-as-recreational-center has been a growing American trend.

Edward Hall sees our obsessively private environments growing inevitably out of the need we feel to Maintain Appearances in public. The Arabs and Japanese, he points out, as well as the British, consider it perfectly appropriate to withdraw, to become silent in public for hours or even days at a time. No one will ask, "What's the matter?"

But living under the compulsion to be sociable, and happy when with others, American face muscles eventually grow weary. "The strain of keeping up a façade can be great," writes Hall. "Architecture can and does take over this burden for people. It can also provide a refuge where the individual can 'let his hair down' and be himself."[36]

"AUTONOMY WITHDRAWAL"

Increasing numbers of us suffer from an "autonomy-withdrawal syndrome," according to the architect-planner C. A. Alexander. Most people, explains Alexander, use their home as an insulation against the outside world, a means of self-protection. Eventually this withdrawal becomes habitual, and people lose the ability to let others inside their secluded world. What begins as a normal concern for privacy soon resembles the pathological.[37]

A woman from Arkansas recently wrote Abby[38] about how she maintained the integrity of her home:

> . . . I have a big poster with red letters on my front door which says:
>
> For all who wish to pass through this door:
>
> 1. No smoking inside. It makes me sick.
> 2. If you bring your kids, either take care of them yourself or leave them outside.
> 3. I am not a bank, so don't ask to borrow any money.
> 4. I am not a grocer, so don't ask to borrow any groceries.
> 5. I am not in the hotel business, so don't ask me to put you up overnight.
> 6. Don't bring me your problems. I've got my own.
>
> Since I have had this poster on my front door, lots of folks have said I was nuts, but I don't care. This is the first time in my life I have had any privacy.*

* Abby later printed a response from a reader: "Dear Abby: I just read the letter from the 28-year-old mother of four who tacked a poster on her door with 'rules' to keep visitors away.

"Well, I'm a 38-year-old mother of six, and I'm amazed that anyone would want that much privacy. We're newcomers who live out in the country, and I'm stuck out here with six kids, two dogs, and three cats. I'm ready to go out on the road and flag down some strangers.

That sounds like at least the early stages of autonomy-withdrawal.

We've come a long way from the time when community of place and community of sentiment were one and the same. It's not only that we *don't* know our neighbors; it's more that we don't *want* to. Generally we have little in common. And if we did, things might be even worse. Who wants to have friends peering through the windows?

"The neighbors are perfect," reports University of Southern California football coach John McKay, "I don't know any of them."[39]

One survey of 4,745 white Lutherans showed that the majority of them wouldn't mind having blacks as neighbors, but *would* mind having them as close friends.[40]

A couple of *Newsday* reporters once toured a new development in Long Island's Suffolk County to examine how "neighborly" the residents were. They found an interesting phenomenon recurring there, a second-wave pulling-in among scarred veterans of too much "togetherness" in older neighborhoods. "The most vehement advocates of going it alone," wrote the reporters, "are men and women who have had it the other way . . . and have decided the disadvantages of socializing with the neighbors far outweigh the advantages."[41]

"Please print my 'poster' in the paper for all to read:

"• You may smoke inside, outside, on the roof, or anywhere you wish, just don't burn the house down.

"• If you're hungry, help yourself to anything you can find. And if you don't find anything, ask one of the kids. They'll fix you a peanut-butter-and-brown-sugar sandwich.

"• If you're here around mealtime, grab a chair and join us.

"• If you want to stay overnight, bring a sleeping bag and we'll move some clutter from the corner to make room for you.

"• Bring your kids. We have so many, a few more won't make any difference.

"• We can't lend you any money, but go ahead and ask anyway. It will make us feel good to know we appear that prosperous.

"• Tell us your troubles and we'll tell you ours. One of our kids can play the violin for background music, and we can all cry together.

"• If you can stand it, we can stand you, so drop in anytime and stay as long as you like. We're people who like people."

A study of seventy-five white, middle-class, male Michigan suburbanites showed that most of their relations with other men on the block took place standing up. This group of men defined a good neighbor as one who "is available for emergency aid; can be called on to trade mutual aid; lends and can be loaned to; respects privacy; friendly, but not friends." Only four of the men said they had neighbors they also considered friends.[42]

This is also what the *Newsday* reporters found. When they would ask people where their friends lived, it was usually a block away or more.

UNKNOWN KILLERS

I'm constantly horrified/fascinated by the regular accounts of crime and carnage perpetrated by "respectable" but highly private men who turn out not to have been known at all by shocked friends and neighbors. A news account of one hijacking attempt reads, "Neighbors . . . described the graying skyjacker as a loner who said little except 'Hello.' "[43]

Recently an insurance executive apparently killed his wife, three children, and mother-in-law, then left the bodies in their $90,000 New Jersey home. No neighbor noticed anything amiss until the newspapers started piling up on the porch and the lights burned out over a month's time. A news account explained that "The disappearance of the family caused little notice in the suburb where executives move in and out frequently without making close friends."[44]

What these men seem to have in common with assassins is the quality of being obsessively private, "unknown" people who finally are revealed in their Act. Finally they are known.

In one tragic case, hijacker Heinrick Von George was gunned down by F.B.I. agents while trying to extort $200,000 from Mohawk Airlines. Von George turns out not only to have been unknown to his neighbors, but also to his wife and seven children. They knew him only as a devoted husband and father with a history of business failures. After he died, Von George turned out really to be Merlyn LaVerne St. George who once served a term in San Quentin for theft of U.S. government property.[45]

We not only use our homes to avoid each other, but we can do the same thing within the home, with just a little help from modern technology.

Convenience: The Dishwasher Gap

I once gave a speech on "The Generation Gap" to a women's club. In the discussion afterward, one fiftyish mother stood up and said: "I'm gonna tell you what brought on the whole thing—dishwashers. That's right, dishwashers. I got to know my kids better, they told me more, when we washed dishes together. One would wash, another rinse, and a third dry. We'd fight but we'd also talk. Now that we have a dishwasher, there's no regular time when we get to know each other."

She had fingered clearly something I was sensing only vaguely: that our household conveniences, our whole drive for a *convenient* life has cut us off from each other. The cooperation and communication which used to accompany life's chores is being built out of our social systems.

The 1970 census found that most American homes had dishwashers, clothes washers, and freezers. In the first three months of 1971, 6.8 million appliances were wholesaled, following a $26.6 billion year for the housewares industry in 1970.[46]

These applicances are a major dividend of progress, one which keeps us from having to clutter up the kitchen with too many bodies. But electrical housewares also remove much of the incidental contact which once took place between family members in the home.

The whole point of conveniences is to make it unnecessary to ask another's help. Dishwashers make that solitary work. Electric knives take the craft out of carving. Blenders make a two-hand job out of one that once took four or more.

This trend has had more than a little to do with the breakdown of our family system. In the past, the nuclear family has been an important economic unit, all members working together for survival. Today our survival needs are met, and there's no real need to do more than help throw away the vinyl bag from a boil-pack supper.

We're not ignorant of the effects conveniences have on our lives. A survey conducted by Harvard's Program of Technology and Society found 78 percent of a cross-section of Bostonians believe "people today have become too dependent on machines." Yet 94 percent find "machines have made life easier."

"It was surprising to find the contradictory attitudes of people," said the Program's Dr. Irene Taviss. "A substantial majority of Americans are very concerned about the way machines control their lives. But they are so 'hooked' on automatic dishwashers and other labor-saving devices that they seem quite willing to accept the bad aspects of technology."[47]

THE SHRINKING KITCHEN

House Beautiful suggests that by A.D. 2000 the kitchen may be obsolete entirely. With the advent of computerized help, modular room construction, and smaller appliances, the magazine envisions "a kitchen that disappears completely into a wall or folds into an island—perhaps, startling enough, no kitchen at all as we're used to thinking of it. Possibilities are dizzying."[48]

Except that there are people like me who prefer sociable kitchens to more formal living rooms. In a kitchen I can stand, move around, talk loud, hide out. Living rooms scare me. They limit the ways I can be.

"I don't go to nobody's home," says actor Peter Falk. "I'm not comfortable sitting in living rooms. I happen to like the kitchen better."[49]

When it played a larger role in our lives, a kitchen was friendly ground for family and visitor.

Billy Delawie says her warmest memories of an Oklahoma childhood are invariably set in the kitchen. Later she married and her architect husband designed their home. The cooking space was designed for efficiency. It was small, and one could reach anything by just standing in the middle. Billy hated that cooking space, hated the time she spent there. It was cold, not social, space.

Today's housework may be more convenient and less time-consuming, but it also takes place in virtually solitary confinement. "When a colonial housewife went to the village well to draw water," points out historian Daniel Boorstin, "she saw friends, gathered gossip, shared the laughs and laments of her neighbors. When her great-great-granddaughter was blessed with running water, and no longer had to go to the well, this made life easier, but also less interesting. Running water, electricity, mail delivery, and the telephone removed more reasons for leaving the house. And now the climax of it all is television."[49a]

Sociologist Jessie Bernard, who recently completed a study of American marriage and family trends, says such isolation leads to a "housewife syndrome," which she views as a leading public health problem. The aloneness of modern housewives, Ms. Bernard explains, "encourages brooding, leads to erratic judgments . . . and renders one more susceptible to psychoses."[50]

"Kitchen therapy" has proved effective for patients at the Las Angeles Resthaven Psychiatric Hospital and Community Mental Health Center. Even intensive-care patients at Resthaven cook together for the incidental benefits of having to socialize. "The kitchen setting," explains Resthaven's activities' director, "helps patients learn to cope with spaces, restores their confidence, [and] provides an area for identifying problems, more than escaping them."[51]

SLOT-MACHINE MEALS

Kitchen appliances are adapting to our evolving forms of food intake. Some toasters now have heavier springs, and wider slots to accommodate Pop-tarts. Electric ranges can be purchased with a built-in super-hot water tap for instant products. Microwave ovens defrost and cook prepared food in minutes, even seconds.

Eating, according to contemporary nutritionists, has become less and less a family affair and more and more a matter of "slot-machine snacking." According to one estimate, 28 percent of our food intake is now in the form of snacks outside mealtime.

"Convenience will continue to be a prime product benefit," advised Dr. Leon P. Ullensvang of Pet Inc. in a speech to his colleagues in the food business. "Homemakers will search for ways to further reduce the time they have to spend in the kitchen. Products will be lighter, more flexible, easier to use, less complicated and more dependable.

"Social reinforcements to well-organized eating will continue to decline and our food and meal patterns will become more diffused. With our permissive society and our search for individuality and variety, food choices will become more a personal matter.

"Attitudes towards the home and family are changing and will change further. Today's family is more mobile, freer and outward, less dependent on the home itself as the center of activity. Tomorrow's family will be even more so. As marketers of the basic food products consumed by this society we must be quick to spot the changes and interpret them into meaningful products and services and then communicate in the new ways their message that will evoke positive responses."[52]

Ever since the first cereal snack-pack was introduced over two decades ago, individually proportioned foods have taken up more and more shelf space in our supermarkets—frozen sandwiches, TV dinners, packaged instant breakfasts, and cocktails in a can, not to mention all the snack-packaged potato chips and commercially prepared fast foods.

The dietitian of one of California's veterans' hospitals told Harvard nutritionist Jean Mayer that while World War I veterans ate meat and potatoes, and World War II's soldiers had more varied tastes, Vietnam veterans tend to skip breakfast and snack on fast foods all day. Such trends in eating, says Mayer, "are doing more to destroy the family structure than most people realize."[53]

Consider, for example, the effect of individual pudding servings in a can. These not only make it unnecessary to work together in the kitchen preparing dessert, but also reduce the need to consider one's family as a unit, to compromise between chocolate and banana cream, when it comes to fixing pudding. All members get their own flavor, right out of the can, whenever they want.

"The basic theme underlying food practices in contemporary American society is *individualism,*" writes Nutritionist Norge W. Jerome. "The structure, timing, and ordering of meals (and snacks) as traditionally defined are yielding to individual patterns of food use."[54]

This evolution of our eating patterns has been hard to document. Nutritionists take for granted that three square meals a day occur mostly in textbooks, but according to one of their number, housewives feel so guilty about not providing their families with the proper nutrition that they lie shamelessly to researchers. "It may be easier to get people to talk with complete frankness about their sex life than about the eating patterns of the family," says motivational psychologist Paul A. Fine, who has conducted several surveys of meal habits for food manufacturers.[55]

Fine says that today's average family eating-pattern includes little or no breakfast, snacks during the morning, maybe lunch (but not for Mom unless little kids are home), big eating after school, a smaller and smaller supper, and TV snacking which may be supplemented by after-bed refrigerator raids. The sit-down family dinner, he says, seldom takes place more than three nights a week in any family.

That seems a shame. Our family meals were warm, together times, times when the talk rivaled the food for attention. My best memories of home take place around the dining room table.

"Food is such an enhancer of communications that I don't know what can replace the family meal as a forum," says University of Washington pediatrician Dr. Nathan Smith. For Smith, the issue is personal. The doctor confesses that with two teenage boys, the only way his family can be sure of gathering for supper is to mark the occasion in advance on a calendar. They succeed about three times a week—the national average. This American trend of eat-and-run tactics is, says Smith, "destroying not only the enjoyment of the old-fashioned meal but also the platform which family meals provided to air the days' activities and problems.

"In the past, conversations around the table meals would introduce a child to the part each member of the family has to play in life. The family breakfast, the family lunch and the family dinner of my generation are no longer with us and they won't return. However, the social needs that were met around the family dinner table are obviously still with us."[56]

A Louis Harris poll recently found that even when families do eat together, in two homes out of three television remains on during the meal.[57]

NOISE

University of Wisconsin psychiatrist Jack Westman once tape-recorded normal daily talk in seventeen Madison homes. He found that members of those families spent an average of only twenty minutes per *week* engaging in ordinary conversation with each other, either separately or as a group. Westman attributes this reticence primarily to noises trapped in the home, most of which are a byproduct of modern conveniences.[58]

Normal conversation usually occurs at 65 decibels. Talk takes place best at 10 decibels above background din. Any noise level in the home over 55 decibels makes communication difficult. Decibel levels over 70 can be dangerous to the body. But the din in modern households regularly exceeds such limits, sometimes shooting up to 90 or 100 decibels.

One study of in-home noise levels got the following decibel readings: TV (average)—68; water running from kitchen faucet —77; electric can opener—79; vent fan over stove—84; vacuum cleaner—84; electric shaver—85; food blender—92; furnace blower —100; 6-inch skill saw—100.[59]

"We don't understand that noise makes us less efficient, less effective and more tense," says Dr. Westman. "Instead, we scapegoat. We take our tensions out on each other. Mothers yell at the youngsters. Parents bicker. Clinical experience suggests that the inadequate management of sound in the home plays a contributing role in the breakdown of communication and loss of pleasure in family living."[60]

But it's not clear that, except for persons living next to airports, Americans in any great number consider noise pollution "a problem." Nor is it clear how many noises they consider "pollution."

Hoover once made a quiet vacuum cleaner, but it bombed. Customers wouldn't believe it was picking up dirt.[61]

For years I couldn't figure out why so many bathrooms have those awful exhaust fans whose roar made going to the toilet worse than riding the subway. Finally I realized: the fans are there to suck out odors. To most people, I guess, or at least to builders, that's top priority. The noise they make isn't relevant.

More than that, I think many toilet-users actually crave that fan noise. It muffles the sound of urine hitting water, or worse.

Our ambivalence about noises, and the convenient life which produces them, is the same ambivalence we feel about community. We don't want to be cut off from each other, and yet we do—and we crave any help in protecting our isolation. Stereo can be an aid, the scream of a blender, or the steady hum of an air conditioner.

Some people living by Los Angeles' freeways claim positive solace from their mask of noise. "I have some damn good fights with my wife," says one such resident, "and the neighbors never know some of the things she calls me."[62]

With our comings and goings inhibiting friendship, a love of seclusion eroding our neighborhoods, and our passion for convenience atomizing the family, it's no wonder we feel a "loss of community."

But the distinctions are artificial. Mobility, privacy, and convenience are like a trio, first one playing, then the other, and all three finally coming together to play their song—at our request.

More than any single thing on the American scene, cars unite the triumvirate of values which are wrecking our sense of community. Automobiles are at once our main agent of mobility, the most private place to which we can retire, and a primary source of convenience. When one asks what it is that we must trade in on community, the answer could very well be: your car.

CARS AGAINST COMMUNITY

Many social critics say that the car is community's Public Enemy Number One. It's made prisoners of men, chauffeurs of women, cripples of the very young and the old.

Kenneth Schneider, a city planner, recently wrote a book called *Autokind Vs. Mankind* in which he pins the blame squarely on automobility for destroying our sense of place, wiping out small towns, choking cities, planting suburbs, alienating man from his senses, trivializing friendship, and cutting off young and old from society. In an interesting contrast, Schneider defines "community . . . the social integrity of the individual," as the antonym of "freeway . . . the mobile integrity of the motorcar."[63]

But cars per se haven't done a thing. The machines themselves are a neutral. What they have done is implement our values better than any other single tool. Cars are at once our greatest convenience, our most certain place of privacy, and our major source of mobility.

I once heard a woman describe her two and a half years on a commune in a most appealing way. More than most, this commune seemed to have kept a stable core of people together over its brief/long life. She talked of their deep feeling of commitment to each other.[64]

But she also pointed out that although most property was held in common, each communard kept a private car—just in case he wanted to split. And if I lived on that commune, I'd probably want to keep a car too—just in case I wanted to split. I prize my mobility, my right to get up and go, as much as anyone—and I love the car which permits it. It's freedom, and in San Diego as on Long Island, the car is an absolutely indispensable tool for survival. Without it you're crippled, a virtual prisoner.

But, in addition to mobility, the car has qualities to offer which no mass transport can match: convenience and privacy. Futurist Don Fabun says that the reason the average passenger car carries 1.5 passengers, "is that the .5 passengers can't talk back."[65]

"If people are to be brought together again," writes Edward Hall, "given a chance to get acquainted with each other and involved in nature, some fundamental solutions must be found to the problems posed by the automobile."[66] But the problem is not one we want solved. Our car population is rising at twice the rate of the human one.

Muriel and I have only one car but wish we could afford two. The other day I sat in a boring seminar to which a friend had driven me. I pondered leaving in the middle, then realized that was impossible without my own car. I was stuck with those people to the bitter end. I hate asking people for rides, don't like "imposing," but often have to. What I'm finding is that I've gotten to know lots of people better as they happily give me rides here and there. We're forced together in a way we wouldn't be if I had my own car and its radio for company. But when I can afford it, I'll buy a second car. I treasure its convenience more than the opportunity to be with others.

The great, overlooked seduction of this earth module, the car, is privacy. Cars and bathrooms are the only places where most urban/suburbanites can be completely and blissfully—alone. And a car is better than the bathroom. No one can knock and tell you to hurry up.

I initally grew interested in the car as private space when friends of mine began screaming inside their automobiles.

The first person to tell me about this, a father of five in his late thirties, explained that within his van, driving to and from work, was the only time he felt free to rage—spit and holler—

let it all out. He called it his Private Therapy Van. Just roll up the windows and howl, go crazy if you like. No one will ever know.

This intrigued me, and I began to talk with other friends, asking what they did alone in a car, mentioning that one guy I knew screamed. With striking frequency faces would light up, and heads nod vigorously as they heard this. "Hey, me too," they'd say. "I scream in my car too sometimes, but I didn't know anyone else did."

I was ridin' in my car
Screamin' at the night
Screamin' at the dark
Screamin' at fright

I wasn't doin' nothing
Just drivin' about
Screamin' at the dark
Lettin' it out

Well, along comes a motorcycle
Very much to my surprise
I said said," Officer was I speeding?"
I couldn't see his eyes

He said, "No you weren't speeding,"
And he felt where his gun was hung.
He said, "lady you were screamin'
At the top of your lungs.

And you were
Doin' it alone,
You were doin' it alone,
You were screamin' in your car
In a twenty mile zone,
You were doing it alone
You were doing it alone
You were screaming in your car
In a twenty-mile zone

I said I'll roll up all my windows
Don't wanna disturb the peace
I'm just a creature
Who's lookin' for a little release[67]

Screaming is only the most dramatic example of private behavior taking place inside cars. Columnist Art Seidenbaum of the *Los Angeles Times* says he knows novelists who construct paragraphs within, an insomniac who finds freeways his most relaxing environment, and one father who uses time driving alone to argue with his family so he can be nice when they're around.[68]

Jack Smith, Seidenbaum's colleague at the *Times*, calls freeway time "the only time we're free; free from the telephone, free from things we ought to be doing, free from any kind of interruption but the occasional necessity of a prudent steering or braking to avoid catastrophe."

Smith got so much response to this position that two follow-up columns were necessary to handle the load. One woman, an anthropology teacher, wrote Smith that she found freeway time "glorious. . . . Those times of privacy and contemplation, of separateness and selfness, when one can be truly alone and thoughtful. I sometimes think freeway driving was made for philosophical thought and problem-solving as no other situation can afford."[69]

My own informal survey has uncovered everything from crying to masturbation going on inside cars, with nose-picking the runaway first choice for entertainment while driving.

One woman I interviewed, a mother in her late 40's, confided that she often sucks her thumb when alone in her car. I asked if that were a life-long habit and the woman replied no, that it began just over a year ago when she asked her six-year-old why he sucked his thumb and he said it tasted good. He suggested that she try it. It was a suggestion she couldn't refuse, so the mother tried it—and liked it. Now this woman reports sucking her thumb regularly, but only when alone. Sometimes this means at home, and more often while driving.

Traffic patrolmen with whom I talked said singing is common within cars, especially among women, and many drivers seem just to be talking to themselves. They say you can tell the difference by whether the driver's head is keeping time with the movement of their lips.

Singing is my own favorite activity for time alone in our Saab. I also yodel, badly, and find other drivers are the only people who will put up with it—so long as my windows are tightly closed.

Sometimes, during thousands of hours trapped on Long Island's freeways, I'd glance hungrily at other drivers. Who are they? Do they love anyone? Might they love me?

Only inches away, I could have reached out to touch them had glass and steel not separated us.

And often they'd glance back, hungry too—but afraid. Then the lines would move, all eyes right, and off we'd drive—jousting for position, hunger forgotten. Had we been on a bus, or a train, or even on foot, we might have talked. But armored by two tons of steel, we battled.

"Automobiles," writes Edward Hall, "insulate man not only from the environment but from human contact as well. They permit only the most limited types of interaction, usually competitive, aggressive and destructive."[70] Which is a big part of their appeal.

I had a friend in college who couldn't wait to get back to New York between semesters so that he could roar around screaming and flipping the bird at other drivers—just to let off steam.

A Viennese newspaper once asked readers aged nine to fourteen to write in about their father's driving habits. Some of the responses included:

- You will not believe such a lovely father can curse so loudly.
- Father shouted at pedestrians, Mother shouted at Father, and they both got so cross my father almost lost control of himself and the car.

• At first it is cold and the engine will not start, so father's cursing starts right away. Then a car passes us, and Father curses the driver. He has to step on the brakes. When he starts again, we continue our excursion and our cursing.[71]

The only problem with criticizing the way cars make us anonymous, unknown, and nasty to each other is the assumption that we'd prefer it any other way. We do, of course, and yet . . . .

It's that ambivalence. We say we'd like not to be so cut off and uncivilized with each other, but another voice within speaks differently. The private car is a place safe to be our other self.

Walter Cronkite tells of being viciously sideswiped one afternoon by a blue-and-white four-door sedan with a dent in the right front door. At a dinner party that night, hosted by a biology professor of impeccable courtesy, Cronkite recounted the incident. All present agreed that even civilized men often can become brutes when protected and hidden by two tons of steel. As the evening ended, the host offered his guest a ride home—in his blue-and-white four-door sedan, which, Cronkite noticed as he got in, had a dent in the right front door.[72]

OF THE CAR, BY THE CAR, AND FOR THE CAR

The car itself has had a lot to do with cutting us off from each other by sealing us in cocoons on wheels and making it easy to drive away from each other. But its greater impact may be in the environments we erect to suit the car, environments built for mobility, privacy, and convenience.

Sociologist Phillip Slater says that the car "did more than anything else to destroy community life in America. It segmented the various parts of the community and scattered them so that they became unfamiliar with one another. It isolated travelers and decoordinated the movement of people from one place to another. It isolated and shrank living units to the point where the skills involved in informal cooperation among large groups of people atrophied and were lost. As the community became a less and less satisfying and pleasurable place to be, people more and more took to their automobile as an escape from it. This in turn crowded the roads more which generated more road-building which destroyed more communities and so on."[73]

The process is self-feeding. The more we drive, the less pleasant it becomes to walk down streets which have become noisy, dangerous, and smelly from cars. The less pleasant it becomes to walk, the more we drive. Eventually, custom becomes law.

In 1971 the City Council of Dallas passed an antiloitering ordinance which made a crime of the following activities:

> The walking about aimlessly without apparent purpose; lingering; hanging around; lagging behind; the idle spending of time; delaying; sauntering and moving slowly about, where such conduct is not due to physical defects or conditions.[74]

Beverly Hills is the logical conclusion. There the police are notorious for questioning anyone caught walking at night. Washing clothes, getting sick, and dying are discouraged within Beverly Hills, since ordinances forbid laundromats, hospitals, and funeral homes within the city limits. There's even a regulation against telephone answering services in Beverly Hills, since these might threaten the resident's privacy.[75]

Life in such environments can be ghastly, a gilded solitary confinement. Maria Wyeth, the heroine of Joan Didion's novel *Play It as It Lays*, lies awake in the evening, separated from her husband and alone with her nightmares in the still of Beverly Hills. When she can stand it no longer, in the dead of night, the troubled actress leaves—by car, driving aimlessly to ease the pain.

> She drove as a riverman runs a river, every day more attuned to its currents, its deceptions, and just as a riverman feels the pull of the rapids in the lull between sleeping and waking, so Maria lay at night in the still of Beverly Hills and saw the great signs soar overhead at seventy miles an hour, *Normandie ½*, *Vermont ¾*, *Harbor Fwy. 1.* Again and again she returned to an intricate stretch just south of the interchange where successful passage from the Hollywood onto the Harbor required a diagonal move across four lanes of traffic. On the

afternoon she finally did it without once braking or once losing the beat on the radio she was exhilarated, and that night slept dreamlessly.[76]

It's no coincidence that Los Angeles, our most automobilized city, is also one of our most fragmented, one of the most private and lonely places on earth.

Long Island, also built to suit cars, is not much better. I spent a lot of our two years on Long Island feeling sorry for its residents —like myself. In all that time I can't remember ever meeting anyone by accident. Or having a place to hang out, a store within walking distance, or anything within walking distance.

The suburbs are simply not designed for congregation. One suburbanite says that in the subdivision where she lived the better part of a decade, seeing more than three people gathered on the street made her wonder whether a disaster had just occurred, and perhaps she ought to inquire.

Like cars, the suburbs themselves are neutral. They have no values. Suburbs do reflect our wishes and were built upon them after World War II when more of us could drive further and did, in search of more privacy and convenience. There, by grouping homes in one place, commerce in a second, and industry in a third, with rigid zoning provisions, suburbanites have made sure that those not mobile enough to get around are crippled—especially the very old and the very young.

I used to feel especially sorry for the kids I'd see trying to grow up on Long Island. No hangouts. Impossible to get anywhere without driving. People scared of you. Okay, small towns are stifling and bigoted, but is this any improvement?

Three-fifths of the suburban kids in a Louis Harris poll said they were "often bored," and almost half wished they lived somewhere else. Yet 40 percent of their parents cited a better atmosphere for kids among their reasons for living in the suburbs.[77]

"On the face of it, the suburb ought to be a very good place for children's play groups," says C. A. Alexander. "Yet paradoxically, this children's paradise is not a paradise at all for the little children." Alexander talks of driving through subdivisions watching little children "squatting forlornly outside their houses—occasionally playing with an older brother or sister, and occasionally in groups of two or three, but most often alone. Compare this with the situation in a primitive village, or with a crowded urban slum: there the little children are out on the street fending for themselves as soon as they can walk; heaps of children are playing and falling and rolling over one another."

Alexander blames the stunted suburban play group on low population density (kids can't walk far), unsafe streets, lack of common land, and their parents' consequent power to dictate who their children play with. "There isn't any natural place where children go to find each other: they have to go and look for each other in one another's homes. For a child this is a much more formidable enterprise than simply running out to see who's on the street. It also makes the children hard to find, and keeps the size of the play-groups down, especially since many parents won't allow large groups of children in the house. . . .

"It is small wonder that children who grow up in these conditions learn to be self-reliant in the pathological sense."[78]

Buckminster Fuller says cars are taking an unfair knock. He says the automobile began simply as an extension of the house, little different from the front porch. "Then, in effect, we put wheels under the front porch, put an engine in it and took off down the street. The kids began to explore the world, spending less and less time around home."[79]

But there's a fundamental difference between the two porches. The old kind was open and stationary, one of our most public spaces. The car is private and mobile, one of our least public spaces. We don't use it to drive toward each other so much as to drive away.

That's the whole paradox of our new environments. More able to leave the home, we have less to which we wish to leave. So we equip our homes with conveniences which ultimately make them a less pleasant place to be. Then we flee, drive away in our private cars, glancing hungrily at each other until we no longer can stand the freeway's loneliness and return once again to the loneliness of our homes.

The ultimate result of a life in which it's so easy to drive away from each other, so possible to hide out in our homes and so unnecessary to ask another's help, is that we become less and less known to each other.

We'd cope with this problem better if we were sure we really wanted to, wanted to become better known to each other. I'm not sure we do.

I *am* sure that we want more feeling of "community." Of that there's no question. We're obsessed with a longing to get back together. But whether we want to be more *known* to each other is a separate question.

As a result what we're doing, is seeking community in ways which ensure that we have to trade in very little of the anonymity we crave, or the privacy, mobility, and convenience which ensure it. The community we seek is one in which we needn't really know each other.

Part II

Seeking Community

3.

"And All in the Privacy of Your Own Home"

HERE'S . . . COMMUNITY!

I got much closer to Dick Cavett after we bought a color television. He seemed more real to me, and quite likable. For a while I joined his crowd nightly. They were a very accepting bunch of people, let me listen, didn't expect me to talk, and never put me down. Best of all, I didn't have to leave the privacy of my home to get in on the conversation.

Once Cavett had Norman Mailer on his show. Mailer is a jerk. I told him so, right to his face. He was speechless.

Television is wonderful. It lets me get involved, feel a part of things, and have a sense of community without sacrificing a second's privacy. Color has made the medium sort of two and a half dimensional, its people almost real.

There's no question that we viewers get intimate with actors over television. That's been obvious ever since we got Ahab, our big collie dog. At first when kids would dash up to pet him yelling, "Lassie, Lassie!" I would patiently explain, "No, that's not Lassie, it's Ahab. It looks like Lassie, but he's another dog." The kids would just look through me, then go back to their petting, murmuring, "Lassie, Lassie."

Now I say, "That's right, it's Lassie. Come see Lassie and pet him." The kids are much happier that way, and so am I.

Children especially seem to get close to their televised friends, and need to see them regularly. Ask any thirty-year-old how he or she feels about Kukla, Fran, and Ollie, or Buffalo Bob. When Buffalo Bob made his recent triumphal tour of the country, old kids greeted him more as a long-lost friend than a celebrity. Bob Egan, just turned thirty, says the reason Kukla, Fran, and Ollie were so important to him was that he knew they would always visit his home at a certain time every day. They could be counted on. With live people he wasn't so sure.

It's a maxim of the television industry that weekly shows must have regular faces to be successful. Anthologies rarely work because there are no recurring characters with whom viewers can get involved.

One woman I know, who has a master's degree in English, watches "As the World Turns" for several days before going home to Phoenix. That way she and her mother always have people to gossip about.

Eileen Fulton for eight years has played a vampish homewrecker on "As the World Turns." She was once approached in a New York street by an excited woman who asked: "Are you Lisa Hughes?"

"I play that part," Ms. Fulton replied, reaching for a pen to sign an autograph. The woman slapped her hard across the face. "You're mean, you're rotten, you're despicable!"

On another occasion the actress was eating out with a date when two old ladies stopped at her table. "You know, Lisa Hughes," said one, "you're a liar. You're supposed to be dying in a hospital. Bob and Mary are worried to death about you. But here you are, laughing and having a good time. You're not sick at all."[1]

Those running television have been slow to capitalize on their surrogate-friendship role, but they're finally beginning to catch on. "Try the friendly Eyewitness News Team in the privacy of your own home," my paper invites me. "If they don't live up to their reputation for being the warmest, friendliest team going, we'll refund your ordinary everyday newscaster."

Eyewitness recently ran a twenty-five-words-or-less contest on "what hearing it from a friend" means to you. The prize: one evening's Eyewitness News broadcasted from your home. "Why such a generous offer? Mainly because that's the kind of guys we are—friendly, human, relaxed."[2]

"THINK OF US AS FRIENDSHIP"
7/KABC TV

This intimate approach to newscasting was adopted for the 70s only after extensive market research showed strong public demand for a more intimate, less anxiety-producing perspective on the affairs of the day.[3]

Marshal McLuhan has an explanation: "The 'friendly teamness' format recognizes the sharing of such experience as a normal feature of our new electronic world by putting a warm personal dialogue at the centre of news processing."[4]

From the way these shows are being marketed, you'd think the producers were veterans of encounter groups and had been personally counseled by Dale Carnegie.

"Roger Grimsby and Bill Beutel. Eyewitness News. People like us because we like us."

"You get the feeling that Roger and Bill like each other as much off camera as they do on camera."

(Four news guys smiling over black woman): "Bringing you the news every night is a pretty tough job. But Melba Tolliver helps make it a lot easier. We like her."[5]

Like like. Happy happy. Westinghouse once even offered me a cut-out picture of a grinning Mike Douglas saying, "Put on a happy face and celebrate Mike Douglas' 10th anniversary. If you'd like to see the world of happy, look through the eyes of Mike Douglas. First glue this ad to cardboard. Cut along dotted line. . . ."[6]

I don't think the approach will last. Its originators are right about one thing: we want more intimacy televised into our homes. But they've missed something more basic: that intimacy follows tragedy more often than joy.

That's the soap operas' secret, the reason that "As the World Turns" and "Edge of Night" are approaching their twentieth anniversaries with no sign of decline. A team of journalism students from New York University once monitored six New York TV stations for a full day in four-hour shifts. They were fascinated by the soaps, by the amount of agony their writers were able to pack into a short span of time. "There is not a single ray of optimism in these stories," said one monitor.

Three daytime soaps in one four-hour span offered two unhappy couples, two illicit affairs, two psychiatric cases, one murder trial, one character seriously ill with an unnamed disease, one amnesiac, and an acid freak-out. Another network had seven serials with four divorces, eighteen marital spats, three hospital cases, and twenty-two kisses.

The team figured that the soap operas, which are geared to lower- and lower-middle-class housewives, concentrate on the miseries of the affluent to make them feel better.[7]

Just concentrating on misery is enough. Winifred Wolfe, the head writer for "As the World Turns," believes that viewers identify with that show's characters because they have worse problems than their audience. "They love to see their serial friends suffer. Whenever things go badly for characters on our show, our ratings go way up."[8]

The soaps may be the only segment of TV—perhaps of life—offering anything close to emotional reality. The appeal of such a commodity must not be underrated.

Free-lance writer and former *Saturday Evening Post* editor Otto Friedrich once spent hundreds of hours over two years' time watching "Peyton Place" reruns. "In the course of more than a million feet of film," he later wrote, "I had let myself become involved in an extraordinary variety of problems—quarrels and rejoicings, seductions and marriages, suicides and murders. The mythical town on the seacoast of New Hampshire, in other words, had become more real to me than the Long Island town in which I actually live."[9]

One older woman who lives alone says she watches the soaps because, "Without these programs going on, I wonder if I would go on. People seem to forget me. . . . These people are my company. My real friends. I have it on because I feel people are talking to me."[10]

FAMILY BY SUBSCRIPTION

T George Harris showed up on television the other night, portraying a western-hatted farmer with a pitchfork, and hoping to get closer to his viewers. George grins with the memory, saying, "That's the way I'd like to be known."

A jovial teddy bear of a man, Harris still retains the broad smile and easy drawl of his rural Kentucky upbringing. The office where he hangs out is a cubbyhole strewn with books and magazines, highlighted by a beat-up typewriter with its mechanism exposed, and a chair permanently set to a lean-back position. When he's there, leaning back in that chair, George invariably wears the same outfit: Levis and a Sears work-shirt.

Harris likes to see himself as a country weekly editor, and doesn't mind saying so. "It's the only model I know," he explains. "A country editor sees readers and deals with them on several different levels." Brushing Pall Mall ashes off his shirt, George looks up and adds, "I want to do the same thing with our community of readers, but haven't quite found the key."

The problem is that his "community" of readers, over two million strong, are scattered all over this country and the world. George edits *Psychology Today*.

He's done more than most editors, answering letters by hand and referring often to "our community of learners." *Psychology Today* regularly surveys its reader's attitudes, hoping to generate both data and a sense of kinship. The magazine provides its readers a general store stocked with books, cassettes, films, records, and sundry merchandise. The Psychology Today Book Club is something they can join.

And it's worked. An outside survey of their subscribers found 60 percent agreeing that they were "typical *Psychology Today* readers."[11]

Roll it off your tongue. "Who are you?"

"A *Psychology Today* reader."

That doesn't sound bad.

Psychology Today is *the* success story of modern magazine publishing. As mass magazines have fallen one by one, this upstart journal out of Del Mar, California, has built up a circulation of more than 750,000 and turned a profit since late 1969.

More than that, it has ushered in an era of specialized magazines.

The failure of mass magazines like *Colliers*, *Look*, *Life*, and *The Saturday Evening Post* is due in large part to their inability to convey any sense of identity to their readers. It's true that the immediate cause of their demise was decline of advertising revenue, but the two are related. "The concepts of identity and reason for being are admittedly vague," writes *Institutional Investor* editor Chris Welles, "but on Madison Avenue and in offices of major advertisers they are considered to be just as important for a magazine as 'image' is for a politician." "The main [long-standing precept of the advertising world] is that a magazine lacking a specific, well-defined purpose is not really 'needed' by readers and therefore is a relatively poor advertising vehicle."[12]

So. "What sort of man reads *Playboy*?" we now want to know. And "Are you a *Cosmopolitan* girl?" When Helen Gurley Brown says, "*Cosmopolitan* is more trustworthy than a girlfriend" she's just being sensitive to trends.[13] When *Esquire* writes me that "you and *Esquire* are a good match for each other, partners, companions and friends of like mind," I'm flattered. Almost.[14]

Identity of course is the child of community. When we ask, "Who are you?" we imply, "To which group of people do you belong?" The smartest magazine publishers know this and are working overtime to provide a sense of family for their readers.

"That was one of the first things we discovered about *Playboy*," explains Hefner, ". . . that it wasn't just a magazine, that something else was going on, an unusual empathy, an unusual rapport with the readers. And that was what led us into all the other things—the *Playboy* products and *Playboy* clubs and so on. As our work uses less and less hours in the week, and as the jobs become more and more automated, you're not able to get that kind of personal identity out of your work anymore, and you've got to find other concepts of what it means to be a human being, a man or a woman. . . . I think *Playboy* is in a unique position to establish ways of spending your leisure time as well as identities and life styles that go along."[15] For years Hefner has been offering his *Playboy* community a heavy identity, complete with logo, jewelry, bathrobes, pipes, hangouts, and himself as philosopher-king.

The identity *Playboy* has so successfully generated cuts both ways. In Houston the reappointment of a liberal, George Carver, as Superintendent of Schools was almost upset when his postman's wife wrote to a local paper that Carver subscribed to *Playboy* and "A man who reads *Playboy* should not have a position in the schools."

(The mailman was transferred, Carver got his job back and showed up for work in a tie decorated with *Playboy* bunnies.)[16]

On the political left, magazines historically have been the most accurate indicator of where one stood. I, for example, could identify myself for years as an "I. F. Stone reader"—radical but nonideological. I'd get into raging fights with readers of *The National Guardian* or *Ramparts*.

James Michener says his F.B.I. file contains the following entry: "This man is nothing but a liberal who subscribed to *The Nation* and *The New Republic*. When interrogated as to what he meant by the word *liberal* he would reply, 'Someone who reads *The Nation* and *The New Republic*.' "[17]

When journalist Michael Fessier, Jr., wanted to make the point that not all residents of California's San Fernando valley are reactionaries, he said: "I know a man who subscribes to *Ramparts* and *The New York Review of Books* who lives in that apartment down Balboa there."[18]

As perhaps the single most widely read periodical among American intellectuals, *The New York Review of Books* is a very heavy source of identity. When a survey showed it the most read journal among humanities and social science department chairmen of American colleges and universities, *The New York Review* told its readers, calling them "a remarkable community of lovers of good writing and intellectual criticism."

They know.

The New York Review also says that 40 percent of their readers move every year (so they'd better get their zip code changes in early), obviously making the *Review*'s community one based far more on interest than place.[19]

A couple marooned in San Diego once tried to convert this interest community into a geographical one by advertising "Couple, 50's, *Review*-oriented, want others to rap with," giving a San Diego box number.

I wrote the couple to ask about their ad, and its responses. The wife replied with a very touching letter in which she said they had placed the ad "because we often feel so isolated and alone. We had only three replies; one from a medical doctor in Chicago who hoped to find people to correspond with his wife; one from a USIU (United States International University) professor and his wife on sabbatical in London and one from a single woman of our age here in San Diego, whom we have seen but found her to be too busy for us."

The couple had previously tried an ad in the *Los Angeles Free Press*, and got about thirty replies from single men "offering to enrich our sex lives."

"We remain alone. Not terribly, and not all the time. We keep trying. It must be easier for the Quakers, the Unitarians, the Catholics, etc. They've bought some kind of binding dogma, religious or not. Perhaps somewhere we'll find a 'community' where we fit—if we don't give up."

The problem may be that people relate to magazine communities precisely because they carry no obligation for face-to-face contact. One doesn't have to trade in anonymity or leave the privacy of one's home to relate to the fellow readers of a magazine.

Playboy tours failed, and their clubs—somewhat more anonymous—are only somewhat more successful. (Many are foundering.)[20]

It's this dilemma which confounds T George Harris. For all of his hand-penned letters, participatory surveys, and TV outreach, there's still an ingredient lacking, something which makes his *Psychology Today* community different from the one where George grew up in Kentucky.

"We smile at 'em," he grins, "but we never hug 'em."

Before he can become a true country-weekly editor, George knows he must convene the community—in the flesh. "Moving to TV makes me more like the country weekly guy who sees the audience," he explains, "but it still leaves me fraudulent on direct contact. There's no way we've ever talked with each other. They can't shoot back at me, ask me questions. Like 'Are you real?' among other things."

But Harris hasn't figured out a reason why *Psychology Today* readers might want actually to touch each other.

So, in the meantime, he scribbles letters to them in black felt pen, up to one hundred a week, blasting back at critics, and getting "Dear George" replies.

He goes on TV, in his work-shirt and farmer hat.

He runs pictures of himself in the magazine, and sometimes of members of his family.

And he builds profiles of his readers, discovering how often they make love, in what positions, and their feelings about death.

Sometimes George makes a hole in the papers cluttering his desk, and starts doodling on a pad the model for a new kind of community. Concentric circles. An outer circle for the TV watchers. An inner one for *Psychology Today* readers. Inside that, those who get the newsletter *Behavior Today*. An extended family of editors and contributors. The staff at home in the center.

But the circles haven't a heart, and George knows it. And he knows that until they get one, until they breathe on each other's faces, the community isn't.

LET YOUR FINGERS DO THE WALKING

The question George can't answer is whether members of his *Psychology Today* community want to breathe on each other's face, and have a country weekly editor, or whether its vitality isn't rooted in anonymity.

His readers, and the readers of most magazines, probably would like to be in touch with each other and be more of a community. They just don't want it to cost too much of their anonymity.

Physician's Management has an alternative approach, as do *Innovation* and *db*. What these magazines have done is invite readers to pick an article they would like to discuss with other readers, send in a $30 reservation for a specific time, then dial a given New York number at that time.

"Now," *Physician's Management* told its readers, "without leaving your home or office you can have this kind of valuable informal discussion" with a "unique telephone conference system that repeals geography."

Economist Milton Friedman recently participated in such a discussion, examining some fine points of the economic situation with colleagues from the comfort of his summer cabin. Later Friedman said he found the conference "more productive than if everyone had been able to get together in the same room."[21]

Friedman's parley, like those of the magazines, was sponsored by a New York firm called TeleSessions, which advertises that "the telephone seems to work some kind of magic. . . . for some reason we don't completely understand yet, there are fewer interruptions than face-to-face. . . . And we've found that people who were complete strangers end up after a few minutes talking as if they've known each other for years."

TeleSessions claims to have spent over $500,000 developing sophisticated conference-call hardware which permits their phone-discussion hosts to keep track of who's participating, do "instant replays," and talk privately with a reticent member who might need encouragement, or a noisy one who needs shutting up. Such meetings are easier to host than ones in the flesh, they say, because over the phone there is no distracting cross-talk. Distractions are virtually nil, and the problem of where to direct your eyes is eliminated.[22]

It's no coincidence that so many of the "phone phreaks"[23]—the electronic wizards who have cracked Bell Telephone's long distance dialing formulas and call each other all over the world—are blind. To them phone contact is little different from in-the-flesh. In some ways it's better, since the telephone frees them from imprisonment at home. "He saw the telephone as his link with the entire world," explains the mother of one blind phreak who said he had been fascinated with telephones since the age of three.[24]

The phone has provided a path into the world for the home-bound.

Information operators find it quite common to be called by lonely people simply wanting to talk. "If it's not too busy, the girls will usually try to cheer them up," says a supervisor in the Glendale, California, office. "When something happens like the earthquake, people seem to want reassurance. If they're alone, they'll call an operator just to hear another human voice, to share an experience."[25]

The employees of one commercial answering service in Atlanta keep a list of senior citizens who live alone. They make excuses to call up the people on their list, and do so every day. Then they put an "x" by that person's name to indicate they're still alive.[26]

There is also Dial-a-Prayer, which in San Diego County gets up to 18,000 calls a month among five services.

Sometimes they get letters.

Dear Dial-a-Prayer: I am bed-ridden. When I start feeling sorry for myself I dial the number and feel spiritually renewed. You have helped me think of others.

Dear Dial-a-Prayer: My mother has quit drinking now. I think it's partly because she called your number every day.

Dear Dial-a-Prayer: Here is $12. It isn't much to thank you for saving my life. One of your messages kept me from committing suicide.

Various local ministers take turns recording Dial-a-Prayer's two-minute messages. "I talk into the recording center just as I would talk to another person," says one Evangelical minister. "In fact, I can feel all the people I am talking to."[27]

But the real appeal of telephone friendship is the lack of actual contact, the privacy maintained.

It's as the little girl explained, about why she preferred Dial-a-Story-at-Bedtime to her dad's reading. "The stories are much better than what Dad tells. And the man doesn't get upset when I look as if I'm not listening."[28]

Anonymity has been the secret appeal of call-in talk shows which are enjoying a phenomenal success on radio. Flourishing since the early 60s, these shows are a magnet for the lonely and afflicted. Call-inners can reveal their innermost selves to listening members of the community, without giving up an iota's anonymity. One woman told a New York talk show audience that she likes to stick her fingers between her toes and smell them before taking a shower.[29]

In California the latest variation is shows for women only, who are invited to call in about various aspects of their sex lives: "Who turned you on to sex?" "Do you have more than one affair going on at this time?" "What's the most unusual place you ever made love?" (Sample answer: "In a bathtub filled with Cream of Wheat.")[30]

ON THE PHONE HE'S THE MOST STIMU-
LATING MAN IN THE WORLD.

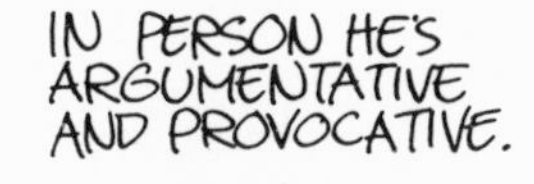

ON THE PHONE SHE'S LOVING AND SUPPORTIVE.

IN PERSON SHE'S COMPETITIVE AND EMASCULATING.

SO WE NEVER SEE EACH OTHER ANYMORE.

BUT WE TALK ON THE PHONE FOR HOURS.

THE SECRET OF TRUE LOVE IS:

NO PERSONAL CONTACT.

On some shows regular call-inners take nicknames: "Acid Annie," "the Old Philosopher," "Zig Zag," "Flushing Flora," "Apollo the Messenger of the Gods." After a while they feel part of a family.

Especially for lonely shut-ins—the aged, the handicapped, the infirm—such a community can be a godsend. Psychiatrist Edward Litin, formerly with the Mayo Clinic in Rochester, Minnesota, feels that "talk radio has definite value for the lonely. It comes into the home as a friendly voice in time of trouble. The listener is encouraged to face up to his problems, and he also learns that others are bearing even greater burdens. It takes his mind off himself and recharges his batteries, so to speak, in making him feel he is not alone but a valued member of his community."[31]

"Jealous" recently wrote to Abby that his wife had gone for another man—a talk-show host. Whenever he was on the air, she'd take the phone off the hook, and carry a transistor radio around during any necessary chores so as not to miss a word. She called her paramour "the man with the golden voice."

Abby's advice: "Let her enjoy the man with the golden voice. It's good insurance against competition who may appear in the flesh."[32]

"The basic principle of anonymity," says the head of a suicide call-in service in Johannesburg, South Africa, "has been the keynote of our success in appealing to the stress-ridden victims of our community."

Like most such ventures, this one discourages personal contact between counselor and counseled, in large part, explains the director, because of "the role that we can assume in relation to the caller's needs. He can imagine us as he would like us to be. We can for a short time give him the relationship he lacks."[33]

Counseling over the phone began as an emergency service to would-be suicides. But people who were just lonely kept jamming the lines, pretending they were about to kill themselves just to get someone who would listen. The trend today is toward more general counseling services, ones which don't require an "emergency."

"We saw Hotlines as a friend," says a founder of the original such service in Los Angeles. "A friend with whom people could relate, and talk, and have someone to listen who would be interested in them."

"We've discovered," adds a Hotline psychologist, "that adolescents will use the emergency phone service to discuss their personal problems in detail—mainly because of the anonymity it allows and because it is available to them immediately when a crisis occurs."[34]

This youth-oriented service began in Los Angeles in 1968. The idea's time had come, and today there are hundreds of hotlines the country around. In 1970 the First International Hotline Conference attracted one hundred participants. The next year, four hundred showed up.

Some interesting data came out of the latter conference. Hotliners said most of their calls came not from desperate people, just lonely ones. In Los Angeles, a city wired with over forty telephone counseling services, "regulars" get the number of many hotlines, and call each one daily. A common "problem" among hotlines nationally is the callers who learn the name, or just the voice, of one counselor and then will talk only with that person. Some people at the conference found this perfectly natural and no problem. Others thought phone counselors shouldn't "play favorites."

More agreement was found on the universal problem of volunteers who prefer the sound of telephoned voices over the phone to those of fellow volunteers. "I believe there is a fairly decent amount of good listening on the phone," said Ken Beitler of Youth Emergency Service in Minneapolis. "Where we don't listen is to each other. I think the first area where we fail is among the staff of our services. You have a lot of phone volunteers and they are all supposed to be good listeners, so why don't they listen to each other?"

Psychologist Carl Rogers, there as a resource person, pointed out that it's often easier to listen closely for a few minutes to unfamiliar voices. "It's when we are emotionally involved," he explained, "that we can't listen."

A volunteer concurred. "Sometimes it's easier to talk to someone you've never met or you don't know. I feel as though there has to be some one person I can talk to, and sometimes the people around me I can't trust, or I don't feel comfortable with."

One hotline staffer found his own solution to this problem. He said he woke up depressed one morning, very out of sorts, and didn't know where to turn. "Now, if I was someone else, I'd call the Hotline," he thought. Then it occurred to him: Why not? He called his hotline, got a very sympathetic ear for a few minutes, and felt much better. He said it made his day.[35]

The Center for Policy Research in New York has been comparing meetings over the phone with live ones. Like TeleSessions they find the electronic kind going more smoothly, with participants sticking to the topic, and butting in on each other less. The Center is interested in what they call "mass participatory technology." To investigate this they have set up a project called MINERVA, Multiple Input Network for Evaluating Reactions, Votes, and Attitudes.

With the emphasis on telephones for now, what MINERVA is working on is means to plug us all in so that we can debate the issues of the day without having to leave the privacy of our homes. "When the system is fully developed," says one of their documents, "every person who owns a radio or a television set and has access to a telephone will be able to follow, react, and participate in discussion and resolution of public affairs. Thus it would provide an electronic equivalent to town hall meetings, allowing dispersed groups to act as if they were all in one central gathering place."[36]

The technology to do this is available right now, not just over the phone but over TV as well. Pilot two-way cable television systems are being tested in different parts of the country. F.C.C. rules require that all new installations of cable include a two-way capacity. Ten percent of the nation's homes are already hooked up to cable, and that figure is expected to at least triple within two decades.[37]

Consider the things which could be done via two-way television: go to the library, shop from catalogues, deposit money in the bank, read a paper, have a doctor look down your throat, talk things over with a counselor, worship, work, study, watch a blue movie. All in the privacy of your home.

Cable TV visionaries keep pointing out the new medium's potential for enriching community life. The Alternate Media people at New York University talk of combining cable flexibility with that of portable cameras for "the freedom to go out of the studio and get into the neighborhood." Community Cablevision's manager in Los Angeles calls cable "another communication system in your home that can be used in many ways to stimulate and enrich neighborhood life."[38]

The unanswered question is whether television viewers want their neighborhood life stimulated. I doubt that they do. I think most of us would rather get close to Walter Cronkite than the guy next door. Cronkite is less threatening.

Merv Griffin dreamed the other night that he should put all of his money into furniture. "I dreamed that in the future everything will be centered in the home," he explained. "No one will go out. Restaurants like '21' will deliver to the home. Housewives will do their shopping from a supermarket on television. People will show movies in the home. Everyone will have their own private communication center."[39]

Through television, cable television especially, the process which began when we closed in our front porches will be completed. We finally will achieve privacy in full, with community beamed into our homes, delivered by mail or phone.

Marshall McLuhan and others say not to worry, that soon

we'll be closer electronically than ever before. But I do worry. It's just not the same. People on TV look similar, but they're another species entirely from those I can reach out and touch.

Bill Moyers, my boss while I was at *Newsday*, later hosted a weekly show on educational television. But I don't think it's the same man. I think it's really Ted Sorensen made up, or someone from General Casting. The Bill Moyers I knew was warm and loose and good-humored. The guy on TV is kind of stiff, and doesn't have much opportunity for humor.

TV distorts. There's no way around it.

Politicians are daily faced with this truth and forced to become actors. Joe McGinnis documented with painful detail in *The Selling of a President 1968* the ways Richard Nixon can work at looking warm and intimate on television.[40] Marshall McLuhan says Nixon succeeded to a large extent, that the "hot" gladiator of 1960's TV debates had become a "cool" media performer by 1968. McLuhan says that for politicians TV produces a kind of mirror image: hot people come across cool; cold people look warm.[41] "To appear natural on television," says Joe McGinnis, "it is necessary to be, to some extent, a performer. Thus: unnatural."[42]

That's why I'm not worried about Bill Moyers. I figure the day he starts coming across the tube warm and loose is the day he'll be cooling off and tightening up in person.

But what am I to make of people on TV whom I don't know? How can I feel the fiber of a man when all my human signals don't work in this medium?

I have this problem now with Dick Cavett. A few weeks after I joined his community, Cavett began to bug me. He kept using the same mannerisms over and over. He was a little too cute, too mock-humble. He has an irritating habit of playing with his shoe whenever he's nervous.

I wanted to tell him all this and work things out, not let our friendship founder on misunderstanding. But I never got the chance.

So I read up on him a bit. Which only made it worse. ". . . my mind is always on what I'm going to do next," Cavett said in one interview, confirming my suspicion. ". . . when guests touch me," he said elsewhere, "I figure they're trying to bug me, they're just trying to bug me. They're trying to see if I'm buggable."

Then I read this anecdote about Cavett: "Once, one of his more raucous lady guests, overcome by mothering instincts, bolted to the desk to smother her host in hugs and kisses. It took Cavett several commercials to reclaim his cool."

Elsewhere, I read his version: "On occasion I'll play a situation for discomfort. When Kay Stevens bolted to the desk and on the air began to smother me with kisses, I looked piqued but rather enjoyed it."[43]

What can I make of that?

And if the people aren't real, then what of the communities I enjoy on television?

An interviewer once asked Mike Douglas what would happen if guests just chatted on his talk show as if they were together in a living room. "The sound of sets being turned off across the country," he answered, "would break your eardrums."[44]

One thing television does give me is friends in common with people I meet the country around. What Johnny Carson had to say last night, and Howard Cosell's latest outrage are instant conversation topics with almost anyone I run into. This is helpful, because so far it's not possible to live completely within the privacy of one's home, and sometimes, many times, we have to move from one home to the next. The moves can be traumatic and any known point of reference in a strange setting is welcome, if only a televised friend.

Televised celebrities of the national community are just one among many ways we're making the country familiar ground for all of us, another means to reduce the trauma of moving and make new environments almost as unthreatening as the ones we left. By so doing we're changing the face of this country to make it safe and familiar, just like the old home towns some of us had and all of us miss.

4.

The National Home Town

When we lived on Long Island, 7/11 was the only store close by —our neighborhood grocery. It was also a hangout for local kids, in this purely residential area. When you went in to buy something, you'd have to plow through compacted youth, like police breaking up a demonstration.

Shortly after arriving in San Diego, we checked out the stores close by. The nearest one was 7/11. On their parking lot, kids were hanging around outside, with identical banana-seat bikes. Inside, the store was just as I remembered it: refrigerated goods in the rear, magazines up front, Slurpee machine by the cash register. All of this made me feel good, secure. There was a familiar place in this strange setting.

It seemed like a fresh insight—that I felt right at home at my local 7/11, almost as if we'd never left. Then I started reading up on franchisers and found that's exactly what they want me to feel.

"Franchising caters to a highly mobile customer public," explains Dr. Charles Vaughn, Director of Boston College's Center for the Study of Franchise Distribution. "It caters to a United States public which is constantly on the move. . . . The mobile customer wants some assurance as he moves from a known to an unknown environment—some assurance that he will get the same quality of product he bought in his home environment, the same or similar quality of service. . . . Obviously, this similarity . . . he identifies readily by a trademark, a brand name and other symbols such as the architecture of the franchisor's buildings. These symbols—franchisor's trademark, the franchisor's brand name, his other symbols—are the franchisor's most priceless possession."[1]

7/11 is among the most successful operations doing this. The distinctive red-and-green sign of this convenience grocery grabs your attention in thirty-six states and the District of Columbia. Though the stores themselves vary somewhat in design, the sign's the same wherever you go. That and the Slurpee machines.

" 'Slurpee' sort of ties all the stores together,' explains A. T. "Red" Robbins, Training Director of 7/11's Western Division. "It's a copyrighted name, advertised all over."

"Slurpee," of course is 7/11's own frozen carbonated slush. It has become a household word in less than a decade of existence.

"How many of you have slurped?" is one of the first questions Red Robbins asks new franchisees as their one-week training session begins. Robbins, sandy-haired and with a ready grin, looks like a classic Irish bartender. The day I was there, only four hands went up, out of fourteen in the class.

"How many of you know how to slurp?" is the next question. This time no hands were raised. "Well there's a technique to it, always start from the top and work down. You'll miss sometimes that way, but how can you make a slurping noise if you don't miss now and then? That's the secret: always start from the top."

The members of this class were a mixed lot: a young couple with a college-town franchise; a former barber there with his wife and two teenaged children; a retired Korean Air Force officer; an ex-bartender. All were gambling $5,000 down (including $1,000 for training) that they'd like being grocers of the future.

Lots of what the trainees were told was nuts-and-bolts: i.e., kids do 20-30 percent of your business, so treat 'em right. More was intangible: "You people have a personality," grinned Red Robbins, "or I hope you do, or can develop it. A lot of people shop our stores because they like the people running the store. We encourage our people to shop the competition. IGA, Mom & Pop, other 7/11s. If the guy running it has a small smile, you're in business. If it's a big one, you'll have to make yours just a bit bigger."

Adjacent to their classroom was a room with several mocked-up 7/11 counters. The trainees were advised to make lots of use of them. "Any time you have the opportunity, slip in and play the role. One be clerk, the other customer. Thank the customer. Smile. Make change. Invite him to come back to the store. Play the role until it's second nature to say, 'Hi. How are you?' "

A sign next to one of the cash registers advised, "Be sure to call your Slurpee flavors by name, i.e., Red-Eye, Sticky-Icky, Fulla Bulla."

SOMEONE YOU KNOW, WHEREVER YOU GO

The less we live in towns, or any one place at all, the more we seem to crave a small town's trusted stores and faces. Without staying anywhere long enough to get familiar with the grocer, or known by a barber, we still would like to know who we're dealing with—hopefully, in advance. The franchisers have done an especially good job of telling us. They've replicated nationally the friendly little places we once knew locally. Now, when you wrench yourself away from an old place to settle in a new, many stores remain the same; familiar faces await you, and merchandise already known. Your credit card is good. Trust.

The rise of 7/11, our national Mom & Pop grocery, has been concurrent with that of the automobile. Since its inception as an ice-store and grocery in Dallas almost a half century ago, 7/11 has become the nation's leading "convenience" chain. The parent Southland Corporation owns 60 percent of the 7/11 stores, and franchises 40 percent. These stores make average sales of under a dollar to customers who park only a few feet away.

Southland maintains a rigid uniformity of plant, product, and style in 7/11's across the country. They build their own buildings, produce many of the products sold within, and require all franchisees to begin with their training course, then submit to ongoing scrutiny from Dallas. The only part of 7/11's appearance which the proprietor can alter is the landscaping.[2]

Maintaining such consistency of product is considered basic to success with the franchising industry.

"What is the franchiser selling?" asks William Babcock, an architect of franchise stores. "He's not selling a hamburger. He's selling a consistent quality level. That means sameness. The more sameness you're selling somebody, the more secure he will feel. The franchisers aren't foolish. They know that."[3]

Thus, McDonald's gives you ¼ ounce of onions on your 1.6-ounce burger across the land. The bun on which it sits is exactly 4¼ inches in diameter. A pickle slice is placed in the same spot on that bun in Portland, Maine, and Portland, Oregon.

"In an age when so many Americans are on the move," explains McDonald's president, Fred Turner, "one of our main assets is our consistency and uniformity. It's very important that a man who's used to eating at a McDonald's in Hempstead, Long Island, know he can get the same food and service when he walks into one in Albuquerque or Omaha."[4]

McDonald's allows virtually no variations for regional taste. They do leave off the mustard on Long Island, and put less ketchup on in Memphis, as a concession to the local palate. But basically, one Big Mac is like another, the country around.

This concept isn't new to franchising, building trust through uniformity for people on the move. That's something the Catholic Church has known for centuries. Until very recently they kept buildings and liturgy enough alike the world around that wandering Catholics could go to church anywhere and feel right at home.

Brand name and chain stores are based on the same wisdom. One capitalist I know calls brand-name goods "the original extended family." Charles Vaughn says they're like an introduction to any new community.[5]

Though the insight that sameness builds trust is an old one, what's new is simply that as more of us are moving longer distances more often, an increasing amount of the landscape is homogenizing to reduce trauma. Franchises play a big role in that process, giving us familiar stores the country around. Television helps by providing common friends and a national idiom. ("Sorry 'bout that." "Try it, you'll like it.") Wire services allow us to read the same news in New York and Pine Bluff. As the differences between regions decline, America itself becomes one big, familiar, dependable environment, a nation where we can feel at home on the move, as we once did staying put in small towns and cities.

Mobility has a built-in paradox. We move on in search of change. But the more we move, the more identical things become in every region. And the process feeds itself. The more we move the more same things become. The more same things become, the easier it is to move.

We fret about this growing sameness for a variety of cultural and esthetic reasons, but without considering the comfort uniformity provides for a people constantly on the move. As Lewis Mumford points out, the common grid pattern of our towns and cities has historically made strangers as much at home as veterans.[6]

Thus franchising is only part of an honored American tradition, with a few novel twists. Selling franchises has proved a rapid way to capitalize outlets and disperse them around the country, since purchasers put up most of the money. By this method franchises spread more quickly in years than the chains could in decades before.

In addition, since they grew up after World War II right along with the auto and freeway explosion, franchises have housed themselves in very visible buildings which have the advantage of being easily seen from a speeding car. When everything else is a blur through the windshield, Holiday Inn's green, red, and yellow logo is a comforting point of stability. Their 1,500 buildings may seem distinct, but that's an optical delusion. There's really only one Holiday Inn, just as there's only one 7/11, one McDonald's, and a single Colonel Harlan Sanders.[7]

A nineteen-year-old college student I know once described to me his fear as a child the night his family was traveling and couldn't find a room available at the Holiday Inn. They ended up at an unfamiliar hotel, and he trembled the whole night.

Holiday Inn has pushed uniformity of plant and product to new plateaus through a complex of subsidiaries which supply most needs of their motels around the world, down to the bologna in their restaurants.

One Holiday Inn patron, who is blind, says that to him the Inn represents freedom. Since the rooms are arranged exactly the same across the country, each one is familiar territory.[8]

And it's not just the decor. After hearing that Holiday Inn offered the only courteous, satisfactory accommodations in the United States, Headmaster Serge Perrot of the Technical Hotel School of Paris came to the Inn's headquarters in Memphis for his own inspection. Perrot later wrote an accolade, saying that the Holiday Inn represented a return to humanism in American hotel-keeping based on "a visible charm; a smile, a gesture here and there . . . a thousand little things that made me feel I was in a different world."

He explained to his French audience: "The working environment developed in Memphis is instituted all over the world (the type of work performed is the same from one Inn to the next . . . as are a number of other things: type of room, decor, furniture and equipment and standardized furnishings . . .). The result is a 'Holiday Inn style' or 'atmosphere' to which the employees can easily relate. It is easy for employees to 'open up' and feel confident in the Holiday Inn atmosphere which is their own."[9]

Inn founder Kemmons Wilson (called one of the twentieth century's one thousand most significant figures by London's *Sunday Times*) is acutely aware of his role in the country's community. Wilson even looks beyond our borders, envisioning Holiday Inns as a force for peace and understanding now that "the whole world has become our neighborhood."[10]

So far, the Inn has proved remarkably successful at becoming the national town's most popular place to meet.

Many of the preconvention caucuses of the Democratic Party took place in Holiday Inns. Driving through Jackson, Tennessee, I heard a local politician say that that was where he would announce his candidacy for something or other.

It was in Room 520 of a Milwaukee Holiday Inn that Ed Muskie met with advisers after losing the Wisconsin primary, to begin planning his exit from the Presidential race. Muskie made his concession speech to the nation standing behind an Inn podium.[11]

George Wallace also had his Wisconsin headquarters in a Holiday Inn, and some people think they saw Arthur Bremer stalking Alabama's governor in his Milwaukee motel's corridors only days before their rendezvous in Maryland. Just months later George McGovern watched himself lose the Presidency in a South Dakota Holiday Inn, the one in Sioux Falls.[12]

Many national franchises without local headquarters depend on the Inn as their community center. That's true of the Reading Dynamics Institute, it's true of Silva Mind Control ("Meet some new people," reads their advertisement for an introductory lecture at the Inn[13]), and it's true of Weight Watchers.

Weight Watchers is the astoundingly successful self-help program for the future formerly fat. They sponsor several thousand meetings weekly, supervised by 101 franchises in forty-nine states, Puerto Rico, and eight foreign countries. Like other successful franchises, Weight Watchers has a rigidly standard format. All franchisees must be former Weight Watchers. Their training is the same. Weight Watchers meetings follow the same basic agenda from New York to San Diego: weigh-in, gain and loss report for members, lecture and discussion. Once a Weight Watcher has paid the $4 registration fee and the $2 weekly dues he or she is welcome at Weight Watchers meetings anywhere in the country. Thus if you're too heavy and belong to Weight Watchers, you can have not only the familiar golden arches of

McDonald's and 7/11's smiling clerk waiting to greet you, but also a club, an instant community whose next meeting is open to you—complete with familiar format and instant friends.[14]

The coming field generally, says *Franchising Today*, is "The Business of Caring." "Business," they explain, "and in some cases government acting through business, is supplanting the family as a reservoir of care. In the 'good old days' the children and the elderly or the infirm were an integral part of the home scene. But with America's families on the move about once every five years, an increasing number of working mothers and a general loosening of family ties, a demand for care services from outside the home has been steadily built."[15]

The magazine advises its readers to anticipate a bonanza in day care, nursing homes, health care, and companionship.

So far, the prediction has been premature. A variety of firms lost their shirts trying to franchise nursing homes. Even more companies have taken a flyer on day care.

Which doesn't mean that franchised care won't eventually catch on—particularly when government subsidies step up. If mobile families are comforted by the same corner grocery and hamburgers wherever they move, think how much more reassuring it will be to transfer elderly parents to the same nursing home, and minimize a preschooler's confusion by placing him/her in a day-care center where the child already knows which cabinet holds the blocks.

In Oakland the Institute of Human Abilities is franchising communes and human growth. They buy up dilapidated houses in the Bay Area, redub them "More Houses," then charge the young and lonely $200 a month to live there and fix up the places. For their money and effort, residents get more than just a place to live. They also get a hero, Victor Baranco, the "heavy" founder/philosopher-king of the Institute; a medallion with the More symbol; a variety of courses in human growth; *Aquarius* magazine, and sixteen More Houses to be welcome at.

The More Houses people know what they're up to. "We *are* like Colonel Sanders," admits Institute president and *Aquarius* editor Ken Brown, fifty-one. "We can reproduce our thing anywhere. The product is words. And the attraction is love."

A Baranco assistant calls More "like a discount house of growth organizations.

"We're like a little town on a trading route, with lots of people coming through. We're like a soap opera, you know, like 'As the World Turns.' "

Adds Brown: "This is a religious institution, really. It's a business, true, but the Catholic Church is too. It's the same hustle in a different package. But we fit into the tenor of the times what with the communes and all."[16]

The counter-culture generally has built up a rather impressive network of familiarity within the national small town. Ranging from informal places to crash, thorough friendly homes listed in guidebooks, communes and spiritual centers—the new nomads needn't feel much stress on the road.

"For the nomad," says one, "the range is communal, shared among everyone: networks of expanded kinship encompass the wanderers to make them always near a known place."[17]

Ashrams serve such a function for today's Siddarthas. Hundreds of spiritual centers dot the country in every major city and many minor ones. Devotees can be passed from ashram to ashram, knowing that a roof always awaits them as well as a loving family who eat their kind of food, wear their kind of dress, sing similar music, chant the same chants, and speak the same language.

The head of one such sect says he achieved enlightenment in 1964 while standing in an A & W root-beer stand.[18]

LAUNDRO-MATING

Laundromats have become an excellent place to meet other citizens of the national home town, straight and hip alike.

Bill and Anne Stillwell recently returned from a trip to Alaska and reported meeting many of the people they passed on the road at the White Horse laundromat.

Usually unguarded, often open all night, laundromats have become a major American hangout. There's something about laundromats which makes them much safer, less threatening space than other public mixing points. It's just hard to seem dangerous with a box of Tide in your hands.

Jan McClain, a student at the California Institute of the Arts spent a few days observing one laundromat in Tujunga, outside Los Angeles. Different types of crowds hung around there at different times. Kids after school would fill up their squirt guns at the bathroom sink, or start up a machine and throw suds at each other. On weekends, Friday night especially, bikers would hang around with their girl friends. Older teenage girls who had moved away from home would show up on Sundays, carrying a small load of wash and looking around for old friends. During the week, groups of women would come in together, put in their wash, then sit down to talk.[19]

"Sometimes I will talk to a stranger who wants to talk," explains one woman sitting in a Los Angeles laundromat, "not about detergents but about their children and the things they have done or not done. Maybe it is easier for people to talk things over with a stranger."[20]

Laundromats were born out of World War II's soap and washing-machine shortage. As more and more people began moving after the war, and didn't want to lug along washing machines, laundromats boomed. Sixteen hundred were reported in seven hundred towns and cities in the mid-40s, twenty-four thousand by 1961, and forty thousand by 1970.

"The social function is what really made laundromats a success," says Donald Muhich, community psychiatrist. "They have become places where people go to meet other people . . . places where people can bring and try to solve significant problems that each is trying to deal with."[21]

The Muhichs' washing machine broke down just before they left Minnesota for Los Angeles, and rather than buy a new one, he took their wash to the laundromat for several months. There the psychiatrist grew intrigued with how much more groups of women seemed to get from their visit than clean clothes.

"SURE, WE GOT A WASHER AT HOME.
BUT MY MOM CAN'T *TALK* WITH IT."

Courtesy Publishers-Hall Syndicate.

"You'd see somebody tentatively bring out an idea," says Muhich, "just kind of bounce it off the table. They'd talk about housekeeping stuff but also about how their kids were doing; talk about their husbands; talk about a whole variety of life problems. Things like, 'My husband, you know, he's chasing around. I don't think he's out with the boys like he used to be.' Then someone else would pick up with, 'Well, what are you gonna do about it?' Then they'd go into this whole group interaction. It's ongoing leaderless group therapy."

In this sense, as a place to gather and share, laundromats differ only in form from the streams running by old home towns where washers used to congregate. But laundromats have many more purposes to serve in the national home town. After the Holiday Inn, they may be our leading community center.

A trial was once held in the Booneville, Kentucky, laundromat.

One of Nader's Raiders recently spent an entire Saturday afternoon interviewing House Majority Leader Thomas O'Neill while helping him wash clothes in a Washington laundromat.[22]

Some laundromats are picking up on their potential as community space, and have installed lounge chairs, jukeboxes, Coke machines, even a fireplace. Margo, the *Chicago Daily News*'s "now" columnist wrote her inaugural piece on "laundro-mating." She called it much preferable to singles' bars.

There are rules for laundro-mating. Weekends are prime time, but only during the day. (Doing your wash on a Saturday evening would be humiliating.) People inside have far more permission to talk with each other than if they were on the street.

"This setup is more subtle than the bars," says one laundro-freak. "The conversation's better. You don't get the typical bull, and nobody's three sheets to the wind."

In her survey of laundromat singles, Margo found some freely admitting they hope to meet people within, others stoutly denying any such intent.

One young lady, asked if she ever dated other patrons, replied, "*Dates*? I'm here to do my laundry."

"And so she was," wrote Margo, ". . . in two pairs of eyelashes, silver-blue eyeshadow, a little brush-on, and a cashmere slack outfit."[23]

TRUST

The reason laundromats have adopted such a successful social role is trust. Self-service laundries are one of the few public places where people usually come for a respectable reason—even a revealing one. A group of people sharing their dirty underwear have revealed a little something to each other, have built a trust.

Trust is what all these comfort points are about—the laundromats, the ashrams, the communes, the franchises. No matter how they clothe it or what they call it, the uniform gathering places—franchises in particular—are basically marketing trust. When we lived on a smaller scale, we would learn which merchants were trustworthy. Living now throughout the country, we can only grope at symbols, and consistency is the best substitute for intimate knowledge.

As one customer says about McDonald's: "You know ahead of time what the stuff will be like. It's always warm and always has the same good taste. You begin to develop a certain trust in it."[24]

Or, as the man says on the radio "You know, it's kinda fun pulling into a strange town, but its never any fun feeling like a stranger. So I carry a special address book. It's got the name of four hundred fifty friends in it: TraveLodge Motels. There's four hundred fifty TraveLodge Motels and I've only been in half of 'em. But let me tell you, I trust 'em all."[25]

I think they know something, the franchisers. That there's a basic problem about trust in the national home town. When you're on the move, who can you trust?

My newspaper says to "Trust Abby."[26]

A recent nationwide poll showed Walter Cronkite the most trusted man in America, trusted by 73% of those polled.[27]

When I think about who I trust, the first things which come to mind are: Pepperidge Farm, *Consumer Reports,* Campbell's soups, Coleman camping equipment, L. L. Bean's, and Levis. Them I really trust. We've built up a relationship over several years' time.

But what people?

It's not that I can't trust people. It's just that it's hard to know who's trustworthy when you move around so often.

UNIFORMS

The last hitchhiker we picked up was a longhair with a guitar, outside Yuma, Arizona. He stumbled into the car, saying, "Far out. It sure is far out to get picked up by a brother and sister," and gave us a quick thumb-lock.

"Hey, whatcha doin' man," he said as we started up, "just truckin' around?"

"That's right," we said, "just truckin'."

"Right on," he said, "just keep on truckin'."

Then he asked if we'd like to smoke a little grass with him. No, we said, thanks, but no. The hitchhiker began to get uncomfortable about this time, especially after his repeated talk of "our people" and "our press" (*Rolling Stone*) and so on didn't get much response. Then the hitcher started telling us about a commune in Arkansas which was "really full of loving people, man. They treat everybody just like a brother."

He said we ought to go visit it.

The problem was that we were giving out double messages: wearing the poor guy's uniform—Levis, work-shirts, long hair, my beard—but not acting like kin. That sort of thing can be very perplexing, because when you're on the move a lot within the national home town, outer symbols are terribly important for knowing who's a brother.

This insight isn't unique to the new nomads. The men of Sudan's wandering Nuers knock out a front tooth. Then, when meeting in their travels, all they need do is smile to find out who's a fellow Nuer.[28]

We're just rediscovering that insight in the national home town, the importance of cues, of uniforms, in knowing who you can trust.

Whenever doing a "kid" story for *Newsday*, I would arrange my uniform with great care. The long hair and beard were a great help, bell-bottoms essential. A colorful vest helped.

Once a group of young drug users had agreed to talk with me, but warned a mutual friend that they were mostly going to "goof." As it turned out, the kids and I had a great hour's rap, without apparent deception on their part. As I was leaving, I told them of hearing that they intended to goof on me. The young faces looked startled, and finally one piped up: "But that was when we expected some guy in a suit and tie."

Later I shared a shopping-center bench on Long Island with a fifteen-year-old girl who explained to me in great detail the variety of passing youth.

"See that guy," she said. "He's basically a greaser. You can tell by his hair. But he's trying to go hip with that headband."

"And that girl. She's trying to look poor-hip, but really she's into money."

How did she know?

"You can tell by her Harwyn shoes. They cost."

She examined a sweet-looking young thing across the way with two Levi-ed guys in Cuban Fence Climber boots. "Now you see, she's probably just a regular chick and she came here and those guys showed some interest in her. No . . . wait! She's a greaser." The verdict was final. "You can tell by the way she's wearing her eye shadow."

A girl passed with long, straight hair, jeans, a poncho, and fringed moccasins.

"Now here's a girl who thinks she's a hippie, because of the moccasins. Moccasins went out about a year and a half ago and she's still wearing them."

Why, did she suppose?

"I don't know. Maybe she likes them. Yes, that could be the reason."

STICKING TOGETHER

With all the time we spend in cars, bumper stickers have become a kind of uniform, a means for spotting kin on the road.

Take WE DROVE THE ALASKA HIGHWAY. Two people pass with that, wave, and feel warm toward each other for an instant. Part of the same crowd. A common shared hardship.

Community.

When we first moved onto our block in San Diego, I didn't know what to make of the people already there. Katy Miller next door flew an American flag and that seemed a little ominous. Joyce across the street had an English accent.

The biggest puzzle was figuring out who the scores of people were in the apartment house across the street. It's built Spanish-style, around a courtyard, and the apartments themselves are hidden back there. Residents park their cars in a lot out front. So mostly what I got to know was their cars, and the bumper stickers.

My favorite was LET PEACE IN THE WORLD BEGIN WITH ME on an Oldsmobile across the street. That seemed close to my thinking, so I went out of my way to meet the car's owner. She turned out to be a middle-aged lady into good things like nudity, encounter groups, and mysticism.

But in the same apartment building there was a couple with AMERICA: LOVE IT OR LEAVE IT and two other patriotic slogans papering their bumper. Them I pretty much avoided. Now they've moved, and the only way we and others on the block remember them is "That couple with all the right-wing stickers."

JUST MARRIED, of course, was the first, and for a long time the only, bumper sticker around. Beginning with Coolidge in 1924, metal bolt-on attachments advertised political candidates. The metal became wired-on cardboard during World War II's shortages.

It wasn't until after the war that Aldine Printing Company in Los Angeles adapted paste-on paper stickers from the adhesive product used to mark airplane fuselages. Car production was just beginning to boom, and—like franchises and laundromats—bumper stickers tagged along.

Aldine's composing chief, Johnny Madina, has worked on their bumper stickers for almost three decades. In that time he's seen the product grow more artistic (sometimes being signed by a designer), colorful, and varied in size to fit foreign bumpers. And—since Vietnam—slogans have dominated stickers. "First it was just Vietnam," says the fifty-five-year-old Madina, "both sides. Then we got orders for twenty or thirty different slogans about guns. Then the dope scene came in and we got all the dope ones. Anything in the news."

Days after Daniel Ellsberg confessed leaking the Pentagon papers, Aldine got orders for:

SUPPORT ELLSBERG, NOT CALLEY

ELLSBERG'S OK

VOTE NO ON ELLSBERG

"People come in here with clippings right out of the paper and ask us to write humper banners for them," says Mrs. Dale Borgos, an administrative assistant at Aldine. "Though we won't actually write slogans, we do give advice: keep it short—you've got only three seconds to read a bumper banner—and keep in mind whom you're trying to reach."

"There was one lady who came in with a slogan several lines long," adds Johnny Madina. "I tried and tried to persuade her to shorten it so the letters would be bigger. But she wouldn't budge." He pulls out the sticker:

I BELIEVE IN THE PARAMOUNT
SANCTITY OF INTELLIGENT LIFE,
AND IN THE LESSER SANCTITY
OF BARELY APPERCEPTIVE LIFE,
AND IN THE NONSANCTITY OF
NONAPPERCEPTIVE LIFE: REGARDLESS
OF RACE, SPECIES OR PHYLUM

Abolish All Abortion Laws

Its' estimated that a bumper sticker on the average urban car will be seen by up to five thousand other drivers daily. There aren't many other forums which can claim such exposure at anywhere near the price. As a result, bumpers are being forced to carry a heavy load, and the stickers on them must play different roles. Messages on the bulletin board. Commercials. Rolling graffiti. Commentary on the issues. Conversation.

HAVE A NICE DAY

POW's NEVER HAVE A NICE DAY

In the old home town, we'd talk as we walked. By talking, even by just observing each other slowly sauntering by, we'd come to know each other. But living in cars as we do today, communication is far more difficult. We still want to talk, to reach out, to know each other and identify ourselves even as we rush by, so we turn to bumper stickers. No matter how many new roles they're forced to play, the main purpose bumper stickers serve is simply IDENTITY. There's just no better way for a bleary-eyed commuter to say, "Hey, that's not your ordinary shlepp you see basting in sweat behind the wheel there, that's: [choose one]

a patriot
dissenter
cynic
Jesus Freak
doper
a, a, a . . . .

The problem with bumper stickers, as with all outer symbols of identity in the national home town, is that they can be misleading. Identity just isn't pasted on so easily, and the trust bumper stickers build may be based on false premises.

Take CAUTION, DRINKING FLUORIDATED WATER MAY BE HAZARDOUS TO YOUR HEALTH

That's available to John Birchers at their local American Opinion Bookstore. Opposition to fluoridation for years has been a right-wing obsession, and putting such a sticker on your bumper put you right in there with General Jack D. Ripper, worrying about Commies tampering with your precious bodily fluids.

But when a group of fifteen California policemen[29] were recently asked to write down their reaction to the antifluoridation message, and predict who would be driving a car with such a sticker, their responses included:

health nut, vegetable person, a hippie
misinformed nut
right on
ecologist worrier
health warning
cynical about advertisements
middle-aged or older person
student

The policemen were part of a training institute for community-relations specialists which was held recently at San Diego State University. I showed them a series of bumper stickers, thinking to discover prejudice against drivers in cars with particular stickers. What I actually uncovered was utter confusion about the meaning of the stickers themselves.

HE'S YOUR *UNCLE,* NOT YOUR *DAD*, for example, was distributed in 1970 by the Republicans. It's in red, white, and blue and has a big picture of Uncle Sam. One cop thought such a sticker would be on the car of a "war protestor," and added, "don't let him dictate to you." Another wrote, "good sticker, makes good point, get your ass out and get a job." Although one policeman thought it identified a "right-winger," another said, "big deal, driver young, long hair." One honest cop "never did understand that one."

ANOTHER AMERICAN FOR PEACE is somewhat confusing because it's also done in red, white, and blue. One policeman thought it identified a "youthful liberal," another predicted "Bircher type person." Or "parent of serviceman."

Other stickers and responses to them included:

PEACE (Picture of Pooh Bear and Piglet)

"Smokey the Bear"
liberal
creep
draft dodger or girl friend—woman or long hair
beautiful lover of nature

PEACE OF CHRIST (put out by a Catholic organization)

nut, religious person
possible Jesus Freak
do not understand
driver older person

GOD AND COUNTRY (red, white, and blue, banked with flag)

good idea, driver straight or long hair
bullshit artist
no opinion
aw! lover of this country, a real American

PIGS ARE BEAUTIFUL (blue and white; pig's head in cop hat)

outstanding, police are all right
capitalist cop selling the sticker
must be a cop
just as bad as "Get Your Shit Together"—don't like term *pig*
law-abiding citizen, conservative
wondered when it was coming, driver cop or his wife
tired of hearing about it
ok, good for a laugh

IF YOU DON'T LIKE THE POLICE
NEXT TIME YOU NEED HELP
CALL A HIPPIE

ok, beautiful, a cop lover
makes good point
another John Bircher

like him
right on, right wing
truth, well-informed, involved American
too much, driver woman

I AM MY BROTHER'S KEEPER BE MY BROTHER	Afro-American Patrolman's League

(picture of raised fist)

radical racist Afro propaganda, freedom rider
black police officer
must be a Panther
a radical that doesn't know what it's all about
militant officers, separated from others
?
hate, bullshit

If You Like Me GRIN

nasty, dirty bastard
ok, driver young female
lonely, insecure person
the owner is on the make
weird
sex-starved, weirdo, needs ego effacement

NO PLACE FOR INTIMACY

There's a basic contrast between the national home town and the older kind. Our new forms may resemble those of the old home town—7/11 as neighborhood grocery, laundromat as stream, bumper stickers as conversation and identification—but the forms are only outer. With all our milling around, there's little time to go beneath the surface. Sometimes our identities get confused. When we're forced to deal with the external, and the most garish, obvious symbols are the ones we relate to most quickly, be it Colonel Sanders smiling face, HAVE A NICE DAY on the bumper, or a Hare Krishna's pigtail. Under such circumstances, revealing too much, getting too close, can just be embarrassing.

"One thing I like about 7/11," a new franchisee told me, "is that you don't have to get so involved with your customers. They're in and out."

This guy had just sold his neighborhood tavern after eight years to buy a 7/11 franchise. Only days before he began 7/11's training program, the regulars in his bar gave him a farewell banquet—complete with beef, ham, and drinks.

"And they gave me this ring," he said fingering a thick gold band with obvious pride.

I said it sounded like quite a place, his old bar. "Yeah," he replied, with a fond smile. "We had a real family feeling."

Why did he make the switch? I asked. The guy looked down. "Ah, it's a rough life. The drunks got to me." He thought a second, then looked up. "The only problem in a neighborhood bar is that you get to know the people too well. You come in and I can tell in five minutes whether you've had a fight with your wife."

Sometimes, people reach for some of that good old intimacy even within a franchise. But it just doesn't work. Too much familiarity is inapropriate in the national home town.

That's what Red Robbins concluded after running three 7/11's in Florida before joining the company staff. Robbins said that wherever he worked, it was no time before he felt like "the chaplain of the neighborhood."

"After six months," he explained, "most people think they're your friend. They confide in you things like who's running around with whom, whose kids are up to what, where babies were just born."

I asked Robbins if he enjoyed that chaplain's role. He winced. "Nope. It was embarrassing."

Intimacy is decidedly out of place in the national home town. The Holiday Inn's blind fan, a "phone phreak" about to be jailed for tampering with Ma Bell's equipment, spent his final free night in an Inn. Later he described the scene: "It was my last night ever at a Holiday Inn, and it was my last night ever using the phone and

I was crying and crying, and the lady at the Holiday Inn said, 'Gosh, honey, you should never be sad at a Holiday Inn. You should always be happy here. Especially since it's your last night.' And that just made it worse and I was sobbing so much I couldn't stand it."[30]

Sometimes, though, you just need to cry—not alone, but in a community. The national home town is not a receptive community for that, because it's scary to see rank emotion bubbling out from people you don't really know. But enough of us are getting so desperate for a place to cry, to reveal, to get really intimate with each other, that we're learning ways to provide, ways which allow us to enjoy intimacy without sacrificing any of our anonymity, individuality, or right to move on. What we're learning is that intimacy in the national home town takes place best disposably.

5.

Handi-Dispoz Community

Ironically, the last encounter group I attended spent its final day in the Holiday Inn room of one participant.

In that room, on Sunday morning, one of the men in the group gave me an "Esalen Massage." The experience made my body tremble and my mouth moan—as loudly as I would let it in the Holiday Inn. It felt great, great to let go, at least part way, and trust that group of people to see me shaking and exposed.

Afterward I exchanged hugs with all the participants, and addresses with a few. We promised to visit, though it was months ago and we haven't yet. I still think we may.

WEEKEND ROMANCE

My first encounter group, in Philadelphia in 1968, has to have been a turning point in my life.

The group was a marathon, going for seventeen hours nonstop. I held back until near the end, asking others questions, saying things about myself in the abstract, but releasing no feelings. Then I got mad at the leader for being too bossy. She suggested that I sounded angry. Why not tell us about that? So I did, repeating, "I'm angry. I'm angry! I'm angry!!! I'M ANGRY!!!!!!!"

And I was—I'm still not sure what about—furious. I went around to each person in the group just saying, "I'm angry, John. I'm angry, Bob. I'm angry, Betty. I'm angry, Jim"—but Jim's eyes were so full of tears that my own dam broke and I ended up sobbing on the floor. Soon the whole group joined me and we all sobbed together, for hurts long forgotten and civilly kept to ourselves.

I fell in love with those fourteen people. Each one. Even though there were some who bugged me, some whom I didn't like, our feelings were so strong that I loved them all.

We parted with tears and regret, and I left a note for the male coleader, signing it "Love, Ralph."

For days I was on a high. There seemed to be nothing separating me—from people, from trees or even the concrete sidewalks. Colors were brighter, sounds more vivid, and I could smell a hundred beautiful odors at once wafting though the air.

The high couldn't last. I had to go home, to my wife and others who knew me, at least my "old me." They couldn't tell what had happened, and seemed scared at my lively eyes and bubbling feelings. But I was scared to tell them, people I knew, about my ecstasy. It was embarrassing.

Soon the high had dissipated, and I was my same old me and I resented my wife and friends for "bringing me down."

Several months later I was back in Philadelphia and went to visit the coleader of my marathon. He was in a hurry to get somewhere and we had only a few words in passing. He seemed distant. That puzzled and irritated me. What had happened to our love?

I never saw him again, nor anyone else from the group.

Since then I've been in several encounter groups, both as participant and as facilitator, and the pattern is usually the same: general wariness at the outset, probing and testing of each other leading to a trust, and a general outpouring of feelings with all falling in love by the end.

But something else is the same too: you rarely see anyone from the group again afterward. In the heat of the moment you often plan to, you assure yourself and each other, "This one is different. These people I really care about and I'm sure we'll meet again." But you don't.

Occasionally by accident I'll run into a past love from a group, but it's usually a stiff encounter, like meeting any old lover. What do you say? How can you recapture the feelings? Do you want to?

A unique breed of "grouper" has grown up in southern California, and perhaps across the nation. With so many encounter groups going on, such people go from group to group getting stroked, enjoying their intimacy *seriatum*. To this group you reveal what a cad your wife is, to that group you cry about your vicious mother, and to the other about your brother. Then maybe trot out your wife again. If you handle the situation right, and it's not hard, each group of people will love and console you. A weekend's intimacy can sustain you till the next group.

I once asked a leader of student-adult groups[1] in a Long Island School District, if they had a gossip problem, since participants lived near each other and could tell tales out of group. "Oh, no," he replied. "We make sure that people in the groups are strangers to each other." Then he leaned forward affirmatively. "It's not the sort of thing you'd want to do with friends and neighbors."

Intimacy, it seems, may be easier to share with strangers than with friends.

This is what intrigued Bert Brown, a Cornell psychologist, when he had college students sing "Love Is a Many Splendored Thing" before several panels of judges. Some of the panels included friends of the singer, others were made up completely of strangers. Brown was testing how far a subject would go to "save face."

To his astonishment, Brown found the singers warbling far longer for an all-stranger panel than they would for one which included friends. He considered this a rather startling challenge to several theories and to common sense, which says we trust friends over strangers.

Not so, says his colleague Eliot Aronson. Aronson, a University of Texas psychologist with an interest in modern friendship, says that strangers have much more to offer than friends. A compliment from a friend we expect, but strokes from a stranger can make us euphoric. Conversely, a stranger is little threat to us. In contrast to a friend, strangers won't have the opportunity to ever do us in. They can't punish. Our confidences, our trust may be best placed with strangers.[2]

ALL MY FRIENDS ARE GONNA BE STRANGERS—AND MY LOVERS

Students of swinging have found that the intimacy of group sex depends on not knowing your bed partners. Gilbert Bartell found swingers in suburban Chicago who had shared sex for two years, without ever exchanging last names.[3]

A surveyer of southern California swingers talked to couples who said they preferred group sex parties to one- or two-couple exchanges because they felt safer with the greater impersonality.[4] One hostess says of swinging get-togethers, "The hardest thing in the world is finding four people who can swing together congenially. Any day I'll give a party for twenty, but don't ask me to bring together a foursome."

Swinging is only the most obvious example of the growing acceptability of intimacy with strangers. Swingers have taken the trend a step further, removing the need even to feel good about the person with whom you're sharing intercourse, or to seek actual closeness in the sex act. "It's fun," explains one New York swinger, "but I don't like most of the people involved in it."[5]

Carolyn Symonds, a San Bernadino sociologist who was spent years studying them, calls swingers "the antithesis of community" because they so rigidly discourage emotional intimacy. But, she adds, "Our thoughts are that much of sexual contact is a desire and a need for physical contact with others, and that sex is a more acceptable way to get physical contact than just going around touching people."[6]

I think this sentiment contributes more than we credit to the rise of swinging and casual sex generally. We seek sex disposably, partly because it just feels good, and partly because it's a safe form of neo-intimacy. Even if you're going to great lengths not to get involved with your partner, echoes of closeness hover around the sex act. When ongoing intimacy is so hard to come by, and so scary, sex—especially transient sex—can be a pretty good substitute.

"I am able to display my warmth and natural affection without misinterpretation of emotional involvement," was the way one San Francisco Bay Area swinger put it. Her comment was made to Lynn and James Smith, who interviewed hundreds of Bay Area participants in group sex. Other comments they heard included:

"People . . . seem to like me more, and more readily."

"A new honesty and communication has come into our relationship."

"I like myself more, and accept other people more."

"We now have friends with whom we can be honest, which helps bring stronger and closer relationships."[7]

Nena and George O'Neill say swinging couples they interviewed in New York (while researching *Open Marriage*) "expressed a feeling of warmth, of acceptance and response from other group sex participants that is often lacking in other social context."[8]

Sex will always retain overtones of intimacy even as the order of things gets turned around. Making love used to follow getting close. Now the sequence is reversed: getting close follows making love.

"Once the barrier of sex is out of the way, a person can relate more freely," explains Los Angeles psychiatrist James L. Grold. "In other words, it is certainly easier to relate to somebody after you've been to bed with them."[9]

Or, as the girl from Berkeley put it: "Balling is a good way of knowing someone."[10]

THE "FREEWAY ON-RAMP" SEARCH

A college co-ed recently told sociologist Jessie Bernard that she had never been more open with men than inside the building she helped liberate while a sophomore. "Here," she explained, "all together, the games I had always felt I had to play with boys fell away."[11]

"In such moments of collective enthusiasm," recalls Daniel Cohn-Bendit, of the 1968 Paris revolt, "nothing could be more natural and simple than a warm relationship between the boys and girls. Everything was easy and uncomplicated."

Easy and uncomplicated.

In general that characterizes the kind of intimate community we seek, the handy disposable kind. It's as the Harvard sit-inner explained: "For those few hours we were brothers . . . we were very human and very together."[12]

Barbara Meyerhoff recently returned to the University of Southern California after a year of anthropological field work in northern Mexico. That year's revolt was at fever pitch at U.S.C. The protestors had occupied some buildings, put up barricades, and for a few days reported the ecstasy of intense brotherhood.

But once the revolt ended and the buildings were abandoned, most of the insurgents spun into lethargy. Ms. Meyerhoff talked to some of them and found them depressed, listless, and disillusioned that their high had to end.

This intrigued the anthropologist, because she had recently taken part in a two-week ritual of an Indian tribe in northern Mexico. It was their annual pilgrimage to a sacred mountain lake, one they had been making for centuries. The time was one of celebration, uninhibited and ecstatic. Though the setting was different, radically different, the feelings resembled those felt by U.S.C. students in the liberated zone.

But there was a basic distinction. At the end of their two weeks, the Indians departed reluctantly, with tears, yet ready to go back to another fifty weeks of drudgery. Their ecstatic experience was built into an ongoing culture, and seemed to make the rest of life more bearable. They knew that in fifty weeks the mountain lake would still be there, and they would be back once again worshipping their gods and celebrating their selves.

The U.S.C. revolt, far from adding meaning to the subsequent life of protestors, only made what followed pale in contrast. They weren't sure when the feelings could be rekindled, if ever.

Meyerhoff calls this the "freeway on-ramp search" for ecstatic *communitas,* which we crave so desperately and seek with strangers, but without knowing what to do for an encore, or how to integrate the experience into our lives. The problem is, says Meyerhoff, that once we stumble on ecstasy, we hope to make it permanent, but run from the necessary commitment. This was true in the student revolt, is true of too many encounter groups and drug experiences. We have no tradition of integrating ecstasy into an ongoing life and, she says, "We just can't accept a fluctuation between ecstasy and doing the dishes."[13]

It's as if we're trying to make our opportunities for intimate community, the times when we'll peek from behind the mask, as handy and convenient as a TV dinner. A time to cry, to reveal, to take off one's shoes and relax is a human necessity. To do so with friends, even with family (especially with family) is scary and risky. It might lead to rejection, even worse—to commitment.

The safest, most convenient alternative is to seek a few day's intimacy with strangers, love and let loose.

"The key word," says Warren Bennis, "will be temporary."[14]

Psychologist Richard Farson says "The only people who will live successfully in tomorrow's world are those who can accept and enjoy temporary systems."[15]

Fewer and fewer of us stay anywhere long enough to know the neighbors, join a club, or become regulars at a bar. Nor do we want that much commitment. But we do need intimacy, something a little deeper than the promiscuous friendship of a smiling 7/11 clerk.

So what we're doing is developing temporary love systems, hit-and-run intimacy, self-destructing communities which are making closeness just as convenient and just as disposable as a two-week guided tour.

I'm frequently confronted by friends going off for short-term encounter or similarly intense experiences, then returning after a few days all high, eyes alive, and bursting to tell me about this "beautiful" community of people they were part of, and if only the rest of us could learn to love and be together as they did for those few days, etc., etc. Some recently returned told me of the "front-porch revival" which took place at the resort where they had been encountering and sitting on the porch—for five days.

Ask when such communities will reconvene and you usually get a blank look and "What does it matter?"

It does matter. It's not hard to get it on and build intimate trust with people you'll never see again. They can't do you in.

Robert Houriet describes the meeting of a commune to decide whether to be open to the scores of visitors coming and going, or closed to the handful of committed. The main exponent of being open kept citing the weekend at Woodstock as his argument. "Man, at Woodstock," he'd say, "hundreds of thousands of people lived together peacefully on less than we have here! They fed themselves, took care of their sick . . . ."[16]

For a total of three days.

Eventually the disposable style becomes so ingrained that even communities we want to be durable become throwaway—communes, for example, friendship or marriage. Marriage, the experts say, is being transformed from a permanent to a temporary commitment. "Serial marriage" is the evolving form. Over three-quarters of divorcing men in America remarry, and two-thirds of the women.[17]

Some accept this reality and don't see it as bad. The teacher of a free university course on communes even sees it as good that so many go under after a few months because "it teaches you that friendship, places of living, etc. are temporary and for a purpose."[18]

QUEUE COMMUNITY

The young especially, though not only the young, have grown deft at making music festivals family for the weekend, audience community for a few hours, and waiting lines friendly in the minutes they exist.

For someone in a hurry, waiting in line can be pure frustration.

But to the high school girl sitting on the sidewalk, waiting on "Woodstock," "It's nice to sit here and talk to your friends." The girl next to her says, "You see different things. Like a little while ago a woman tripped. We noticed that, but the man she was with didn't see it."

The *New York Times* got wind of this development and sent a staff member out to cover movie lines. He reported: "The longer the line, the younger, more modish it is likely to be, and the more bemused—and thus not bored—by itself. Almost invariably, the predominant conversational gambit has to do with similar evenings at the movies; not remembered great films but remembered great lines."

"*Romeo and Juliet* went around the block. *Easy Rider* was fantastic."

One mother and her seventeen-year-old daughter stood next to each other for an hour and a half at a Long Island theater waiting on *The Godfather*. With nothing better to do they talked. "You know how people say parents never talk with their kids," said the mother. "So we've been talking. And I really listened. After seventeen years, I finally got to know my daughter."[19]

The English historically have been great queuers, and are probably far beyond Americans in their approach to humanizing waiting lines. Author Calvin Trillin once wrote of a fictional queuer-hobbyist in London:

> . . . Penfold decided to spend that evening queuing about. He often spent his evenings that way, joining one queue, then another. He had a closetful of items that he had purchased without really needing them, souvenirs of the times when he had been enjoying himself so much that he neglected to leave the queue before arriving at the counter and had to buy something or risk being accused by those behind him of having queued frivolously. Once, on Regent Street, he had been rather embarrassed when he joined what he thought was a short

queue toward a shop door but turned out to be a German tourist ducking out of the wind to light a cigarette. But he continued to find queues irresistible, and he often spent an entire evening strolling from bus stops to cinemas to news dealers and back, queuing happily.[20]

More of a "family" is to be found on unemployment lines, where people huddle together for months, at appointed times, and among kin with the same letter beginning their last name.

"You just don't stand in the 'E' or 'A' line anymore," writes one observer of the unemployment scene in Manhattan. "You meet old friends, make connections, get dates, take phone numbers, everything but finding a job . . . ."[21]

Muriel's grandmother, her "Bubby," was on a Mahattan unemployment line for a year, her eighty-second. Bubby said people on the line came to know and care for each other, sometimes more than her own grandchildren perhaps. She was the line's oldest member, and younger members would hold her place so she wouldn't have to stand. If a regular didn't show up, people on line worried.

Once, Bubby was transferred from her old unemployment office to a new one. There, members of her original line who had also been transferred greeted her with hugs and cries. "I love to look at you," one woman said as she held Bubby. "Let me look at you. You remind me of my grandmother."

Bubby remembers her unemployment lines and their members with great nostalgia. "Everybody gave me respect."

AUDIENCE

When a queue becomes audience, its possibilities for intimacy are enhanced. Until the Rockets sold out to Houston, one of the few community experiences relating me to San Diego used to be going to their basketball games. Yelling with that big a crowd, sharing tension, joy, and tragedy was a real communal experience for a few hours. Sometimes, in the heat of a moment, we'd talk to one another.

A hardhat-looking guy even flashed me a "V" once as we left after a Rocket victory.

Some audiences can take on characteristics of an ongoing community. A friend with season tickets to the San Diego State football games says that one of the side benefits is getting to know the people in adjoining seats.

In Oakland Janice Mitchell, who held a 1969 season ticket to Raiders' games in Section 403, Row 17, Seat 4 of the Oakland Coliseum, later married Rodger Schmitt, who had Row 17, Seat 3, Section 403 during the same period.[22]

But it can cut both ways. A woman in Bellevue, Nebraska, recently asked a judge to modify the terms of her year-old divorce decree. She wanted two of the four season tickets to University of Nebraska football games, which she and her mate had owned jointly. The ex-husband objected. His former wife just wanted to sit next to him at the games, the man said, to embarrass him.

The judge ruled that each would get all four tickets on succeeding years.

A season ticket is a much bigger commitment than a night at the theater. It can lead to love and marriage, or hate and divorce—just as in any ongoing community.

A safer intimacy is to be found in participatory theater. The great discovery of this dramatic form is that audience and cast can be blended into intimate community within hours, minutes even, night after night. In those few hours, some of the feelings which used to be built over a lifetime can be grabbed at in passing by loving strangers.

Sociologist Bennett Berger, noticing the increasing propensity of audiences to participate in the production, from dancing in the aisles at *Hair* to shouts of "Bullshit" at lectures, wondered what was going on. He had a fantasy for himself coping heroically with such an incident in one of his lecture classes.

> My heroic fantasy goes like this: some aggressive student shouts "bullshit!" at some innocuous fact that I mention. A hush falls over the class as they wait with barely suppressed delight for my response

to this assault on my adequacy. Aware of the character of the crisis, I pause, letting the silence grow in intensity. Then, very deliberately, I raise myself up to my full five feet six and one-half inches, lean forward, rest the heels of my hands on the edges of the lectern, and shout with full volume (and just a hint of absurdity), "It is not bullshit," then pause again and say, "Are you going to say it is so bullshit?" then I'll shout louder, "It is not bullshit. Where do we go from here?" Then as I watch the student's face collapse and shatter in five pieces, I turn gently and fatherly and say, "If all you mean is that you disagree with me, perhaps we can talk about it."

But Berger went on to guess that his antagonist wanted something considerably different. What we really want, in school as in theater and life generally, is to break down the teacher-taught, player-listener, performer-audience roles so that "isolated experience between audience member and performer is replaced by an emphasis on 'getting it together,' on collective experience, on unity between performer and audience-as-constituency. The occasion, the encounter between performer and audience is transformed from one of segmental exchange into a celebration of ritual solidarity."[23]

One reporter calls the moment that Mick Jagger steps on stage "the moment when the community is born."[24] Night after night, in city after city—each audience a community.

JUST ADD HOTDOGS AND STIR

In California, the state's Park and Recreation Department is trying to pick up on this style, to make camping more of a celebration. "We intend to build around campfires a completely new kind of experience," explains one of their officials, "one that will be emotional and dramatic, exciting and interesting, and using all of the opportunities available to us—sound, color, music. . . ."

The Parks people have a problem. Yesterday's tenters used to average ten days per stay in a state park, but today's campers-on-wheels average only two and a half days. This aggravates the poor rangers no end. "We don't feel that we should spend money just to provide a place for someone to stay overnight," complains one of their officials. "What can we do to slow down these urban dwellers so that they will spend more than one day in a state park?"[25]

What they did was hire a company to consult with them on how to learn from rock festivals and the like, to make camping more handily disposable.

Camping once was a little adventure in outdoor deprivation, uniting nature lovers for a time in primitive togetherness. No more. There is virtually no comfort of home that cannot be installed in the rolling split-levels which dominate campgrounds. Wall ovens, toilets, 8-track stereos, televisions—just about any convenience imaginable can be built into the four million recreational vehicles which now travel ten billion miles a year in the United States. (This figure is expected to double by 1980.)

Once flush toilets were installed in campers, the whole nature of the experience changed. Convenience transformed both the physical and the psychological nature of camping. The new vacationers travel much more in search of community than the outdoors. A disposable community, to be sure, quick, intense, and disposable, but community nonetheless.[26]

I think Starcraft Campers understand best what we're looking for. Starcraft promises, "The Excitement of a New Neighborhood Every Time You Set Up."[27]

I'm fascinated, driving down the highway, by the number of campers which are complete with name-and-address plates just as if it were home. "The Newmans," a plate will say, "Bayside, Texas." Sometimes a little message will be added, like, "Y'all come see us."

And the new campers find the community they seek. Their changing cast of neighbors will be gone in a few days, so there's little risk in getting close.

Chuck Powers of *WEST* magazine recently toured state parks in California and caught the spirit. He said they had begun to resemble crowded parking lots with a constant coming and going.

Powers described what ensues as "Instant communities—just add smoke and charred wieners and the people stir themselves."

In these settlements, anyone who stays longer than a weekend automatically becomes a town father. He knows where the water hydrant or restroom is, and can tell a newcomer. He knows a bit of the community's history.

Powers lingered at one park, and said it was only days before the campsite felt like home. But the feeling was shattered when he and a friend returned one night to notice something wrong. Sweeney, one of the town fathers, was gone. His truck, his tent, lantern, ax—all the symbols of a staked claim were gone. Where Sweeney had been was now just a hole in the woods.

But within a minute another van pulled in and filled the hole.

And Powers wondered what it all meant. "Over the weekend," he later wrote, "we had defined the campground by its residents, who replaced the river and the meadow as camp landmarks. We knew faces, not trees. But it was easy to believe we knew them better than we did. Did Sweeney, the retired pipeline worker with eight children, live in an old white two-story house? Did Bob Smith, the aerospace worker from Lancaster, live in a tract, pre-fab with bicycles in the driveway? You didn't ask, but somehow you thought you knew. It was one of the deceptions of the experience; you watched the family fry their morning bacon and believed you knew them."[28]

Throwaway community is very much within the American tradition. Ever since the first wagon train moved out, we've developed increasingly sophisticated ways to make sure our intimate gatherings have built-in endings. New ones can be easily rebuilt elsewhere. "American communities," writes a New York housing expert, "can be disassembled and reconstituted as readily as freight trains."[29]

Phillip Slater is a sociologist who's been diligent in teasing out the implications of our evolving social forms. Slater is sure that temporary systems are the wave of the future, but warns that this implies a certain interchangeability among people. Once we're no longer rooted in a place, or tied to our relatives, all communities must be temporary. Inevitably one person becomes as good as another for the disposable groupings.

Slater sees this evolution bringing us closer to the "flocking" done by animals, the kind studied among geese and ducks by ethologist Konrad Lorenz. "Lorenz points out that species characterized by flocking do not recognize individuals at all, and any permanence in specific relationships (such as mating) is entirely dependent upon stability in extrinsic situational factors. While it is doubtful that humans will ever lose altogether the ability to discriminate among individuals, the evolution of interchangeability can be viewed as a legitimate cultural analogue of flocking."[30]

That scares me, because I do want to be known in particular, and I want intimacy with friends, real friends, the ongoing kind, not just weekend lovers. Which scares me even more, real ongoing commitment with people who might stay with me for years. Can they? Can I? Or am I better off sticking to transient relationships?

A TEN-BLOCK COMMITMENT

This is a lot of the appeal of hitchhiking. "It's a special feeling," wrote one guy hitching across the country. "Meeting other people and throwing in for a while together. There's a trust."[31]

I once discussed this with Julie, my sister-in-law. She's a Berkeleyite who enjoys hitching around that town. Julie likes meeting people and talking with them. I commented that I really used to resent it when people would pick me up just for company, especially when I didn't feel like talking.

"Well, how far were you hitching?" she asked.

"Usually hundreds of miles," I replied.

Her face brightened. "Oh, I see the difference. I'm usually just hitching around town. Anything over ten blocks is a heavy commitment."

When I pick up young hitchers, I'll sometimes ask them about this, the social aspects of hitching, the quick strokes. They're usually right on to what I mean, and dig it. "It's a good way to meet people," is the constant refrain.

It works both ways, for picked-up and pick-upper. I know at least two people who drive around picking up hitchhikers when they have nothing better to do. "I just get in my car and rap," explains one of them, a twenty-five-year-old editor. "There's something about the milieu that because you're not going to see the person again you can rap out heavy things on your mind. A lot of my friends are beginning to realize what a neat thing it is. A friend of mine took five days off from work and just drove around the state picking up hitchhikers. His mind was blown. He met chicks. He had all kinds of good times."

"I'M COMMUNITY—FLY ME"

Airlines understand our hunger for intimacy in passing better than any sociologist alive. Disposable community has become their bread and butter.

United wants me to fly their "Friendly Skies," in "Friend Ships."

Southwest Airlines calls itself, "The Somebody Else Up There Who Loves You." Passengers boarding one of their flights are greeted by a stewardess saying, "Hi, I'm Suzanne, and we're so glad to have you on our flight. You-all buckle up your safety belts and don't dare get up. We don't want anything happening to you now, because we love you."[32]

747 jumbo jets have broadened the opportunities for community in the sky. Soon after these flying suburbs took off, airlines executives began to notice how much time passengers were spending in line at the bathrooms. The queuers didn't seem to mind, and in fact were quite sociable. The executives suspected that some people in line probably didn't need to use the bathroom at all. But the passengers did seem to need an excuse to leave their seats and get involved with each other.

Since the airlines were having trouble filling their 747 jets anyway, some began ripping out a few seats and creating lounges by the bathrooms.

These early lounges soon overflowed and it wasn't long before more and more seats were pulled so that bigger and bigger lounges could be built in ever more fancy forms. The great lounge war was on.[33] Continental made theirs into "pubs" where one could become a regular for a few hours. American introduced "a friendly little piano."[34]

"It was a piano that brought together a Baptist minister and three gamblers the other night on an American flight between New York and Las Vegas," writes someone who was there.

"Anyone who knows even 'Chopsticks' is invited to audition, and so the minister sat down to play. He was joined by the three gamblers, the types with the wide lapels and loud neckties.

"The gamblers asked for a pop tune, and soon the trio and the minister were belting out, 'On a clear day . . . .'

"After this they doffed their hats. And obviously in deference to the minister did a few bars of 'Onward Christian Soldiers.'

" 'Amen,' said the minister."

747s as a toll for reconciliation.

One recent passenger described his 747 experience as "not actually a plane. It is a flying Holiday Inn on the eve of a Rotary convention."

The passenger, Ken Sobol of *The Village Voice*, described the boarding process. "Before I could pull it back, the captain had grabbed my hand, shaken it firmly, and claimed he was glad to have me aboard. . . . His sentiments were quickly echoed by a regiment of social directors, motel/hotel liaison men, supervisors, stewards, cooks, stewardesses and a representative of Chico the mechanic, wearing overalls so resplendent it was obvious he hadn't been in the shop for weeks."

I upset the stewardesses when I bolted into the lounge as the movie started and refused to be persuaded to go back with the rest, or buy a drink, or plug myself into my seat and trip on the Doodletown

Pipers, or arrange for a hotel/motel reservation, or ask a question about the airplane. "Isn't there anything you want to know about the 747?" they pleaded. "No, I replied, "there isn't." And there wasn't.

At one point, as I sat in solitary revolt in the lounge, I received a visitation from the most obvious fed I had ever encountered. He glanced over my inappropriate attire, unnarrowed his eyes as best he could, and dropped cat-like and iron-bottomed into the opposite chair. After a perfunctory glance out the window he turned to me and confided, "Makes you feel mighty small, don't it?" "No," I replied truthfully, "it don't." After a while he left, no doubt to cable the FBI to make more room on my file.

Like the plane itself, I could go on and on. Especially about how they kept trying to sell me things—movies, music, tenderloin tips, drinks, information, cheerfulness, what have you. The most tenacious stewardess, who pushed good fellowship with an uninsultable vigor, thought she had my number at one point, and informed me hopefully that she just adored New York and always went to Charlie Brown's. When even that good news failed to enliven me, she asked for the last desperate time if there was anything I wanted to know about the airplane. Actually, this time there was. A few minutes before I had gone to the bathroom and, after wiping my hands, searched in vain for a place to throw the towel. Finally I pressed a likely looking button and was immediately deluged by a year's supply of sanitary napkins. By the time they stopped falling out the pile was up to my knees. I asked the stewardess why that had happened and she replied that they still had some bugs to iron out.

I think it is probably the other way around. If I know the airlines, they still have some bugs to iron *in*. There is no gift mall as yet, for example, and a singles dance over Iowa is a natural for C deck. I also feel there is a crying need for a charcoal sketch artist or at least a house photographer with a selection of exotic backgrounds.[35]

One year after this was written, United Airlines put a caricaturist on their Tuesday 747 flight from San Francisco to New York. He alternates with a wine-taster on Wednesday, and a guitarist on Thursdays.[36]

As usual, the government is out of step with the nation's lust for community. The Civil Aeronautics Board (CAB), which still views flying as transportation, has been pressuring airlines to add more seats on planes so they can lower prices. This could mean the death of lounges.[37]

The C.A.B. doesn't know what the airlines do: that flying, like most of our social services, no longer *serves* the community, because there's no longer a community to be served. The communities where we used to belong have been sacrificed to mobility, privacy, and convenience. Our alternatives are based on the same values—community sought anonymously, from the privacy of our homes, in passing on the roads of the national home town, and with tears shared in intimate moments with strangers. None of this satisfies and we end up seeking community everywhere, like promiscuous lovers.

Airplanes are forced to *become* community and serve up intimacy because their customers' hunger is so great. The airlines know that, that they had become the comunity they once served, long before most of us had a notion. But we're beginning to catch up. That transformation—from *serving* community to *being* community—is revolutionizing our social institutions.

6.

Serve the Community, Be the Community

Sometimes the jeweler leans against the corner of his store, watching and wondering. What are they up to? Why do they come here? What do they want? "They just walk up and down all day long, wearing their shoes out," he says, "and what have they accomplished?"

It wasn't this way when he was their age, back in the 40s. Then he and his friends would go down to the Sugarbowl, get a Coke or a malted, stick a dime in the jukebox, and kill a couple of hours before going home to crack the books.

But these kids today, the ones who hang around shopping centers. What are they up to?

The kids themselves aren't talking, at least not to the jeweler and his kind. They just walk on by, studying themselves in his window, waving cigarettes like swords, whispering of conspiracies untold.

They pass by the guard in green, grimacing at him and mumbling unpleasantly. But he knows their game, knows why they're on the mall.

"It's nothin' but a perfect hideout for crooks," says the guard in green.

During the six months he's worked at the Walt Whitman

Shopping Center, the guard feels he's learned the habits of his prey. They break glass, turn over trashcans, curse, arrange to fornicate, pick up dope, leave off dope, and generally make his life miserable.

"You can look at their eyes, shining like everything. You see, they been in school all day and they probably had nothing to smoke. This is their meeting place for the stuff."

Cull one of the marchers and ask her about *that* and she'll grab your tape-recorder mike, roll her green-shadowed eyes, grin wildly, and shout: "Here we are in the heart of the mall! The drug scene is all around! And Susy Creamcheese, the head pusher, the head of all heads, is about to be busted!"

CENTERING

It's a bit of a comedown from what architect Lawrence Israel had in mind when his firm designed Walt Whitman's covered and climate-controlled mall during the late 50s.

"The enclosed mall was always thought of as a place for people to promenade, to preen themselves, to look at one another in the manner of the old city boulevards," explains Israel. Then he sighs, and adds, "I'm not sure we anticipated what's happening with the younger groups."

Especially on Saturday you see them, streaming off the buses from Plainview, from Bethpage, from Huntington Station, Halesite, and points north, south, east, and west. The kids come roaring, screaming across the asphalt, beelining for the shopping center—the big top in sight.

Once inside they dart down the mall, stopping only to buy a Coke at the soda stand, cotton candy at McCrory's, or a big hot pretzel—two for a quarter.

Some of the stores open directly onto the midway, and there are lots of things to look at inside. Negligees at Macy's. Rhinestone chains at Abraham and Straus'. Helium balloons at McCrory's, piercing the air with their *hssssssssssssss*.

Outside the stores stand vigilant merchants, the barkers.

And everything is framed by din from loudspeakers: "LOST KIDS! POLICEMAN NEEDED IN FRONT OF A & S! SPECIALS TODAY! STEP RIGHT UP!"

This wasn't how shopping centers were intended. The early versions, which sprung up after World War II were just sets of buildings planted together helter-skelter. Customers were moving to the suburbs, so stores began to follow and found it convenient to cluster.

But by the 60s, shopping centers had mushroomed in size, become the regional centers of today which cover acres of asphalt with scores of stores, and serve customers who drive for miles to get there. More significantly, beginning in the frigid Midwest, shopping centers put a roof over their malls, heated up the insides in the winter, and cooled them off during the summer.[1]

This proved to be a more revolutionary act than the original designers realized. "We discovered that the enclosed mall changed the concept," explains Vice President Paul E. Leyton, of May Stores Shopping Centers, who has worked in shopping centers in California and on Long Island since 1954. "The idea of having an enclosed mall doesn't relate to weather alone. People go to spend time there—they're equally interested in eating and browsing, as well as just shopping and leaving. So now we build only enclosed malls."[2]

The trend is national and not limited to cold climates. Covering malls is so profitable that open ones are being shut in at the rate of fifty a year. Of the twenty-nine malls larger than a million square feet which opened between May 1, 1971, and April 30, 1972, all were covered.

One downtown area of a Knoxville, Tennessee, suburb has even put a roof over its street, trying to compete.[3]

Under the covers, shopping centers have become bazaars. Leyton says they're now competing for the recreational dollar as much as the retail one. A whole subcommerce has grown up to help: carnival rides, traveling art shows, Hawaiian luaus, dog contests, children's beauty shows, concerts.

San Diego's Mission Valley Shopping Center has one or more extra-commercial activities scheduled almost every day of the year. Recently their parking lot was jammed with boats for a boat show. "At first the dealers felt they should be on the water," explains Leyton, who manages Mission Valley, "but we pointed out to them it was really people they were interested in, not water. And this is where the people are."

Since shopping centers are where the people are, those who seek the people are following.

"When Paul brought the gospel, he went to the marketplace," explains the director of a mall chapel outside Pittsburgh.

Chapels-on-the-mall are increasingly common in this country. The Rev. Robert W. Verley, Director of Marketplace Ministries in Alexandria, Virginia, points out that one nearby center gets thirty-two million people-visits per year, the kind of audience which just can't be ignored.

At the Plymouth Meeting Center outside Philadelphia, one Protestant ministry began in a storage corridor. Then it moved to a kitchen. Now regular services are held in the Center's community hall for the 300-member congregation. Church school classes meet in stores—kids in the lobby of a jewelry store, adults in a bar, teens in Sal's Pizza.

"The shopping center is potentially the real center of community life," explains Rev. Mr. Verley. "The church is finally waking up to this. We're moving where the people are—and there's no better place to meet them than in the marketplace."[4]

Politicians know. Shopping centers have become their favorite place to press flesh. Candidates for office go to shopping centers for the obvious reason that lots of votes stroll up and down the malls. Also, the centers are easy to get to and have loads of parking. "But best of all," says one campaign planner, "everybody knows where a shopping center is. For downtown rallies we had to circulate maps in advance."[5]

It was in the Laurel, Maryland, Shopping Center that Arthur Bremer finally caught up with George Wallace. And days later a gunman shot five people rallying for Senator B. Everett Jordan at a shopping center outside Raleigh, North Carolina.

Courts at different levels have been asked on several occasions to decide how open shopping-center space must be to political activity. Most recently, just after 1972's Democratic Convention, the Supreme Court ruled 5 to 4 that shopping centers are "private property" and have a right to control what goes on within. Justice Lewis Powell, who wrote the decision, stressed that the public can have only limited access to shopping centers, largely for commercial purposes.

Earlier decisions, in state and federal courts, had taken a different tack, arguing that shopping centers had become more "downtown" than actual downtown areas for many suburbanites. California's highest court ruled 6 to 1 in 1969 that a San Bernadino center had no right to expel antipollution petitioners. Justice Stanley Mosk wrote for the majority that shopping centers were little different from business districts, and "Indeed, in many instances the contemporary shopping center serves as the analogue of the traditional town square."[6]

Shopping center managers looked askance at that sort of decision, but were elated by the recent Supreme Court ruling which restored their control over what goes on in the mall. Paul Leyton is a maverick in this regard. He agrees with the Mosk decision, even though it limits his rights as a property owner, because it clearly defines shopping centers as part of the community—just like downtown.

Ah, but they're so much more. Shopping centers aren't *part* of the community. They *are* the community.

In a sense, the Powell decision is more sophisticated than that of Mosk, even though more reactionary. Shopping centers aren't "part of the community" because there isn't any community to be part of. Their resemblance to downtowns of old is purely visual. Once shopping centers put a roof over their heads, shut out the weather, hired their own police force, and struck up the band, they had for all practical purposes seceded and become communities unto themselves.

In Torrance, California, the new Olde Towne Mall is nearly completed. The 140 shops within will adjoin a winding street paved in antique brick. The enclosed mall will be lit by reconditioned seventy-year-old standards from Long Beach. "We're creating nostalgia," says developer Robert Brindle, who has built forty shopping centers before this. Olde Towne, he says, will draw its inspiration from Disneyland, Ports O'Call, Farmer's Market, the Laguna Art Festival, and Universal Studios. Along with an antique merry-go-round and roving entertainers on the street and in balconies, puppet shows will play for the kids in a Frog Ampitheatre and an old-time gazebo will be host to the Olde Towne Band.[7]

Shopping centers are much closer to villages of old than downtowns of new, their managers like despotic princes.

One shopping center in Detroit flies its own flag. Another in Florida generates all its own power, and is linked to the outside world only by telephone wires and a natural-gas pipeline. In California's Orange County, where Anaheim, Garden Grove, and Santa Ana meet, a new mall calls itself simply The City.[8]

We may not like this evolution, but it's happening. As any environment resembling "community" crumbles for those of us in city and suburb, those institutions which used to *serve* community now *are* community.

Journalist Michael Fessier, Jr., "searching for L.A.," in the San Fernando Valley, ended up in Topanga Plaza. There he caught the spirit.

In 1963 the Plaza opened and it was an instant success; the ants had found their anthill.

Without announcement or legislative decision the Plaza became more of a *de facto* city than the West Valley had ever known. In place of the zoo which it didn't have there were exotic birds and monkeys in modernistic cages down near May Company; instead of the Cultural Center it didn't have it had the Rain Fountain court where Greek Tourist Agency dancers recently performed; instead of the art museum it didn't have it has art exhibits all year long, the artists sitting there on the slab benches watching the people look at their paintings of fluorescent surf, snow-capped mountains, large-eyed little girls and conquistadores in gold helmets. While its 90 or so assorted shops, stores and restaurants were selling nearly $100,000,000 worth of goods per year the Topanga Plaza became a civic center as well—the place to register to vote, to meet candidates in elections (Barry Goldwater, Jr. lurking amiably around Kinderfoto hoping to snag someone to talk to). Students from Valley State College came to protest the war in Vietnam and a year ago during the teachers' strike pro and con groups came in to present their case.

Plaza manager James Charter would thus become far more a mayor than Sam Yorty. . . .

Here is our Broadway, our Picadilly Circus, our Champs-Élysée.

It would, all in all, seem a perfect setting for some modern Jeremiah to run about screaming at the top of his lungs, "Flee this synthetic world. . . ."

But where would we go? The city-mall, a midwestern invention, has spread throughout the country and in at least half of them you will find a Rain Fountain.

What you should do then, is to settle to enjoying it.

Relax. Listen to the music. Look there in the skating rink. . . . Very nice.[9]

That sounds like what I found at Whitman. An honest-to-goodness community, dominated by kids but not limited to them.

The heart of this community wasn't the dip-in-and-outers, the dilettantes who only showed up on Saturday. The *real* Whitman community was the people who hung out there virtually every day, and had for years, the people with some commitment to the place.

One widow, seventy-eight years old, had her breakfast every morning at 10 in McCrory's, then sat around on the benches before having some milk at 1 and returning to an empty house. She'd been coming to Whitman for four years, and really enjoying the kids. "I could love all of 'em," smiled the grandmother from a mall bench. "They're so cute, the kittle kids, fourteen and fifteen. They tell jokes and sit around."

And the kids return the affection. The old widow is kind of a mall hero, one of the few "good" grownups around.

Ellen is another mall regular. The pale, sunken-cheeked blonde had been coming to Whitman constantly since even before it was finished, and recalls with pride hanging out at Whitman when there were mudholes where the trees are today. Now nineteen, she had to skip a few days the year before to have a baby, but two days later Ellen was back. "As soon as I could take him out of the house he was down here seeing what was happening," she said.

What *was* happening? Or what *is*?

Well, kids still talk about the time a few years ago when some of them came down in bathing suits and splashed around in a fountain.

That shook people up.

Or the time a girl's mother flipped out and did a barefoot dance on one of the benches before they took her away.

That was really something.

Two years ago someone got stabbed. And just last month some of the mall people got busted.

It all gives the kids something to talk about as they walk up and down the mall, lingering a few minutes to listen to sounds coming out of Goody's, stopping off in McCrory's bathroom, going down to Vend-O-Snack for a hamburger. . . .

PARTICIPATORY JUSTICE

It isn't members of a larger community who walk a mall; it is isolated individuals in search of a community. The family they find is tied to no larger gathering. Sufficient unto itself, shopping centers offer their own community to replace the one once served. These communities float freely with their own members, their own life, incidents, and drama.

That kind of evolution is taking place throughout our institutions and social services. Any gathering of people is liable to become community for the community-less people participating.

I spoke earlier of juries as a social institution once composed of people *known* to the defendant, then being open only to those *un*known to the defendant. Thus juries and their parent court went from being *of* the community to being *for* the community. Even in the latter form, our system of justice was considered to be part of the community—aloof, but part.

Now courts and juries have entered another incarnation and are floating free of any community except the one they have become themselves. Today's jury *is* the community, a family even.

Consider:

• Angela Davis is acquitted. Bedlam erupts in the courtroom. Angela cries. Several jurors cry. She embraces them all. Several hug back.

At a celebration that night most of the jurors toast Ms. Davis with champagne. A young female juror, a clerk at Sears, boogaloos with one of the defense lawyers. She tells reporters the trial caused a "big change" in her life.[10]

• After Charles Manson is convicted, jurors discuss their 9½-month ordeal more as a social than a legal phenomenon. One member hints broadly at "promiscuous" goings-on in the hotel where they were sequestered. Others talk of the practical jokes, the running in the halls, the parties, the singing and dancing, and playing cards till all hours.

"I miss the friendship," says a forty-eight-year-old juror afterward. "I always felt like I could go knock on someone's door and talk any time of the day or night, just like when I was in the Navy."[11]

• Three members of the Washington State jury which acquitted San Francisco Mayor Joseph Alioto show up later as spectators when he is tried later in Federal Court. Asked why they are there, the three reply that they have become good friends during their jury duty together, and are still interested in Alioto's case.[12]

• A year after New York's Panther 21 were acquitted, jurors, defendants, and defense lawyers who took part were still holding reunions. Nine jurors showed up for the first anniversary gathering with some of the defendants and their attorneys. Twelve jurors (out of sixteen, including alternates) had attended an earlier reunion. Several of the jurors and Panthers have become friends, visiting in each other's homes and exchanging Christmas cards. "It was almost as if the jurors had been sitting there growing fond of the people they were being told such terrible things about," sniffed one spectator at the trial.[13]

That's a popular perspective, nauseated revulsion at the emotional goings-on, the shocking fraternization between juror and judged in our courtrooms. Kissing the defendant! Crying in the courtroom! Boogalooing with the defense attorney! Indeed!

But it's just not the point. The flashier goings-on in our nation's courtrooms are only symptomatic of a larger trend: the communalization of justice—every trial a community, each jury a family.

Consider what happens to a group of twelve people sequestered for a long and emotion-charged case. They're stuck with each other. The jurors can't move on and must learn to live together. Their privacy is limited. They're cut off from the outside world and must deal only with one another. The controversy, the emotions of the case force a dropping of masks. Jurors must in some degree reveal themselves and become known.

No wonder service on a jury can be such a moving communal experience.

"If jury duty actually is a way to swing, and now everyone knows about it," wrote Margo after the Manson trial revelations, "we can expect some changes in the system. Whereas in the past a lot of people tried to get exempted from jury duty, I think we're going to see a resurgence of civic spirit. Everyone's going to want to do his duty."[14]

Just a few months later, *New York* magazine ran an article suggesting jury duty as a good way to meet people. "It's a paradise for single girls down here," one female juror was quoted as saying. "If you don't meet someone in the jury room, there's all those lawyers who hardly ever see a woman unless she's on the witness stand."[15]

The article gave advice on what to wear in case you are called.

And so the circle is completed. When we lived on a smaller

scale, juries consisted of community members *known* to another member on trial. As we grew larger we sought refuge in the objectivity of anonymity, of jurors *unknown* to the person being tried.

Now we're in the third stage. The courtroom is a community, the judge a father, each jury a family, and the defendants prodigal sons. Trials provide the opportunity to come to *know* each other once again, to become community. Justice has been communalized.

The evolution is from bureaucracy to brotherhood. Do you dislike waiting anonymously in line? Get to know the other people and make the queue family. Is the multiversity giving you "just another number" blahs? Shut it down and become a community.

This evolution of our social institutions is pandemic. As whatever sense of community we have had is sacrificed in tribute to cars, seclusion, and dishwashers, those institutions which used to *serve* a community of people now must *become* a community of people in order to function.

The magazines which once provided reading material for a community of people, now have become that community. Magazine staffs once considered themselves a family serving their readers; now that family *includes* the readers.

Planes which used to provide transport from one community to another now provide community transported from one place to another.

Participatory drama today *makes* a community of the theater which used to serve one.

Once cable television starts building smaller, more intimate viewer-communities than are now offered by mass impersonal networks, it will be their turn to *become* community.

FROM BUREAUCRACY TO BROTHERHOOD

The process of which I'm speaking actually takes place in three stages. In the first stage, when we lived small scale in tribes and villages, community members all knew each other whole, and services were rendered by members *of* the community. Education was part of day-to-day life. Artists drew pictures of community events, and musicians sang their legends. A story or a play would be performed by familiar faces. Merchants lived nearby.

In the second stage, as population grew and we spread out on the land or grouped in cities—as society grew mass, goods and services were offered to the community by people detached from it. The grocer, the doctor, the teachers of our children became less and less known to us. They were no longer *of* our community, they were *for* it.

Eventually this separation of services, this sense of being *for* a community rather than *of* it, grew habitual, even venerable. Professors shielded themselves with podiums, and called themselves more objective. Policemen hid in cars, and said it made them more mobile. Clergymen's altars drew higher and further away from the congregation, as did actor's stages.

A study of dance-band performers early in this century found that they felt uncomfortable without some barrier—even a line of chairs—separating them from the audience.[16]

"Professionalism" is what this distinction from the community is usually called, this quest for objectivity through detachment. Psychologist Donald Klein explains of him and his colleagues, "Much of our training has taken place at universities, hospitals and other settings that in most instances are relatively isolated from other institutions. We may even have lost whatever sense of the local community we once possessed. Most of us no longer are 'locals.' . . . If anything, we tend to avoid involvement in community affairs even when issues affecting us and our families arise."[17]

Now, in the third stage of the evolution, people are reclaiming the services, walking out on the detached professionals who have treated them with detachment, and building their own communities of people gathered to serve. Services which once were *of* the community, then *for* it, now *are* the community.

After trying all manner of diets for years, Jean Nidetch ended up at a public Obesity Clinic in New York City in 1962. A skinny nutritionist asked the group how they felt when shown a smorgasbord table. The woman next to Nidetch said, "I feel like diving in. Don't you?"

Nidetch thought, "Ah, a friend."

Then the nutritionist told the class that *she* got sick to her stomach at the sight of a smorgasbord.

"What she didn't know!" Nidetch said later. "She didn't know that if you feel lonely enough or worried enough—and if it doesn't move—you can eat it. She didn't know that if you need a jelly bean bad enough, you can go looking for it in your son's pants pockets, and even if it is covered with dirt and crayon, you can eat. She knew nothing; she got sick to her stomach from food!"

Nidetch ended up following the clinic diet—except for cookies. But she lied about them to the skinny nutritionist. "How can you tell a woman who gets sick to her stomach when she looks at food that you have to have cookies?"

So Jean Nidetch gathered some fat friends at her home to confess her transgression. They all ended up confessing their "Frankensteins"—the one food they couldn't resist. "We not only kept discovering things about ourselves," says Nidetch, "but, because we were confessing to the others, we could help ourselves stop doing what we knew we shouldn't be doing. Besides, we had fun."

From this gathering, Weight Watchers evolved.

At an early public meeting in a rented hall, one schoolteacher confessed that, seven years before, one of her pupils had thrown a half-eaten doughnut in the wastebasket. This doughnut fixated her until school let out. When the class was finally dismissed, she fished the piece of doughnut out of the trash can and ate it. "It's troubled me for seven years," said the woman, "but I've never been able to tell anyone about it."

"At that moment," writes Nidetch, "every single person at the meeting was the schoolteacher's ally. Everyone in the room knew what she had gone through and how relieved she was to tell other people about it. And right then and there I knew what Weight Watchers was all about.

"Here at Weight Watchers you could talk. You could say, 'I hide in the bathroom and eat cookies, because I'm afraid I'm going to get caught.'

"When everybody understands you, it's easy to talk. When I talked honestly to the people who came to my loft, they discovered that everybody had the same experiences, and that made us all friends."

Ms. Nidetch calls their approach "a combination of mutual support, lavish encouragement, week-by-week accountability, re-education of eating and thinking habits, undeviating honesty and rewards." She believes that fat people are intimidated by skinny people, who are referred to as "civilians" and not allowed through the door of a Weight Watchers meeting.[18]

Professionals, doctors, have an admittedly bad record at weight control. They know what diet to recommend but there's something intangible, a motivation, a group support which is more difficult to impart. In fact, professionals can't. What the self-help groups—Weight Watchers, Overeaters Anonymous, Take Off Pounds Sensibly (TOPS)—can uniquely offer is a sense of community, the community of the afflicted.

"I could not agree more that this organization is part of a 'quest for community'," says Dr. Albert Stunkard of TOPS. A psychiatry professor at the University of Pennsylvania, Stunkard and a colleague studied twenty-two TOPS chapters in the Philadelphia area. They found that the *average* weight loss of their members was comparable to the *best* results reported by doctors in medical literature.[19]

The basis for success of so many self-help groups is that they've taken over duties once handled within the community, and brought along a sense of community as well. This is true of groups helping the obese, the alcoholic and drug-addicted, and explains the need for them. Your actual community may turn its back on you, ignore your problem, or turn you out, but there is a separate community of those alike who welcome you in.

One mother of a chronic drug user in Los Angeles found herself unable to face members of "the community." When her son was convicted of drug possession, the mother pulled the curtains, turned her TV low, and refused to see any friends.

Then she heard of Families Anonymous, a new self-help group for families of drug users which is organized in fourteen cities. She began attending their meetings and found great relief. Families Anonymous was a community that understood. They all shared her problem.[20]

Families Anonymous is just one of the self-help groups which are springing up in this country like dandelions after a rain. Many are anonymous, patterned after Alcoholics Anonymous. These range from Survivors Anonymous (for those left behind by suicides) to Pussy Anonymous (for men who are compulsive philanderers). Other groups, without being "anonymous," are bringing together Vietnam veterans to talk out their fears, POW wives to share frustrations, or unemployed aerospace engineers to share despair. A 1962 survey listed 415 such groups, and hundreds if not thousands have begun since then.[21]

By joining such efforts people are taking part in the same process which is transforming our shopping centers and courts. They are making a community rather than serving one.

When problems like illness, insanity, and death were dealt with within the community, there was no question of embarrassment. Everyone knew everyone else's misfortunes. Then professional services grew up to segregate treatment of such problems: doctors for physical illness, psychitrists for mental illness, and undertakers for death. What such professionals couldn't offer was actual sympathy. To be professional is to be detached, to be unknown to the person who is revealing things to you.

So the victims of various afflictions are today forming communities of the afflicted, neither part of a community nor serving one, but self-help groups which *are* the community themselves.

Within these communities they seek a sympathy more authentic than bedside mannerisms. Reach for Recovery, a self-help group for mastectomy patients, says part of its reason for being is the insensitivity of male surgeons to the emotional needs of women about to have a breast removed.[22] Weight Watchers calls itself in radio spots "a church made up of the sinners."

Sociologist Nathan Hurvitz has studied a variety of Peer Self-Help Psychotherapy Groups (PSHPG) and admits "nonprofessional enthusiasm" for their results. They key to their success, he says, is the intimacy which follows public confession. "Peers," writes Hurvitz, "disclose their secrets in public and have complete knowledge about each other. . . . Peers do not represent 'significant others'; they are significant others.

"The purpose of PSHPG's is to change people and these amateurs succeed in a considerable number of cases, apparently more often than professionals do."

Hurvitz says that professionals often look down their noses at PSHPGs because of the revival aspects of their meetings—the semirituals, the code words, the public confession.[23]

Margaret Mead says social scientists generally can't grasp the real purpose served by the American passion to join groups. "Not until he has been marooned," writes Mead of her colleagues, "his train missed, no taxi available—and driven sixty miles across bad roads in the middle of the night by someone who belongs to another chapter of the same national organization does he begin to realized that the tie of common membership, flat and without content as it is, bolstered up by sentimental songs which no one really likes to sing but which everyone would miss if they weren't sung, has an intensity of its own; an intensity measured against the loneliness which each member would feel if there were no such society."[24]

The Encyclopedia of Associations lists more than 16,000 nonprofit groups in this country, ranging from "Left-Handers Against the World," through "The American Peony Society" and "Lions International."[25]

"It helps us not to be lonely," explains the president of one Connecticut women's group, about their reason for gathering. "I've just been sick, and if it had not been for our worthy organization, why, I would have been awfully lonely. They brought me flowers, and sent me all these 'get well' cards, and came to visit me. If you don't belong to an organization, why you are all alone in the world."[26]

Without any one community to call our own, where we can take off our shoes and get comfortable, what we do is seek community everywhere. If no gathering is really community in our lives, then every gathering must try to be.

DeTocqueville anticipated this development a century and a half ago. Like most observers of the "American Character," before and since, the French aristocrat noted our propensity to congregate at the slightest excuse. "Americans of all ages," he wrote, "all conditions, and all dispositions, constantly form associations." DeTocqueville saw our drive to associate, even in the early 1830s, growing inevitably out of our rootlessness and the lack of relatedness he considered inherent in a democratic society. "I have shown that these influences are almost null in democratic countries; they must therefore be artificially created, and this can only be accomplished by associations."[27]

This perspective helps me understand why I found Long Island so meeting-happy. In that most alienated of living environments, people seemed driven to MEET: about politics, about drugs, about mental health—you name it. The gatherings never seemed to accomplish much, or at least what they were supposed to. But they did do something. The meetings, and the organizations sponsoring them, were a community for the gatherers, a point of intimacy replacing that no longer felt at home.

"Americans will join anything in town," said Will Rogers. "Why two Americans can't meet on the street without banging a gavel and calling the other to order."[28]

"FAMILY"

The only thing new in our drive to belong is the degree of disconnectedness Americans feel, and the added weight we put on our associations to be not only community but also family.

A biker says of his gang, "Our chapter is like a brotherhood. Strong. Strong. We're real tight. One of us cries, we all cry. One laughs, we all laugh. That's the thing about the Aliens. We're a family."[29]

The Aliens. A family.

After completing the Dale Carnegie course, an insurance executive boasted, "Now there's a lot more cooperation in our department. . . . We enjoy working together so much we're really more like a family."[30]

A family.

When Oregon's Governor Tom McCall decided against running for the Senate in 1972, he explained, "My prime commitment is to Oregon and the Oregon family. I feel I can do the most effective job for Oregon by finishing what the Oregon family reelected me to finish two years ago."[31]

The Oregon family.

I don't know much about lexicography, but when a word becomes that popular and that diverse in the ways it's used, some of the original meaning has obviously been lost.

At New York University, there's a psychologist who teaches a course on how to build a "second-chance family"—through encounter-like exercises, with people he assigns.[32] In Gary, Indiana, the largest criminal syndicate calls itself "The Family."[33]

Lacking a real community or family doesn't mean we can live without one. To the contrary, we need it more, and seek it everywhere—in shopping centers, at laundromats, in court, through the Lions or Weight Watchers, Dale Carnegie or the Aliens—any gathering today must provide some family feeling for its participants, or risk extinction.

Reese Paley sells membership in families. The son of an Atlantic

City jeweler and a trained economist, Paley deals in art and objets d'art. He points out that people buy such things not for the object itself so much as the sense of belonging. A purchase of Tiffany glass, for example, makes the owner eligible for books written on the topic, clubs, dealers, catalogs, brothers and sisters. "A good merchant," explains Paley, "recognizes that people are fundamentally disconnected, lonely (and the more successful the more lonely)—and a good merchant recognizes that he can't sell an object to people with too many objects. Another car, pool, or set of clothes will not make him less lonely."

So what Paley sells is fine art to a small population, and Boehm porcelains to a larger group.

"It's the entrance fee into the tribe," says Paley. "That's the *real* reason people collect." But the tribes detest each other, and must be serviced in different ways. For the fine-art collectors Paley last year chartered two 747 flights to Paris. The porcelain people get a *Boehm Collectors Newsletter* which addresses them as "Dear Boehmnick."[34]

An important asset of such interest groups is that—like the tribe or village of old—they virtually *have* to take you in, without judgment of your *persona*. Exile is a serious step under such conditions, and not done lightly. The only criterion for membership is commitment to the community hobby, and whatever fee may be involved.

A car salesman in Oceanside told me of the community awaiting him there when he moved from Germany—Citizen's Band Radio users. He's one, and to scout up his brothers and sisters, all the guy had to do was get on the air and announce his presence. Now, only months later, the salesman feels close to many of them and sometimes they get together at Sambo's for coffee. "They're some really great people," he explained, "and you know you've always got a friend."

But such membership is good only so long as you share the community interest. When your pretense for gathering is the club's stated goals, where can you gather once the pretense is gone?

Dave Walden once belonged to the sports car community. He

worked on cars and officiated at rallies. Dave had friends within the community, friends who really cared. When he had to go to the hospital, they visited.

But then Dave lost interest in sports cars, and soon lost all contact with that community, as they with him. Their commitment was only to the sports car buff, not the person. The community was only in part.

Gene Man belongs to a "time-of-day community," the people he meets while jogging every morning at 7 o'clock—milkmen, paperboys, other joggers. But that community exists only in the early morning. They're the people who nod at 7 A.M. but never at noon.

That's the problem with most of the new communities we've built. They always include an escape clause to make sure one needn't get known whole.

Club members usually share only their common interest. One participant in an old-time movie club, whose members met weekly and sometimes dressed up in Laurel & Hardy outfits, told me that no friendships had really grown from the experience, though he was "hopeful" that some might.

The mall bums are more "family," yet they know very little about each other. I was family with them for a few days, but mostly as "the *Newsday* freak."

The jury families seem much more intimate, but they're disposable.

Even in self-help groups you're known in some of the scariest parts of you, but rarely in the whole of you. In "anonymous" meetings, for example, you confess your transgressions but not your name. You exchange your outer identity for the inner one.

Edward Sagarin, a sociologist who has studied the anonymous and other self-help groups for "deviants" that have grown up in in the past few decades, says mobility and anonymity are necessary antecedents. ". . . a man could organize and join an association, go to its meetings, and then return to the quiet surroundings of his home and neighbors with few people knowing about his membership. Thus the anonymous society—as opposed to the secret one —was born."

Sagarin met one man who was attending meetings of two different Alcoholics Anonymous chapters, as well as two Schizophrenics Anonymous meetings every week.[35]

The risk we've avoided by making "community" of our clubs and self-help groups, juries and shopping centers, is the risk of getting known whole. By belonging to several such "communities," including the disposable kind, we can stay divided, become known a little bit here, a little bit there—here our name, there our face, why we might like to die in yet a third place.

It's not the same as being known whole in one community. The parts don't add up. The sense of community which we once knew whole has been shattered, the pieces scattered, and they never seem to get put back together.

Bobby Fischer intrigues me. The world's chess champion is such a sharply etched portrait of how we've lost community and the ways we're seeking a new one. According to news reports: Fischer has no home. He lives out of two suitcases. When he collects enough money, the chess champion says he plans to buy not one house but several.

Fischer is painfully sensitive to noise. Children rattling candy wrappers and the whirr of TV cameras were among his major grievances during the world chess tournament. To help him sleep at night, Fischer plays records of "white noise."

Bobby Fischer is cut off from his parents. He hasn't seen his father since the age of 2 and no longer communicates with his mother. An intensely private person, Fischer seems barely able to communicate except through the medium of chess. "His secret defense," writes a friend, "is a privacy more closely guarded than a monk's. Day after day he spends most of his waking hours alone with his chessmen. . . . His most frequent visitors are the voices that come to him through his portable radio, and I suspect that he prefers their company because he can abolish them with the twist of a knob."

Chess is Fischer's community. He gets scores of chess magazines, plays in chess clubs all over the world, eats, sleeps, drinks chess. However, he also has a newly-found family, the Worldwide Church of God which is a fundamentalist sect based in California.[36]

Bobby Fischer may seem a little odd. But really I think he's just a bit more exaggerated than the rest of us in the community he's lost, and the one he seeks.

We do seek community. There's no question about it. But also we're scared of it. So we seek a safe community, one in which we needn't be fully known. We want to preserve as much as we can of our privacy, our conveniences, as well as the freedom to pick up and move on.

And we continue to crave something more binding. It's that old ambivalence. We're scared of ongoing community, of letting ourselves be known whole, yet hungry for it.

We've always warred with ourselves on this issue—venerating Rugged Individualism on the one hand, and being the world's champion joiners on the other. That's not a paradox. The conviction that one should Go It Alone if not too weak, leaves us lonely, so we join things, always being sure to reserve our basic right to Go It Alone. It's really a community tablet we seek, the social equivalent of a cold capsule, to treat the symptoms of our malaise, but not the cause.

AGAPURGY

The logical conclusion, the direction we're headed, is what Henry Burger calls "agapurgy" the industrialization of affection. An anthropologist at the University of Missouri, Burger says that although America has done badly at providing enough "tender loving care" to go around, we do have a demonstrated genius for mass production and sophisticated technology. Therefore, why not apply the strength to the weakness: build love machines; Friend-O-Mats; or, as he calls it, "the mass production of affect."[37]

We're already in the primitive stages of agapurgy.

Courtesy Chicago Tribune-New York News Syndicate, Inc.

A University of Michigan economist reported recently that over four out of ten people who work with machines call their mechanical coworker "a friend."[38]

"Love" was once defined by Sonny Barger of the Hell's Angels as "the feelin' you get when you like somethin' as much as your motorcycle. Yeah, I guess you could say that was love."[39]

Americans have always had a highly erotic relationship with their cars. We choose them on looks, caress them on Sunday, and fondle the stick shift. Now electronic hardware is coming up fast, as our language illustrates. We casually use a startling amount of electrical terminology to describe human experience: "turned on, tuned in, plugged in, getting feedback, on the same frequency, scanning." Someone in the know is "well wired."

I know how involved we can get with our machinery, because I've had such an affair. It was scant years ago that I worked at a printer's and grew to love my mimeograph machine. I would tenderly fit the stencil holes over beckoning shafts. A few gentle tugs on the inking level gradually lubricated the roller with a glistening, oily blackness which eagerly awaited the caress of my fingers, barely protected by a stencil. A quick turn of the crank and the stencil would slide smoothly onto the roller. Then and only then was the machine ready to be turned on. A twist of its dial and the motions commenced, slowly at first, then faster and faster until the mimeograph machine was caught in a frenzy of movement which neither of us could stop until the cycle was complete.

Sometimes the roller would be overlubricated by ink and cause the stencil to slip around. But the closer my mimeograph machine and I grew, the less that seemed to happen. We learned each other's rhythms.

But this involvement was primitive. Burger says the future steps of agapurgy will range from the simple coordination of human services to actual dispensing of mechanical love. ". . . factorial affection," he explains, "may, with sufficient permutation become 'creative' affection. In such an elaboration, sensations are codified

into an alternative decision procedure, an algorithm. Then, d
pending on the incoming stimulus, they can produce highly var
able reactions."[40]

A mathematician at the University of Miami is already trainin
a computer to be a marriage counselor. He has it programmed fc
the 65,000 mood variations possible in a marriage, so that a coupl
can get help from the computer in pinning down the componen
of their spats.[41]

Burger describes a computer being developed at Massachuset
Institute of Technology which, he says, can "engage a psychoti
patient in typewritten dialogue to provide at least the simpler stage
of Rogerian therapy."[42]

A speech therapist at Virginia's Hollins College has programme
a computer to work with him as cotherapist. At first he had th
computer compliment stutterers when their speech improve
When they kept stuttering, it would type out, "That was an awfu
sound, you dummy!"

This proved a little unsettling to patients, so the computer no
greets errors with silence and progress with "Okay."

The therapist, Dr. Ronald L. Webster, hopes to program h
computer to diagnose speech deficiencies by itself, and print ou
prescriptions for treatment. He dreams of eventually establishin
a telephone network which stutterers could call from home, so the
could work on their speech with a connected computer.[43]

The seductive thing about getting close to machines is tha
you needn't sacrifice one iota of anonymity. Also, they're con
venient: available when you want them, shut off when you don'
Machines can not only be trusted as much as a human, they ca
be trusted more.

A Stanford psychologist who recently studied fifty junior hig
school students found that they often preferred computer to huma
instruction. Students said the computer seemed more fair to then
than teachers, they trusted it and "sometimes attributed to it a
almost human role."[44]

Similarly, medical testing clinics are finding that patients often eveal far more to a computer than to any live doctor. "When we irst installed this equipment," says the director of a medical center n Atlanta, "I discovered very quickly that if I was in the room, it ut down on the patient's response. But as soon as the patient and nachine were alone together, things worked out fine.

"An almost human interchange takes place. A real rapport is stablished. . . . After a few minutes, patients forget they're pushng buttons and begin to talk freely with the machine."

A medical testing center in Cincinnati includes a question tovard the end asking the patient whether he or she lied about anyhing. The clinic's director says most will confess if they have.[45]

Machines could prove to be the most trusted friends of all.

LONELINESS, LONELINESS, LONELINESS

It won't work. Agapurgy won't work any more than TV and nagazine communities work, or dialed counseling, franchised riendship, bumper-sticker conversation, thumb-lock trust, encouner-group love, tribal clubs or self-help groups. None of them work s community because none is a place where we're known whole.

We want to be known, whole, and yet . . . .

Ambivalence plagues our search for community. We're desperate o come together, to really know each other, yet do so in ways vhich guarantee we'll stay apart. The common strain in all the ays we seek community is that they allow us to stay unknown to ach other. The forms we seek are risk-free. But getting close sually follows mutual risks. Community is dangerous. Intimacy is ot safe. By always playing safe, we confirm our lack of community.

If any or all of our approaches worked, we wouldn't be suffering uch an epidemic of loneliness.

"The most dangerous sickness in America," the *National Enuirer* calls loneliness. They may run more articles on this topic han any other.[46]

Mother Theresa, an Albanian nun who's worked for decades with the afflicted of India, Pakistan, and Bangladesh, says, "the big gest disease today is not leprosy or tuberculosis but rather the feel ing of being unwanted, uncared for and deserted by everybody."[4

"Loneliness, loneliness, loneliness," says a Social Security official "this is the word which best describes what we came up agains when we sought to locate old persons and tell them about Medi care. We found people hidden away in cold, lonely rooms, deserte by their children, often ignored by their neighbors. They wer frightened old people—and they yearned for companionship."[48]

A Fuller Brush saleswoman told my mother that lots of elderl people on her route buy things just to make sure she comes back.

But it's not just the aged who feel alone.

A sociologist at St. Petersburg Junior College once ran a news paper ad offering to talk to lonely people for $3 an hour. The firs day he says he got fifty responses, from people twenty-five t seventy-six. This expert on loneliness identifies two basic varietie of the malady: the physical isolation of the elderly; and the psy chological isolation which young people can also feel, even i groups.[49]

Nor is loneliness limited to the poor.

New York magazine, whose readers' median income is $19,80 runs articles on the advantages of paying extra for a butcher wh knows you by name, the best telephone counseling services, an window-peeking "as a way to break down city loneliness."[50]

Of Marin County, one of California's richest, a voluntee worker recently wrote, "In this wildly assorted mish-mash o California, loneliness is epidemic and it doesn't really help to sa we were born alone, blow our noses alone and die alone. We ar looking for people to blow our noses with. We are all deliverin a double message: love me and let me be."[51]

We sit alone, or hidden in a crowd, and wonder how it wa that we got so cut off. With luck, we have someone else to blam it on—Dr. Spock perhaps, or Richard Nixon. Perhaps a progran takes our mind away: if only we had a revolution; if only bette people got elected; if only all would return to God and the fla Then I wouldn't be so lonely.

But it doesn't work. Because it's we who cut ourselves off, by the things we value which make it unnecessary to bump into each other: the cars, the computers, the suburban castles.

But these are just tools, reflections only of something more basic cutting us off from each other, which is fear. Fear. Pure and simple. Fear of intimacy. Fear of rejection. Fear of getting too involved. Fear of ourselves, fear of what they might find if we let others peer too deeply inside. That's the basic fear, the fear of being known.

Part III

Building Community

7.

Known at Last!

V. H. Auden recently left New York City and returned to Eng-
ınd, to Oxford. The British poet said he regretted leaving his
dopted home of more than two decades, but explained: "It's
ust that I'm getting rather old to live alone in the winter and I'd
ather live in community. Supposing I had a coronary. It might
e days before I was found."

At Oxford, he said, "I should be missed if I failed to turn up
or meals."[1]

Auden fingered what, for me, is the minimum criterion of being
a community, for being known: that my absence, as well as my
resence, be noted.

Some of us have at least the latter. The bar where they start
) mix your drink as you walk in the door. Or the poker clubs in
ardena, (Los Angeles) where regulars get slipped into games
head of the line. Collections are sometimes taken in these clubs
or afflicted members of the community.[2]

Such a community is more than many of us have—a place
here we're recognized as a unique name, face, and set of quirks.
Vhere we can go every day and be sure of finding familiar faces.

But there's that next level, the one Auden mentioned, of also
eing missed when absent.

Like the old-timers who hang around Brooklyn's state court house and get concerned when one of their number fails to show up for a day or two.[3]

Or the regulars on radio talk shows who worry when a familiar voice doesn't call in for a while.

In Los Angeles a woman has organized her bus around the riders' birthdays. She takes up collections from other passengers then on each person's birthday brings a cake so they all can celebrate while riding. If a regular rider doesn't show up for a couple of days, this woman calls to make sure he or she is okay.

Hokey, to be sure. Yet such groups feel closer to communit than being called "brother" by someone who might not recog nize my face a second time.

The minimum question about whether a group of people i really a community for me is: "Would anyone notice if I didn' show up?"

THE FEAR OF BEING KNOWN

It's a frightening question, perhaps the most scary one I coul put to a group of people. I'd dread so what the answer might be

Better not to ask it at all—anywhere.

This fear, I think, fuels a lot of our frantic rushing around— the feeling that if we just keep moving we'll have an excuse neve to raise such a question with any group of people.

The fear of being rejected also fuels our lust for seclusion. B living in splendid isolation we can beg the question of whethe anyone else would want us around. Not accepted, at least we'r not rejected. Nor do we risk getting known.

Sociologist Georg Simmel said that the luxury of being able t hide out, to keep secrets and not be known is a modern one. I the small bands where man has spent most of his history, "th formation and preservation of secrets is made difficult even o technical grounds: everybody is too close to everybody else an his circumstances, and frequency and intimacy of contact involv too many temptations of revelation."

In contrast, "Modern man, possibly, has too much to hide to sustain a friendship in the ancient sense."[5]

Yet we want it, want that old-time intimacy. We're just loath to take the steps to get there, to reveal any of the secrets.

Even Spiro Agnew talks of "the detachment of modern-day life, the fear of really getting to know one another."[6]

What is that fear? Why are we so scared of each other?

Morty Goldstein, who led a couples group which Muriel and I attended on Long Island, used to say that most of us deal with life as if we were half-crazed people who would have to be put away if we let out too much.

Psychologist Sidney Jourard says: "Many of us dread being known because we fear that if we were . . . known by others—as intimately as we know our own experience—we would be divorced, fired, imprisoned, shot or otherwise harmed."[7]

My fear is a little more mundane.

Once anyone knows me—knows not just my bright side, but also the dark one—will they still like me?

And can they forgive me?

Those are scary questions, but they're ones I know I must ask before attempting to build any real community.

When we lived on a smaller scale and were stuck with each other, there was no choice but to accept and forgive. Being known wasn't so scary because there wasn't much alternative. Like it or not, we played out our lives in full view of the community. People watched us grow and came to know us, intimately. The only alternative to such intense intimacy was exile, which under the circumstances could be worse than death.

Today we're free to choose and reject, be chosen or rejected. This right to choose is a liberation, and also a tyranny. It's much easier to be thrust into community from your mother's womb, with the alternative only to leave. The opposite choice—to ask to be included in community—is terrifying and excruciating, a choice rarely made.

The problem is that it's my option, up and down the line. To reveal or to hide out. It's rare that anything slips out by accident.

So invariably I'll show only the good—the nice, the likable, the happy me. The rest I'll hide, even from friends, till something forces me to drop my guard.

To risk being likable and acceptable *in toto*—grim and cheerful, bad and good, hateful and lovable—is so hard, so painful and frightening that I, as most of us, will go to any extreme, accept any watered-down, simulated intimacy before risking being actually *known* anywhere.

I think that's why we're so ready to accept questions like, "What do you do?" or "What's your sign?" as synonymous with "Who are you?" Such inquiries are so much less taxing, less threatening to answer.

And yet we would like to be known more fully. We're hungry for it. That's why we've developed such ingenious ways to reveal ourselves, to get known, without taking any risk.

NEW APPROACHES TO INTIMACY

It's no longer enough to hide out behind an inscrutable mask. In our evolving social forms, one must give at least the appearance of candor, of revealing something, though hopefully with minimal risk.

When Muriel and I were shopping for a car, of three salesmen we dealt with, two told us about their recent divorces and the third discussed his tendency to come on defensive, since his military parents moved around so much.

That's one approach: to share intimacies with anyone at random, but no one in particular.

While working as a reporter, I used to marvel at the unsolicited confidences which would pop out of people's mouths. Ask someone whether they had seen an auto accident and you'd get a stream of data about how they felt about their spouse, their kids on drugs, and a rotten boss who wouldn't let them take any initiative. It seemed so seductive to have a listening ear, and an anonymous one.

Another popular tack is to split yourself up among enough different people that no one will know all the parts of you. In other words, share your sexual confidences one place, your religious confession a second, and how you feel about your mother a third. If your confessees never meet, you're safe. A guy once described this approach to me with great pride, and said there was no one alive who knew all the parts of him, including (turning to her) "my wife." She smiled and said, "That's okay, dear." But I don't think it was.

Another alternative is to share your intimacy with crowds but not with people.

It's probably easier for John Lennon to scream about his mother to millions of his record listeners than to her, or even to a friend.[8]

It is definitely easier for me to be personal on paper than with someone I know. (I'm far more concerned about the typist's reactions to first-person revelations in this book, than the reactions of the millions of people who, I hope, will read it.)

This secret is one politicians and entertainers have long known. Joan Baez says the easiest relationship for her is with 10,000, the hardest with one.[9]

Once, on a record jacket, Baez told me she loved me.

What's new is the number of us who have access to this approach, to a media which can disperse our confidences to the wind.

"It constantly amazes me," says Bob Eubanks, host of "The Newlywed Game" on ABC, "that these newlyweds can go on national television and reveal the most personal things about themselves, their mates and their marriage. For instance, there was the lovely young girl who announced on the show that she was pregnant. Her family didn't even know about it yet. They talk about how they sleep, how they eat, how they kiss, their ex-boyfriends and ex-girlfriends, their mothers-in-law, everything. And without hesitating."[10]

Bill McIlwain, who was editor of *Newsday* while I worked there, recently wrote "A Farewell to Alcohol," in The *Atlantic*.[11] I had known he was an alcoholic, everyone knew. But I had no notion of what was going on beneath his cheerful exterior. The

Bill McIlwain I knew was a happy-go-lucky guy who treated people very gently, and with high good humor. I liked him a lot, the Bill McIlwain I knew. But his *Atlantic* article revealed someone else, a brooding, disintegrating man who hated that phony exterior and wished he'd had the nerve to tell people off. I never knew. Bill McIlwain revealed more to me in that one article than in over a year of personal contact. Reading the piece made me feel bad that I never sensed his despair, and that we couldn't have shared it in person.

HAPPINESS

Former Congressman Abner Mikva (D.–Ill.) talks of the secret anguish a politician endures until he's "on Cloud Nine when he gets a standing ovation. . . ." More often he lives with "the hidden section of the iceberg—the always happy, always smiling, always waving, always friendly officeholder who pays the piper with his personal relationships. His family are the first victims, then his friends. . . ."[12]

Happiness is a good way to avoid being known, and a common one. "Keep a smile on your face" is one of Abby's rules for being popular.

I know a woman who smiles all the time. She was recently divorced, after ten years of a miserable marriage. She says that during the period only one other person (not her husband) knew what was really going on inside.

> Everybody says I always look so happy
> They all tell me you're so good for me
> They never see the worry that I try to hide
> Cause I keep it covered up so they can't see.
> Appearances can often be deceiving
> And even though the truth one can hide
> But underneath it all, the truth is hurting
> And as long as I've got make-up, I've got pride.[13]

"Only Me and My Hairdresser Know," words and music by Arthur Thomas and Walter Haynes. © Moss Rose Publications, Inc., 1966.

In a recent discussion with some friends, we got into the different ways we're known, and not known.

John Wood, who had just ended a long-term relationship with a woman, said he felt they never really talked honestly, didn't reveal themselves to each other, until the point of parting. Then the risk was low, and there was little danger in letting the other person know everything.

Bill Stillwell talked of the year he spent doing anthropological field work in Mexico. People there would ask him if he were a Catholic. When he would say No, they then would ask, "Well, do you believe in Jesus Christ?" At first Bill would reply, "I'm not sure." But that never seemed to satisfy his questioners, and finally he took simply to saying, "Yes." It seemed more important to his questioners to get some common point of identity than it was to Bill to maintain 100 percent intellectual integrity.

But he spent the year feeling unknown in many ways.

Betty Meador said that being known for her faults was far more important than being known for her virtues. She feels that anyone can accept and love her good parts. That's not hard. But the only people she trusts as friends are the people who know her wholly, the worst as well as the best, yet still accept and love her.

That's close to my feeling. I find that I can't trust the friendship of anyone who hasn't seen the worst of me. Not that I distrust such people. It's just that I can't be sure anyone will stand by me until they know the most compelling reasons not to, yet still choose to be my friend.

It's a paradox. We bend over backward not to display anything but our best side, but the only people we trust are those who have seen the worst, have seen us whole, and still accept us.

And it's not just the worst we're afraid to share, the "I'm unhappy's" or the "I don't like you's." It's also the best, the "I really like you's" or just the "I care about you's." They're revealing too, a tip of a mask.

After Janis Joplin died, her father described in an interview the time his daughter found a lonely Louisiana girl working in a Los Angeles restaurant and persuaded the waitress to return home, even giving her the bus fare. "That's the side of Janis no one ever saw," said her father. "She would only do that if no one was around she knew, if none of her friends were around. She didn't want to reveal her true feelings."[14]

Psychologists say that a clear sign of emotional instability is an exaggerated inability to reveal anything. Lee Harvey Oswald, for example, like most assassins, was an intensely private man. Arthur Bremer hides behind an eerie smile.

"An obvious factor in the background of any neurotic or psychotic sufferer," writes Sidney Jourard, "is his tendency to conceal his authentic thoughts and feelings, in order to live a cosmetic life of pretense." Jourard and other psychologists are compiling a growing body of data which document the centrality of self-disclosure to mental health.

"And yet," adds Jourard, "I have known people who would rather die than become known."[15]

Or, as may have been the case with Oswald and Bremer, kill to *get* known.

TRAGICALLY KNOWN

Stewart Alsop is a *Newsweek* columnist for whom I've always had mixed feelings. I've liked his imagination in seeking stories, and the literate way he presents them. But Alsop's columns are usually written with a lofty disdain which is somewhat irritating.

Last year Alsop found out he had leukemia. He's since written several columns about how it feels to be facing death, his hope that he isn't, and the ways he now perceives the world. For the first time his disdain is gone, and I've felt close to Stewart Alsop and concerned for him.

Alsop says that the only good part about having leukemia is finding out how nice people really are. "Most of us live out our lives behind a thick outer segment, or carapace, that separates us from other people," he wrote recently. "The threat of death breaks that carapace. It makes you deeply dependent on other people—

in my case, my wife, my family, my doctor, my friends and colleagues, above all my wife. Once the carapace is broken, you realize how amazingly nice—there is really no other word for it—most people are."[16]

Tragedy, for most of us, is the only thing that rips off the mask. Once that happens, we're amazed at how many friends we find, how much more loved we feel, and loving.

One family recently decided, as an experiment, to send an honest Christmas newsletter to friends—one describing their auto accident, their sicknesses, their children's problems. They were surprised to find that it was much better received than the ones they had written telling about their good luck. The mother later commented, "I guess people love you more when your luck is down."[17]

And you can love people more.

Lyn Helton, who died at twenty from cancer of the leg, said a few months before: "I think death is sort of beautiful. I've learned to love people. I'm not afraid to say, 'Hey, I love you.' "[18]

Without such a tragedy to rip away our façade, most of us amble along with enough roles, enough masks, and communities-in-part to keep us from revealing anything more than is socially necessary. Yet enough of us are suffering from the awesome loneliness, the hollowness which results from such hiding out, that we're groping about to find some means of rebuilding community, of being able to say, "Hey, I love you," before facing death.

That's the path I've been attempting, trying to find a community where I'm known whole just by saying to friends—the people with whom I feel safest—"I want you to know me better, and I'd like to know you better. Maybe we could be a community for each other."

Having to say such a thing never used to be necessary. When we lived together more closely, worked together and moved around less, our inner selves were revealed to each other gradually and naturally. A sense of community evolved inevitably from our ways of being together. This is true for less and less of us.

For me, it feels necessary simply to accept that truth along with my basic need for community. If this be the case, I have a clear choice: to build a community for its own sake, because I need company to survive; or to limp along with no community, or unreasonable facsimiles.

There are many who feel just as much need for community as I do, but see no such dilemmma. Other community-seekers find it more promising to build anew the forms of community life, to recreate the settings in which we might once again come to know each other as part of our daily life. Such an approach to building community looks more to nostalgic alternatives, or political ones, utopian ventures or ones based on mutual work.

TURN BACK THE CLOCK

Village Park, a San Diego development, says they're "Building a sense of community—from $21,000."

In San José, California, The Villages ask: "Remember how neighborhoods used to be? Where your neighbors really knew one another. Where friendliness was a way of life. And where people waved to one another.

"In today's world, that kind of warmth is hard to find. But you can rediscover this welcome way of life at The Villages. The adult community where neighbors actually know one another, rekindle the warmth of community living and enjoy one another in ways that you probably thought were long gone."

Much of our raging social nostalgia is just such a yearning for community, and the hope of its rediscovery in the forms of another time. "Real Live Butchers to Serve You," advertises Hometown Markets. "A great size for a small group," says Carnation of their quarts of "1880 Old-Fashioned Ice Cream," "The Good Old Days Are Back."

"REMEMBER WHEN KITCHENS WERE MORE THAN JUST PLACES TO COOK?" asks an ad in my Sunday paper.

"Remember coffee clatches with neighbors? Kids playing scrabble on a rainy day? Those 'Mom, nobody's-asked-me-to-the-Prom talks? First aid and sympathy for endless bumps, tears and scratches?

"It all used to happen in the kitchen. It still does in Village Park. Because we've put the 'family' back into family homes. . . ."[19]

The thirst for social nostalgia, if not the marketing of it, may be a sincere hope for a simpler life, a fuller sense of community. But resurrecting the artifacts of another era can't build today's sense of community. Sociable kitchens, butchers up front, and dependable neighbors all contributed to a sense of community when they were needed. Today, such forms are empty shells, social museum pieces. It's no accident that we pay a premium for big kitchens, real-live butchers, and the extra eggs in 1880's ice cream.

We can't pour today's community into old molds. There's no sense in restoring Mom & Pop stores when 7/11 is doing their commercial job better. The point is to make sure that the human contact which once took place within small stores, inside kitchens, on the block, and with the butcher occurs elsewhere. It doesn't, and that's the problem.

Betty and Bruce Meador tried going all the way back once, to their home state of Texas after years away. Betty said there's a kinship she feels with that part of the country which can't be described or duplicated. "I can walk into a café anywhere in West Texas," she explains, "and tell you a lot about the people sitting there right off, without even knowing who they are."

The Meadors thought such roots might be enough to hold them, but they weren't. The pettiness, the oppression of small-town Texas was just too suffocating after years away. The bond wasn't strong enough. So the Meadors are back in La Jolla, California.

Millions of us have gladly rejected the suffocation of total community, and even the partial oppression of churches or clubs where we were once known, and scrutinized. We feel rid of that kind of oppression. At least I do. But we forgot to provide anywhere for the fellowship that went hand in hand with suffocation. The sermons may have been a drag, but the potlucks weren't so bad.

Rather than moon about the old potlucks, though, we'd do better to build a new community now, at home. We keep remembering the small towns and stores because we want back some of their qualities—manageable size, familiar faces, a sense of being known. Few of us will ever again know the kind of total community which intermingled place and kin, work and friends, and fewer of us want to. Feeling guilty about this is no help. Far more helpful is to find out where it is that we do feel community *today*, and to set about enhancing that feeling without getting hung up on obsolete notions of what a community should be.

WAITING ON UNCLE SAM

Some see the building of community as a job for the government, the best path a political one. This can be either within the government through reform, or against it in a revolution. One woman told me that her definition of community was "fighting for my freedom, fighting with my brothers and sisters against the pigs and really getting it together." Ed Muskie, for his part, promised that he would use the Presidency to help build America's "sense of community."[20]

There is much that the government can do to create a climate more conducive to community. The government, for example, could evaluate all social and political programs according to a Community Index, one which would judge programs purely in terms of their effect on human intercourse, whether they brought people together or drove them apart. A Community Index should not be the only one, but should weigh more heavily than it does now.

Urban renewal, for example, might get a "0" for putting beauty, high-rises, and freeways above neighborhoods, people, and community.

Local laws which prevent unrelated groups of people from living together rank at the bottom of a Community Index.

Breaking the rigid zoning practices of most suburbs is top priority, so that living, commerce, and work can again intermingle, leading to environments where people might again like to walk.

Some trends in America are encouraging, such as the growing "community-based" orientation in mental health, corrections, and education.

Most of what's going on in the ecology movement is an encouragement to community (for unrelated reasons) and ranks high on the Community Index. Anything which helps develop alternatives to cars has to be good. In Santa Cruz, for example, ecology-minded University of California students are subsidizing the local bus line. An unexpected result is that students are getting friendly with townspeople whom they meet on the bus.[21]

Still, neither political reform nor revolution can bring about the kind of community I'm concerned about, the kind where people really know each other. The job of government is to mediate among millions of people. This gives them a set of priorities in which community-building ranks low, and should. Feeding the hungry must come first, redistributing income, and keeping us from killing each other.

Take the issue of busing. From a political standpoint the cross-town busing of schoolchildren may be a necessary tool for integration and social justice. From the standpoint of community, busing is a disaster, another wrecker of our neighborhoods. In this case, as in so many, political priorities are at variance with those of community.

Building a sense of community will always be the work of those who want it. The government at times may be able to lend a hand, but only a hand.

TAKE TO THE HILLS!

Some who are ready and eager to build a community, and have forsaken the political route, feel it necessary to leave home, to go elsewhere in search of a richer soil where community may flourish.

Over a century ago, Nathaniel Hawthorne spent a few months among such community-seekers at the utopian experiment of Brook Farm. Later he based his novel *The Blithedale Romance* on that experience, and within it wrote:

> On the whole, it was a society such as seldom met together; nor perhaps, could it reasonably be expected to hold together long. Persons of marked individuality—crooked sticks, as some of us might be called —are not exactly the easiest to bind into a fagot. . . . We were of all creeds and opinions, and generally tolerant of all, on every imaginable subject. Our bond, it seems to me, was not affirmative, but negative. We had individually found one thing or another to quarrel with in our past life, and were pretty well agreed as to the inexpediency of lumbering along with the old system any further. As to what should be substituted there was much less unanimity.[22]

A century later Robert Houriet said of the abortive commune Oz: "In general there was tacit agreement on the kind of society Oz did *not* want to duplicate. And a wide assortment of escapist fantasies. But when the chips were down, the commune was paralyzed, unable to convert fantasy into workable realities."[23]

The main problem with taking to the hills in search of community is that it very rarely succeeds. Going "somewhere else" to build a community can be a fleeing rather than a confronting, a running from as much as a running to. In one sense today's communes are like yesterday's suburbs, a search for a removed, controlled setting in which to build "togetherness."

By such a quest we too often confuse the outer and inner meanings of community. We assume that by creating the structure of community, by moving in with each other away from home, a sense of community will inevitably follow. That's not necessarily true.

I do know of successful communes, ones which sound closer to my conception of "community" than anything I have, or have known. But such communities are good, I think, not because the members took to the hills, but for other reasons, having mainly to do with courage, the courage members have found to stick it out and deal with one another.

"The act of building a physical community is not adequately cohesive to hold people together," write three psychologists with an interest in intentional communities. The problem often is, they write, that "the members begin living together . . . before they have a community."[24]

One suburbanite, a middle-aged man, spent five months driving forty miles of freeway weekly to meet with some people planning a residential community. But the meetings began to interfere with work on the home he was building, his gardening and meditation. The man's present life was being sacrificed for a hypothetical future. So he and his wife quit the group to search for community at home.

"Today," he writes, "I feel that I *am* living in community: the close-knit small business where I spend at least forty hours a week and the varied and always interesting customers; the townspeople and neighbors I see and relate to—these people are quite different from me, but I enjoy their uniqueness; all the groovy and beautiful young people who live in these hills and dig somebody older who knows what they are about; our personal friends, few who live quite like we do or exactly share our interests, but who are leading very worthwhile lives. . . .

"If I had to choose between a close-knit little group closed off from the world, and going on the way I am, I would opt for this life of variety. My coworkers and I are friends. Customers both old and young can be beautiful. My neighbors are unique.

"I feel community can best be realized by tending my garden, building my house, raising my children, and waiting for fulness."[25]

LET'S GET TO WORK!

Stanley Krippner, a psychologist who has studied communes here and abroad, sees a far more significant trend in the groups of people who remain in their homes, but build nonresidential communities based on cooperative projects.

"I think this will have greater impact than the residential commune," says Krippner. "One can still have the nuclear family but also have the advantages of a commune. You can buy wholesale in bulk, babysit for each other, keep certain goods in common, share your children, give classes to each other."[26]

Of all the possibilities I've mentioned, this is the one I'm most ambivalent about, the need for mutual work.

Doing a job together gives people an occasion for gathering, and a means to submerge differences. Out of such work a feeling of community may grow.

The problem is that joint work requires only that you share the part of you necessary to get the job done. Work demands roles, masks to hide behind. Revealing anything unrelated to the job at hand is not only unnecessary, but can be counter-productive. "Since there's work to be done, couldn't you please postpone your nervous breakdown until we get this fence built?"

A community based on mutual work can't be a whole community. It can't—at least for me—be the place where I'm comfortable to be known.

In addition, like soda fountains, mutual work is a social artifact. It's less and less necessary, too much like "made-work" of the New Deal.

Even when authentic work can be shared, the questions remain: How do you really feel about each other? Can you trust one another? Is your community a comfortable one? Is it a safe place to let yourself be known there, fully known?

For me, such questions are more basic to community than tasks to share.

My thought is to reverse the usual process: to say, "I need company." Then, having said this and got it out of the way, find out what things might be nice to do together, without using these tasks as a distraction from the real reason for gathering: the human need for community.

Then common tasks become a terribly important way of knowing each other—working together. There are times in a community when having a job to get done can be basic to keeping it together, just as the work of raising children can maintain a marriage.

A common task is only counter-productive when it becomes your sole reason for being together, just as kids contaminate a marriage held together only for "their sake."

As one among other reasons for being, common tasks may be basic to community. I'm still not sure of the issue. But I feel more each day that I would like to be working with people I like, the people I've asked to be my community.

The basic problem of rebuilding community is that there is so little *need* to be together any longer. At one time a sense of community, of knowing each other, grew naturally out of the activities we had to share. With little left that we *must* do together, we're faced with the prospect of living alone; seeking community in weird ways which keep us apart; rebuilding the external forms of community in hopes that a sense will follow; or taking the direct approach: basing a community on the need for community, getting known by risking getting known.

I prefer the latter approach, and see it as the only real alternative for whole communities of urban/suburban people.

Yet of all the approaches, seeking community directly may be the hardest.

WHAT'S "COMMUNITY"?

Not the least of the problems is knowing in advance, when asking people to be your "community," just what it is one means by that term.

Sociologist George Hillery says we assume that although "everyone 'surely' understands what is meant by 'community' . . . everyone 'surely' does *not* understand! And indeed, the opposite is 'surely' more correct: when you use the term 'community,' you should understand that anyone with whom you may be attempting to communicate probably does not understand what you understand."[27]

It's absolutely basic to define community in advance, to determine how much company one wants, before seeking it. Excepting hermits, we all need some company, some community. But how much we want is a matter of taste. It makes no sense to seek the mother's clutch of a commune if all one really wants is the camaraderie of a bar.

A big problem in defining the term is that too many of us tend to perceive "community" in its most pedestrian meaning—a group of people in the same place; or else we confuse it with "communion"—an ongoing group ecstasy.

We forget that the communities into which we once were born, and today romanticize, included all sorts of people sharing a wide range of feelings, from joy to despair and everything in between. So many of us choose only to remember the good, the love, togetherness and joy, and idealize our definitions accordingly.

The term "community" is neutral. "Community" must mean a group of people undergoing a variety of experiences together, positive and negative. With luck the people will trust each other, and face whatever happens to them as a group. But to assume in advance that "community" will be all good, will be love and ecstasy, is to burden the experience with more than it can bear. Seeking only a community of love dooms the search.

PRESCOTT

I taught a course recently called "Losing, Seeking, and Building Community," with fifteen students, at Prescott College in Arizona.

We met the first day filled with high hopes about being a community of the class for our month together. Some hoped we'd be nearly a commune. Others were skeptical.

"I don't think community is possible," said one eighteen-year-old outdoorsman. "I don't see how you can really be involved with more than yourself." Still, he had felt some sense of community on a recent camping trip, and wanted to extend it.

"I'm really hoping that this will be a very open, loving experience for us all," said a sophomore guy. "I'm hoping that we can be open with each other and I can be open."

We seesawed back and forth, trying to pin down what community meant to each of us. One girl saw it as shared love and joy. Another thought this was impossible, that you had to be self-sufficient and couldn't count on others. A freshman said that any group of people he was with could be community—his dorm, the cafeteria, friends at home.

We worked hard at being a community—reaching out to each other, playing together a lot, rocking and rolling, sharing low-level confidences, going on a four-day camping trip.

Tensions began to build and we met to discuss them. I and others went through periods of utter paranoia about "the group," sure we had blown it entirely.

One night around a campfire during our outing, we got into some mini-hassling, first about chores, details, than about more basic feelings. One student said he was "fed up" that we weren't "doing more" in the class, working together producing something. I got to arguing with him, then with a couple of other students, and finally went to bed. As usually happens after such a scene, it didn't take me a minute to figure, "Oh, oh, you really blew it this time Keyes. You're through with this crowd."

But come morning, people had forgiven and forgotten far more than I had.

We held a weekend encounter group to bring out and resolve tensions. To a degree this happened. Tensions came out and the confessors especially grew euphoric with the lightness of unburdening.

My sharpest memory from the group is of the girl who kept telling us that she could make it on her own, and that everybody had to, since you couldn't count on anybody sticking with you.

But her pained, lined face said differently, and people in the class kept reaching out. Each reach must have seemed a stab, because the girl just recoiled in her corner, almost like a threatened rat.

Finally, having held off the crowd, she said, "There's only one thing I have to say to you people, only one thing I want." People grew quiet. "I want . . . I want—you to *help* me."

She was more surprised than anybody by her words. And by the number of people who reached out to touch her.

Later, the girl wrote, "As time passes the more valuable my 'breakdown' with the group becomes. It was one of the very few times where I was verbally completely honest with myself and exposed it to others. And you people showed such compassion and warmth. I was really in touch with myself, the very gut of my soul was out in the open. What a feeling! I walked around in wonderment for a while, savoring the moment until I backslid and closed up again. But that's okay because it will happen again to me and to others whom I can share with and feel with. That moment was community."

The class morale slid straight downhill after the group. I'm still not entirely sure why. Expectations had been high. Those who opened up were scared and pulled back. Those who stayed closed felt left out. People realized that they just didn't like some others in the class, and didn't want to.

But mostly—and this was the issue on which I slipped up the most—this was a group of people living in a larger community (of the college), and having to deal with each other over an extended period of time. I came in cold and the class was my main community at Prescott. I would be leaving shortly and risked little in revealing myself, in taking chances to build a temporary community with this group of people. The class members had to deal with friends who resented our cliqueishness. And they had to consider that anything they said to each other might be held against them in the future. As such a habitual comer and goer myself, I don't think I'm ever sensitive enough to the compromises people make when they have to live together.

In reflecting on our experience later, the thing which struck me the most was that people who came into the class with high hopes that we might be a commune or something, left the most disillusioned.

One such girl stated loudly and often her expectation that we'd find love and joy together. We didn't, and I retain a vivid image of her during one of the last class periods expressing disillusion by reading the latest *Mother Earth News* during our discussion.

"The course was somewhat disappointing to me," said the sophomore who had hoped we'd be open, "because I put all my energy into 'building a community' and we failed in a way that doesn't clearly show me how to attempt again—or whether it's worth it."

He felt our main problem was "that we had no other objective than 'being a community,' and that there was not total commitment to the group. If I were going to try again, I think I would find a common project to work from."

The guy who began the class saying that "community" was whatever group you happened to be with, at the end wrote: "I no longer want to define community as just a group of people who are incidentally related. The dorm I live in is this sort of community and since I don't value it, I won't discuss it. The type of community that is important to me is one that I *feel* I am a member in and want to be.

"I think a community is simply a group of people who share and what they share determines their community. A dorm 'community' shares a geographic location, maybe more. A class shares a common interest or goal. A club may share a goal or project and a football team shares an interest, activity and goal. A community of friends probably shares all of the above at some time and basically just shares themselves. This is the type of community I desire."

The most interesting response come from the young outdoorsman who had started out saying community wasn't possible. Later he wrote, "I find myself more willing than before to believe in community, to believe in the possibility of intimate contact. For one thing, I am not so insistent on Perfect Truth between people and Perfect Comprehension of self and others. Perhaps I am willing to settle for less. Beyond that, though, I believe I did experience a modicum of 'intimate contact.' I did consciously make myself vulnerable in a way that I haven't done for a long time. I'm used to looking at the world from the end of a long tunnel; I feel that I've taken a few furtive steps toward the open air. I rather like that.

"And yet I don't like it. The ambiguities, the ambiguities—there is a conflict between my old and new self-images, and it hurts. . . .

"The old self is the Autonomous Man, the *Übermensch*, the independent who is proud of his self-control and his ability to live alone in the world. The new self is . . . well, I don't know much about it yet, beyond that it's a community man, more sensitive, more spontaneous—but less independent, less in control.

"The old self doesn't like losing control and autonomy. From its point of view I am falling from the lonely, stoic heights of independence into the disgustingly soft nest of men. From that perspective, I am merely undergoing a failure of nerve.

"From the point of view of the new self, though, I am thrusting out from the blind security of a self-made cocoon . . . yes, laying myself bare but facing reality by doing so.

"Well, what I mean is that I'm straddling the fence between autonomy and community, and I am not sure that I'm either willing or able to complete the crossing. The process involves at base nothing less than a polar reversal of values."

STAGES OF COMMUNITY

In my own flounderings for community, and in watching others, I've seen the same process recur too often to be accidental. It goes something like this:

At first, all is hope and good will. A "community" is to be built. A common purpose will emerge and bad vibrations held to a minimum. With luck, we'll all fall in love. This stage can't survive the first friction between two or more people, the realization that all will not be as expected.

If a second stage is reached, meetings are held to iron out differences. This is done with a renewed optimism that all can be worked out, which at first appears likely. The novelty of airing rather than hiding problems keeps hopes buoyant. Euphoria follows confrontation.

But after a time the group meetings get to be a drag. "Oh, no, not another one," becomes the refrain. As "the community" begins to take individual shapes, you look around the room, becoming dimly aware that you don't really like everyone present, and might not *want* to be in community with them.

This realization is generally fatal. It's the insight on which most communes founder. It doesn't take very long to reach, and can happen within two weeks of constant meeting. Commune experts say that those which survive six months, the minority, jump this hurdle and enter a "second generation" of existence.

This second-generation stage is the point at which a group of people can in fact become a community. It's very much like marriage. After romance wears off, you decide how much you're willing to settle for in each other. It's the same thing in community, except many times harder.

Elaine Sundance, who has spent three years in an Oregon commune, said she was ready to split "and find a better group of people" once the novelty wore off after a year. But she looked around and realized the group she was with were pretty good people. So Elaine stuck it out. Now she talks about the "ecstasy in getting to know other people so deeply. I see people from all angles—morning, night, sick, happy, depressed. You see people doing the same routine on others as they do on you. I find certain inflexible parts of everyone's personality. Like I'll always be nervous and a worrier.

"But then you say—hey—these are human beings. The trick is not looking at someone else and saying, 'I want you to be different. I'm going to make you different.' The trick is to look at another person and say, 'That's who you are, this is who I am.' "[28]

It's identical to the principles of a good marriage. And it's why successful communities are as rare as successful marriages.

DEFINING "COMMUNITY"

An ideal community would be like a good family: the group from which one can't be expelled. Or like Robert Frost's definition of home—the place where when you have to go there, they have to take you in.[29]

But that's ideal, and few of us will ever build such a community.

I've defined my attainable community as "the place where it's safe to be known." This has meaning for me, because trusting people to see me is so hard, and it feels so good when I do. It feels like community. And that kind of community can be built in a range of settlings, from a commune to a bar or a church.

Bill Coulson has settled on "Community is when you're stuck with someone." This has meaning for him, because after years of jetting around the country seeking community among strangers, or in a "Project on Community" in La Jolla, Bill has concluded that his family of nine is community enough for any man. They're the people he wants to make it with, the people he's stuck with and can't run from, his community.

For Bill McGaw, lack of judgmentalism is basic to community. Like so many of us, Bill clams up when he feels others are judging him. "But if I feel understood and accepted by another person, then I'm really in community with that cat."

Bill feels that the basic task in building community is to create ongoing group settings where each member feels safe to drop masks, to let down hair, and not have to play any of the roles demanded by work or family.

"I just wish there was a place I could go to be me," is the way one girl puts it, "just accepted. I don't need to have my back patted all the time, but I sure don't want to have to explain myself all the time either."[30]

NONRESIDENTIAL COMMUNITY

Some people around the country have already begun to build such communities in different ways.

Stanley Krippner said he was impressed by Open End, a nonresidential community of three hundred adults and their children in Marin County, California.[31] Open Enders gather in a great variety of ways, from sexuality workshops through potluck suppers. O.E.'s tone is spiritual, their (paid) coordinator an unorthodox Episcopalian priest.

One Open Ender, a woman just emerging from a messy divorce, said, "I wish I could express how much this warmth and feeling of closeness meant to me at this time in contrast to being isolated in a charming but lonely apartment."[32]

Frank Potter, Open End's coordinator, recently formed a group he calls "Well-Being" to promote similar experiments around the country. He's found a hundred or so members, and is in touch with at least twenty nonresidential communities which are being tried in different parts of the country with names like New Forms Community, Living Room, The Caring Community, The Extended Family Program, Full Circle, Therefore Choose Life, and Transfiguration.[33]

At the Center for Studies of the Person, in La Jolla, about forty of us meet weekly to share ourselves as freely as we can, gather socially in different ways, and sometimes work on projects together. The Center's somewhere between a tribe, an extended family, a professional group, a club, and a gang—with elements of each.

I was trying to explain the Center to a guy once, and mentioned writing letters on its letterhead when I want to seem "official."

"Oh, I get it," he said, his face lighting up. "You're just like a teenage gang and your letterhead is like their jackets. It makes you feel tougher than you really are."

Exactly.

The Center as a whole makes each member feel tougher than he or she might feel alone.

At a recent weekly meeting, Bill McGaw opened by telling us of the death of another member's parents. Bill had just returned from the funeral in Los Angeles, and was still filled with feelings—sadness at the deaths, happiness at the way the daughter was carrying on. The meeting felt sober though not heavy, as each of us sat with our feelings about the passing of a friend's parents, and perhaps with feelings about our own deaths.

Eventually we moved to a discussion of the upcoming election of a new Center Director, or "non-Director" as we like to think of the job. Betty Meador, who has just served for a year in the job, said that was long enough, that the demands of being director were detracting from her personal growth, and she hoped someone else would take a turn. Four interested members were mentioned and they discussed their availability for the job—wanting it, but not wanting to compete.

Steve Doyne, a Visiting Fellow up for membership, talked of his desire to be elected to the Center, and his anxiety over the upcoming vote. "I'm hopeful you'll want me to belong," said Steve, "but I realize you may not. I wouldn't like that, but I could live with it." (He was later elected to full membership.)

We discussed for a while with Betty Meador some new directions she was trying in her work as a therapist, acting as "mother" for one client, in conflict with most accepted counseling theory. Then John Wood broke in to say he was still with Bill McGaw who, an hour after discussing death and funerals, still seemed subdued and red-eyed. Bill said he was okay, that he felt good about the way the funeral had gone, but thanked John for his concern. I had noticed Bill's red eyes too, without being sure whether they were for the dead parents or something in himself. But I hadn't the courage to say anything.

Gaye Williams was lying on her stomach on the floor, Dave Mearns giving her a back rub. Elizabeth Allison joined her and Pat Rice went to work on Elizabeth's back. Then Orienne Strode lay on her stomach on the floor for a while without hands touching her back. Finally Orienne said, "Well I sure am opening myself to a rejection down here like this." We all laughed and I got down beside Oriene to rub her back. Then she did mine.

People started whispering to each other in two's and three's and the meeting broke up.

The direct approach to a community-building means getting together with friends, without a distracting excuse, and saying simply, "I need you. I'm tired of keeping to myself. I want to share myself more and hope you'd like to do the same with me. Maybe if we try together, we can be a community."

That's all. Yet that's probably the hardest, the scariest way to get a community started—the direct way. One guy laughed when I suggested he try it. "When you ask directly to be needed," he explained, "you risk directly being told No."

It's a big risk.

8.

Blocks in Building Community

I may not be the best person available to comment on building community. It isn't my forte. If community came easily to me, I probably would not have spent so much time thinking and writing this book about it.

Being part of a group has always been hard for me, and I've yet to fully open myself to a sense of "community." As an American, a writer, and would-be cowboy, my Rugged Individualism is just too precious for easy trade-in on Membership.

Perhaps that's why the issue intrigues me so, the quest for community—because it's difficult for me. And in stumbling around the problem for so many years, looking in on groups of people and wondering how to get in, I think I've developed a sense of what helps pull people together and what doesn't. That sense could be sharper, the insights clearer to an outsider like myself than to an insider for whom community is "easy."

The elements which strike me as especially important for building a community include manageable size, a willingness to be exclusive, acceptance of oppression and some modicum of commitment.

MANAGEABLE SIZE

I wrote the final draft of this manuscript in a little California town called Comptche. To call Comptche a town is a presumption. Downtown consists of one small store and a post office. The post office closes from 2 to 3 every afternoon so the postmistress can take a break. Comptche's few-score residents are scattered on outlying farms.

Though I'd find it hard to live here the year around, several things impress me about Comptche. The store owner asks for no I.D. to cash a check. She knows who I am. Though the post office is tiny, and the postlady anything but a model of brisk efficiency, I find myself far more sure than in the city that she will get my letters where they're going. The postlady knows me, my name, where I live, why I'm here, and the fact that I'm always getting magazines Postage Due. I get a much greater feeling of trust from that than from the brisk professionalism of the vaguely familiar faces at one of six counters of my post office in San Diego.

One time a sign appeared on the post office bulletin board saying: "The wedding is on for July 21st." The next day that sign was down and another had taken its place, reading, "The wedding is postponed till July 28th." Nothing more.

That's being known.

The benefits of small scale have been ignored too long by Americans, been too long out of style. A manageable size has been considered irrelevant to the quality of our human institutions. The convenience of collected resources, the efficiency of long assembly lines, huge hospitals, and school factories have taken priority.

One analysis of a variety of writings on America found that love of size, of bigness, was something generally agreed upon as unique to this country.[1] It has a lot to do with our loneliness.

We may have come "together" to fight World War II; Texans may feel an intense relationship to their state; when I went to see the Rockets play basketball, I felt very much a San Diegan. But such feelings of "community" are all in the abstract, and generally pass. The other members don't know me, nor I them.

Exhortations about "the family of man," or "the world community" or "our basic interconnectedness" don't help when you're feeling lonely. "It is easier for man to be loyal to his club than his planet," explains E. B. White; "the bylaws are shorter, and he is personally acquainted with the other members."[2]

Size is of the essence. Manageable numbers are basic to any group of people hoping to get close. Trust can only be built among familiar faces.

Dr. William Barclay of the American Medical Association says that although our highly specialized technological society requires the concentration of people into large urban groups, "Biologically, man appears to have been designd to function best in small groups. In small groups he appears to be psychologically conditioned to be supportive; in large groups he tends to isolate himself from the needs of others. . . . Constant awareness of potential threats to his security, lack of support by a small peer group and aggressiveness toward large groups of strangers may be the basis of many illnesses, such as peptic ulcer, hypertension, alcoholism and drug abuse."[3]

It's been only in the last few thousand years that man has clustered in groups larger than his original hunting-gathering bands. John Calhoun, a social psychologist interested in population density, has projected from his studies with mammals that these early bands, man's gathering place for perhaps two million years, most likely had an optimum size of twelve adults and related children.[4]

Though we obviously can survive in larger groups, for the healthiest state of mind, each of us needs one or more smaller support communities where we can take our ease.

At least I do.

Decentralization is an absolute prerequisite to humanizing our institutions. Yet even breaking up the social factories we've built doesn't quite reach the level I'm talking about—the maximum number of people among whom it's safe to reveal yourself, to let yourself be known. A real community for me, a safe one, can't be comfortable with too many members. There's definitely a limit to the size of the group in which I can feel comfortable.

There's a simple experiment which can be done with a group to discover one's "comfort peak." Break down in pairs and chat with one other person. After a few minutes, join with another couple to become a foursome and chat some more. Then become eight and talk again, then sixteen and thirty-two if you have enough time and people. The point at which you become uncomfortable, even stop talking, is probably your "comfort peak." For me, it's anything over twelve. In a group larger than that, I start behaving in very odd ways, if I don't clam up completely.

I have a hunch that one reason juries get so intimate is their legal limit of twelve members.

For my class at Prescott, I had hoped to have ten students. That limit got upped to twelve because so many wanted in. Then, after registrations, dropouts and implorings, we ended up with fifteen members. It was too many. Just those extra three faces over my comfort peak made all the difference. It seemed as though there were always at least three people at any time not being paid attention to, and off somewhere else in their heads.

I've set my limit for intimate community at a dozen members. Others have different figures. Interior designer Walter Kleeman says nine is tops in his experience, the maximum number of people who can see what's going on in each other's faces, while sitting in the average circle.[4a] In his book *The Corporation Man*, Anthony Jay comes out for the "10-unit," as closest to the size of most hunting bands, of basic military units throughout history, of athletic teams, juries, and the Jewish minyan. "Indeed," he writes, "once you look around at human groups with the hunting band in mind, the number leaps out at you. . . . it is the driving force behind all creative corporate achievement."[5]

John Calhoun says any group numbering more than twelve adults requires an increase in conceptual size to compensate. Because of this we developed villages, then states and nations with their roles for members to play. Calhoun points out that when a group grows beyond a dozen members, the intensity of interaction each person has with another is reduced.[6]

In other words, you have just so much attention to give to other humans. The more people in your community, the less attention each one gets.

My point isn't that I want to restrict my contacts to a dozen people, or that we should bring back the hunting bands. But—even when living in city or suburb—I want to keep my total human contacts manageable, live on several different levels, and make sure that at the heart of these levels is an intimate, small, support group.

Social metaphors help me pin down what I want—a basic small community around me, a family of friends with whom I can share myself fully, numbering no more than a dozen.

I want an extended family, or neighborhood of friends, maybe fifty people or so, who know me and recognize me, with whom I can share good moments and fond glances, but not feign intimacy.

And I want a larger clan, or town with no more than five hundred people, who know my face and among whom I feel safe but don't pretend to feel close.

Muriel's mother says that her most pleasant memories are of the years they summered in Shrub Oak, New York, a community of about five hundred people in eighty-four homes near Peekskill. "We had some close friends," she says, "many casual friends, but we all knew and greeted and cared about everyone. People didn't lock their doors." Today Reba shares a high-rise with thousands of others on New York's lower East Side, and knows only her next-door neighbor. Her door has three locks.

If some size around five hundred is the optimal boundary for social intercourse, that obviously leaves out most of us, those of us in cities and suburbs.

For a long time I accepted this as truth: that community could never be reborn except in a small-town setting.

I agree with sociologist Robert Park, who wrote earlier this century:

> In the little worlds where people come close together, human nature develops. The family, the tribe, the local community are instances. To the extent that we have intimate relations, we get responsiveness to one another. The definite personalities that we know grow up in intimate groups.[7]

But Park lived in Chicago.

Later, I read and concurred with biologist René Dubos that "During evolutionary development, the human species probably functioned in small groups, each member knowing the other personally. Many may have need for larger gatherings now and then, but certainly not as a constant diet."[8]

Dubos lives in Manhattan.

And I live in San Diego.

And at this time I have no intention of giving up either life in the city *or* my quest for community.

So. Does this mean I must sacrifice the latter for the former?

I don't think so. I think the kind of community I'm talking about can occur in city or town, if one makes it happen. I'm talking both of Norman Rockwell's intimate small towns, and of the New York City of Jimmy Breslin, Pete Hamill, and Jane Jacobs—a city of bar-communities, hangouts, and grocers who will keep your key while you're away.

Mademoiselle once asked some of its editors to give their prescription for survival in New York. Planted among the usual remedies like smiling more, keeping your cool, and one deadpan comment that "During the week I find tranquilizers a great help. . . . Weekends, alcohol and grass," was the best prescription I've read for survival in a city.

> Make friends with your butcher, cleaners, grocer . . . the florist who'll throw in a couple of roses when you buy your biweekly bunch of daisies. . . . I cope with the city's noise, pollution and ugliness by living in the least citylike part of the city—little traffic, or noise, 200 feet from a small park, 100 feet from a big river. . . . Live in the slums or

semislums. It's more human, sometimes horrible, but always personal. You *have* to get to know your neighbors, the kids, the grocers. You live with them. It's safer too. If "the block" knows you, they watch out for you. . . . I live in my area because it is fairly empty on weekends, and that makes me feel like it's my own private city. . . . I guess I've come to live best in New York by converting it into a small town—an East Side neighborhood just a few blocks square; some really close friends I've known a long time; a homey Irish pub around the corner, where I'm on a first-name basis with the bartender, that even my mother (her maiden name was Murphy) would love. From this microcosmic base, I make occasional forays into "other" parts of the city—to the theater, art museums, a club, the homes of friends—but I suppose only in that one small part of town do I really feel at home.[9]

EXCLUSION

There's a pitfall inevitable in building a small support group in city or suburb. If it's a good group, an intimate collection of friends with a family feeling, lonely people will flock to join. Then the community must decide whether it's okay to exclude.

This is a major problem with which communes have had to cope. Word of a good, "together" group spreads fast. Soon all manner of castaways start peering in the windows, scuffling on the roof, and screaming through the keyholes.

Elaine Sundance said it took her commune in rural Oregon a full year of agonized soul-searching before they reached a consensus to exclude. The group at first refused to turn away anyone wishing to join. But by the second summer, after a stable group had been together for a year, it felt right to close membership, to tell newcomers—truthfully—that there was no more room.[10]

This decision is inevitable. Communes deciding not to exclude, to welcome all, end up running crash pads.

For a long time I was sure that it was 100 percent wrong to exclude anyone from a community. The thought of belonging to an "in" group, a clique which kept others out, brought back too many painful memories of groups which have left me out.

But in practice, communities open to all quickly become like hotels, a collection of casually friendly people with little real trust.

The need to exclude is one of the harshest realities with which would-be community builders must cope. It grates against every humanistic instinct to openness, hospitality, and tolerance.

But there's no alternative path to a truly intimate community.

If you did or have done the 2-4-8-16 experiment mentioned earlier in this chapter, check yourself out. Did you resent the intrusion of newcomers once you had some rapport built with one or more others?

I usually do.

And I find that once I've built some trust with a group of people, once I feel they know me and I know them, the presence of even one stranger can make me awfully uncomfortable.

My trust is not indiscriminate.

We've had to struggle with this issue more than any other at the Center for Studies of the Person. Though most members theoretically accept the okay-ness of being exclusive, in practice we've always made plenty of exceptions because we are, after all, decent people—humanists. But then, when all kinds of strange faces start floating around, we've found our contact with each other less and less intimate.

Recently the group put down its collective foot and held the first series of members-only meetings. We were as exclusive as a secret society, cliqueish as a fraternity.

And it felt good. There were only thirteen of us present at the first such meeting, attention was paid to each person, tempers got lost, joy was shared, and the talk was straighter than in any "open" meeting I've attended.

I'm not saying that it's necessary or even good to exclude *all* outsiders. A community with completely stable membership would get as dull as *Main Street* very quickly. But the crucial point for an intimate community is that it controls it's own access, chooses new members, and is not just like a hotel.

Being open or closed was a big issue for us in the class at Prescott. A lot of students not in "the community class" resented our cliqueishness and sometimes tried to sit in on our sessions. We did decide to exclude, but never really decided it was okay.

One girl, by the end, stoutly objected. "A Community needs an outsider," she wrote.

"We thrive on them. Our exclusiveness became an obsession. . . . Rather like the school kids with their chant of 'Tick-Tock, the game is locked, And nobody else can play!' "

But another student, the one who began by defining community as the world and all its people, ended up almost walking out of a class with some strangers present because their very presence made his stomach queasy.

The strangers made me uncomfortable too. Show-offy. I wasn't myself.

And the girl's right. It is snobbery. Since realizing the incredible complexity of building a community, and the delicacy of the trust required, I've come to have far more respect for those "parochial" members of clannish societies whom I've always sneered at for being so suspicious of "outsiders."

Maybe they were onto something all along.

In her study of a small Tennessee Appalachian community, characterized by intermarriage and rigid clannishness, Elmora Matthews described this scene:

Strangers occasionally attend a local auction and are sometimes successful bidders on small items. By valley terms, these are not "rank strangers," for a "rank stranger" is a person never seen before. These "strangers" have been numerous times at county-seat auctions. If a stranger bids on land, the auctioneer often says he has a "secret bidder" who will top the stranger's bid, or he speaks to the stranger at intermission, saying there is a sentiment attached to the land and that the children will give much more than it is worth. Sometimes he makes a public plea as: "Here is a sister who wants to live by a sister." If the strangers should persist, the land may be withdrawn, or the stranger may even be involved in a brawl. Everyone in attendance is made aware of the importance of neighbors, and outsiders sense that they would not fit into the community. One outsider admitted, "I wouldn't think of buying that land. I would feel continually embarrassed like I was living in someone else's home where I didn't belong."[11]

Not too long ago, that would have sounded awfully quaint to me, dumb and backward.

Today I rather envy such solidarity.

I'm just beginning to realize that there is a basic difference between intimate or "primary" relations with people and casual or "secondary" contacts—even friendly ones.

I think back on the many times I've entered groups of people with a history, acted in my most affable manner, and assumed we became "friends"—intimate, trusting.

Now I can see it was nothing of the kind, that I just had no feeling for the subtle kinds of intimacy people build only over time.

I hope I can do the same. And I know that to do this, I will have to exclude.

OPPRESSION

Recently I've been reading about an outfit called Leadership Dynamics Institute which has developed a weird cross between encounter and the Inquisition. Participants in LDI's four-day groups are beaten, deprived of food and sleep, and subjected to hours-long harangues from other members until they break down, confess their shortcomings, and plead for the group's forgiveness. Conservative businessman William Penn Patrick, father of this method, says all but a few of the two thousand participants in his $1,000 weekends have loved it—"a claim," says one news report, "that hotelmen who have sponsored the seminars somewhat incredulously support."[12]

But it's not incredible at all. Individualism is a terrible burden, and when ripped away from us in exchange for submersion in a group, we're ecstatic, reborn, free at last from the tyranny of our selves.

There is an inescapable relationship between brotherhood and oppression. Any group setting out to build community must anticipate this relationship and deal with it. Being in community doesn't make you more free; it takes away some of your freedom in exchange for the warmth of membership. Ignoring or denying that trade-off just makes it harder to confront.

William Whyte was, and is, one of the few social critics to give this dilemma the sensitivity it merits.

In his book *The Organization Man,* Whyte described the post-World War II suburb as essentially a utopian experiment. To him Park Forest was directly descended from Brook Farm.

Listing the apparent and subtle control which suburbanite groups put on their members, Whyte wrote: "I am not for the moment trying to argue that yielding to the group is something to be admired, but I do think that there is more of a moral problem here than is generally conceded in most discussions of American conformity." He continued:

> If he goes along with them he is conforming, yes, but he is conforming not simply out of cowardice but out of a sense of brotherhood too. You may think him mistaken, but grant at least his problem. The group is a tyrant; so also is it a friend, and *it is both at once*. The two qualities cannot easily be separated, for what gives the group its power over the man is the same cohesion that gives it its warmth. This is the duality that confuses choice. This duality is a very unpleasant fact. Once you acknowledge how close the relationship is between conformity and belongingness—between "good" and "bad" participation—you cannot believe in utopia, now or ever.[13]

To deny the relation between community and conformity, to call them two different things, is to make community that much more difficult to achieve. To be in community requires the sacrifice of at least part of your individuality. To belong to a group you must accept the group will at least sometimes, like it or not. That's as true at Esalen as it is in Levittown. For me and for anyone seeking community it then becomes a question of how much autonomy to trade in. Is the community I want Synanon or a radio talk show?

An actual commune or any other total community holds little

appeal for me, at least at this time. I'm too jealous of my liberty, my individuality. There's precious little in me I'll turn over to any group on demand.

I don't want to belong fully any more than I want to be fully free. I do want, within any community, to be able to say, "Hey. I know I have to give in to the group sometimes. But that's hard for me, and I can't do it too often. So: just this once. Or: lay off."

A self-described twenty-year veteran of the Hippie Movement wrote to *The Whole Earth Catalog* that in his experience communes based on freedom failed within a year, and that only authoritarian communes had the power to survive. "I am not pleased with this conclusion," he wrote, "but it now seems to me that the only way to be free is to be alone."[14]

I don't know what to do with such a truth except acknowledge it, and, with Whyte, renounce any hope for utopian community.

That renunciation actually is a kind of freeing thing. Utopian visions sell man short, I think, for they make him something other than what he is: subtle, complex, jealous of his individuality. Once I've given up hope of a community either fully brotherly or totally free, then I can get on with building a real community of complex people.

Which sounds much more interesting.

COMMITMENT

The other day I looked around at the twelve other faces in the Center meeting and wondered what I was doing with such an older and settled bunch of people at my tender age. I should be out with the counter-culture—hitching around, slipping in and out of communes and relationships.

And a big thing struck me. These people were here last year and they'll probably be here next year. Their kids are in school, they own houses, they've slowed down a bit, some have jobs.

Also, they feel at least a little rooted in San Diego, and at the Center.

Roger Ledbetter came back recently after traveling the world for the better part of a year for the Peace Corps. He'd been to Nepal, Jamaica, Hong Kong, Bangkok, Calcutta. It was great to see him walk in the door. And great to feel together with the others welcoming Roger back, just as I liked having the Center welcome me back after only a month away in Prescott.

And I'm conscious that the Center's "family" feeling has grown up only after years of being together in varied ways, good and bad.

It's made me realize that a basic means of finding out who is in my community and who isn't is simply commitment and time. There is no alternative for building trust.

The Center's main work since its founding in 1968 has been in encounter groups. We're skilled at helping others get close quickly, to find trust and love during a weekend or so.

For ourselves, the task has been more difficult. We'll be together next year, as last, which tends to tie the tongue.

But it also results in a deeper form of trust and intimacy. I can blow it today, and know a community will still be there tomorrow where I can work things out.

Recently some Center members put on what may have been our last full set of weekend encounter groups, our "Weekend with Carl Rogers."

In the post program discussion, it turned out that practically every Center member participating independently reached the same conclusion: "It was a good weekend, but I don't want to do that any more. I wonder what we can do next?"

Rogers himself, a Center member who once wrote that he considered encounter groups the most significant social invention of this century, said: "Though I'd still do them, that's not my choice. You can leave with a real high, but there's no follow-up. It's more costly, less dramatic and more lasting to reveal something to someone you've known for years."[15]

A community simply cannot be built from people crouched and ready to take off, like foot racers awaiting the crack of a gun. Commitment is basic. There is just no way that a community can be forged from people trying to make up their minds about whether to belong, community-seekers who keep their bags packed and ready.

Fear of commitment may be the biggest barrier to the rediscovery of community, including marriage.

When I say "commitment," I don't mean a signature in blood, nor even a long-term contract. What I do mean is a willingness to stay through friction, to work on problems when they occur, to be a little stuck with each other. That may not be "commitment" according to Webster, but it's more than many of today's "communities," even today's marriages, enjoy.

In his book *Getting Back Together*, Robert Houriet describes with great perception the scores of communes he visited in America's east and west during 1969-70. Throughout his months of travel, and few days' stay at a variety of settlements, Houriet comes through as sensitive, involved, sometimes even in love with the communards he visits. He describes with tolerant disdain some of the friction that occurs between commune members, especially the "up-tight" types who resent nonworkers and want a little more privacy.

When Houriet returns to Vermont, though, to wife, children and friends, his tone changes. Some of the communards he got to know come by to visit, and a handful stay. At this point Houriet himself becomes tense and irritable. The constant borrowing of his car bothers him. He resents one guy drinking all the Hi-C, and posts a note on the refrigerator saying "JUICE FOR KIDS (UNDER 7)."

And Houriet is honest enough to let us know that he's a different person when visiting a commune temporarily, from the one trying to live a commitment at home.[16]

Without confusing temporary and committed community, some opt for the former. That's the approach of Richard Sennet, a young sociologist, who says that his kind of community is best found in the disorder of a city. "In the adult society I envision," writes Sennet, "there would be no expectation of human love, no community of affection, warm and comforting, laid down for the society as a whole. Human bonds would be fragmented and limited to specific, individual encounters."[17]

That's an honest vision of a society in which I wouldn't want to live, one in which disposability infected every relationship. But it's an alternative not masquerading as anything other than a community of transients. Confusion of that alternative, of disposable communities, with ones based on commitment is what creates problems.

Two sociologists have written that our speeded-up styles of friendship formation have made our communities-in-flux comparable to a more stable kind. "Even though a person has a shorter time span in the group," they write, "because of rapid integration he may have the same social span as individuals in groups with a more stable population."[18]

That's like confusing hothouse tomatoes with the kind grown more slowly outside: they seem the same only until you bite into them.

A basic problem I had at Prescott was intermingling my temporary community with the student's permanent one. For me, the community of the class was disposable. I was in town only for a month, at which point I'd return to my "real" friends in San Diego, perhaps never to see the Prescott friends again. They, on the other hand, could expect to be around each other for up to four years. I knew this, in my head, but don't think I ever really confronted the difference in my soul. For me to be honest and revealing wasn't hard; I'd be going home soon. For them, any drop of the guard was a fundamental risk to take with people who would hold them accountable.

Many people of the future don't accept the fundamental difference between ongoing intimacy and the disposable kind. I think that's why so many communes are unintentionally disposable and disposed. The "high" of a short time together just can't be sustained.

Harvey Cox has said that the case I'm making, for a certain rootedness as part of community, is a reactionary one. "The desire to combat mobility," he writes, "to encourage residential and occupational *im*mobility, is a romantic distortion which springs from a reactionary mentality."[19]

So be it. In fact, though, I can't argue against mobility and in favor of commitment for its own sake. I enjoy moving around, and like temporary relationships too much for that.

What I am saying is that for the kind of community I've missed in the process, the intimate kind where people *really* come to know each other on many levels, I know that I'm going to have to stay put somewhere for a time.

Having sat tight in San Diego for the eternity of three years, I've just slowly begun to realize some things about enduring friendship which were never clear to me before.

Mostly what I've learned is that it's okay to make mistakes. People who expect me to stick around allow me to screw up more than I allow myself. Our friendship isn't dependent on my being nice and likable every minute we're together.

This may sound obvious, but it's never been so to me.

And I've found also that my expecting people to be here next year, and remain friends with me, makes me more relaxed, more trusting, better able to share deep parts of me than I can with friends whom I see only occasionally.

The other night, at a meeting with some Union Graduate School students, I was tired, drank too much wine, and was acting cranky and preachy, as I will when I'm tired and drink too much. The next day I saw John Wood and asked how I had seemed to him. John said, "I noticed you were acting strange. Angry, kind of. But then I remembered that you get that way when you're tired."

That felt great, to know a friend knew enough about my moods to adjust what he could see to what was probably going on inside.

I've not been sure of this with most friends, who had trouble seeing beneath my moods mainly because I wouldn't let them.

Something I love about the southwest is the barren mountains with their painted layers (the "purple mountains' majesty").

The coloring in these mountains changes throughout the day with the sun. Before the sun rises, colors contrast poorly in dull browns and tans. As the sun comes up, tans become pink and browns change to purple. Shadows define the bold lines of crevices. By noon, the mountains have become another range altogether. Colors bleach and blend into a gentle orange. At sunset, desperate last rays struggling not to go down cause the terrain to explode in a last, futile, beckoning red.

That's the way those mountains change during a day. I don't know how they change over a year, or over the years. Certainly less dramatic and more profound changes are always taking place. The only way I could know about these more subtle changes would be to hang around the mountains every day for years.

That's true of me too. I change by the hour, by the second. I'm different this year from what I was last. And my April me is different from my March me. If you weren't around to see it, you missed the show. I can only give you a recap, tell you what I think went on. But it loses a lot in the translation.

I never realized how true this was until I stuck with a few people for a while, as they with me, and saw my different hues reflected in their eyes.

It's been exciting, something totally different from dipping in and out of people's lives.

Last year, Howard was my closest friend, and we saw each other almost daily. We'd barge in on each other laughing, depressed, or in tears.

This year, Howard moved twenty miles north. We still see each other from time to time, but it's not the same. Him telling me what went on last week and vice versa is not the same as witnessing it. We won't be close in the way we were until we see each other that often again.

I'm just beginning to understand the difference betwen friendship on the move and friendship in place.

It's the same word, with two different meanings.

We don't *have* to be together as we once did, so now we must *choose* to be together and find the courage to say so, to look around at a group of friends and say, "I want you to be with me. I need you to be my community. And I'm willing to make some sacrifices for it."

Once we've made that commitment, with a small group which will stay small, one which is willing to trade some individuality for company, an infinite variety of tools can be found to keep a community alive.

9.

Tools

SOURCES

Some of my friends say a "new man" is evolving—flexible, open, sensitive—one who will discover new tools for community. I have yet to meet such a man, and find myself more often poking around musty old basements in search of wisdom about community: country and western bars, ethnic groups, Weight Watchers, shopping centers, churches.

Elaine Sundance says she's been reading books about nuns because she finds their problems in convents are the same as hers on a commune. "The biggest problem is just living with other people."[1]

Andrew Greeley, a sociologist of ethnic groups, says we have much to learn about urban survival from the weddings and cotillion balls of immigrants, as well as from their life in general. ". . . the ethnic collectivity," he says, "represents an attempt . . . to keep some of the values, some of the informality, some of the support, some of the intimacy of the communal life in the midst of an impersonal, formalistic, rationalized, urban industrial society."[2]

They did this by huddling together in neighborhoods, in hangouts, with uniforms to spot each other, ritual, songs, dances, and their own media.

Clifton Bryant says we ought to be paying more attention to carnivals. Bryant, a Kentucky sociologist who has spent time among them, says carnival employees have a lot to teach the rest of us about living in community.

"Carnies" work together in a complex but unbureaucratized system. They feel a strong social bond and give each other help—physically, financially, and psychologically. The carnival provides opportunities for young people to meet, court, marry, and raise children within a small community setting. The marriages themselves are more stable and egalitarian than most, usually a working partnership.

Carnival workers are very conscious of being a community apart, and have an elaborate vocabulary of their own, which includes words like "chump heister" (ferris wheel), "simp twister," (merry-go-round), and "dentist's friend" (candy apples).

But the main thing Bryant says we can learn from carnies is tolerance. Their community includes a wide variety of the physically handicapped, mentally retarded, psychologically misfit, addicted, and afflicted. Though carnivals are full of "freaks," nobody is rejected as too odd, and work is found for all.

"This therapeutic atmosphere is a long way from the more sophisticated occupations where an employee's role is firmly fixed and the tolerance of eccentricity is almost nil."[3]

Convents, carnivals, ethnic groups—the tools for community are where you find them.

A HANGOUT

When Jim Hubbard started his free school, he felt that a common space was unnecessary. Liberated from the confines of classrooms, or any rooms, his students would be free to roam the city, come and go, coalesce or not—as they chose.

Now, a year later, Jim's mind has changed. "When you have

no place, everything must be planned," he explains. "No accidents happen. People don't run into each other by accident."

That's been my experience. I don't have a community hangout, and miss it. I like "just running into people," but have no place to do so.

Before we jettison place entirely as a factor in community, I think we'd better consider what values it can have, and what community needs may best be met in a fixed location.

Phillip Slater goes so far as to say, "A community life exists when one can go daily to a given location at a given time and see many of the people one knows.

"This effortlessness is central to my definition of community life."[4]

Slater is concerned that dwindling numbers of us have such a place, that there are few hangouts for urban/suburban people, and most socialization takes place in homes, by special invitation.

To an affluent mentality, the notion of such "a hangout" can sound quaint—one step above a kid's clubhouse. One reason the Beverly Hillses of this country are such lonely places is that they've zoned out anything which might become a hangout.

But for those who don't live within community—most urban/suburban people—a place where one can run into friends may be the most basic tool for building community. The people who are beyond "hanging out"—well-to-do, urbane, years out of school—may be the ones who need most to hang out.

Hanging out is not as simple as it may look. Journalist Pete Hamill says it's a learned skill, "a complex, sometimes tedious, but absolutely necessary element of the human experience. The human who has mastered the art of Hanging Out has at least a small shot at survival and perhaps even at happiness."

"To Hang Out is a special thing. There is no specific way to define the experience, but everyone who has ever done it knows what it is all about. It means, first, that you have friends. . . .

"But aside from friends, there must be a Place. I suppose this is the Great Good Place that every man carries in his heart, the place of safety, the place where the harshness of the real world is fended off, through the guile or stratagem or the high wall of aloofness."

Ethnic groups tend to place a heavy emphasis on hangouts. When such a group gets itself together amid the city, a "place" is usually one of the first things they sponsor. In New York, the Puerto Ricans have so many clubs that they're organized on the basis of hometowns on the island.[6]

Though less true than it used to be, a range of ages can still feel comfortable in such clubs—three generations and more. Jim Hubbard says the thing he liked most about going to San Diego's Mexican nightclubs with his wife was feeling the presence of so many generations.

Elmora Matthews' Tennessee hill people hang around the local grocery. Usually open 6 A.M. to 9 P.M., it stays open later on Friday and Saturday nights, when the last families leave around midnight. "It is a meeting place for young and old of both sexes, a news center, an every-evening social gathering place. Families have the habit of visiting at the store after supper and during slack workdays. . . .

"If one asks the whereabouts of kinsfolk, the answer is, 'If you go to the store, you're sure to catch some of them.' The men gather around the wood stove in the back of the store by winter or on the porch and in the crossroads by summer, while the women sit at the front of the store year around. Messages and articles and children are left and picked up at the store. Individual dates and groups of young people meet there."[7]

I know of no hangout like that around here, especially one which welcomes such a diversity of generations.

The supermarket and the laundromat have bulletin boards, but I rarely know anyone else reading the notices.

Our milkman just started distributing a flyer which will be coming biweekly, and includes ads from one customer to another. So the milk truck now serves part of the function that hangouts used to serve, saving us the trouble of leaving the house.

Except I like to. To me, looking at messages or getting a cup of coffee somewhere is almost incidental to the "bumping into people" that can happen where messages and coffee and people come together.

SHARED HARDSHIP

The Center for Studies of the Person (C.S.P.) grew out of the Western Behavioral Sciences Institute in 1968. The parting was painful, preceded by months of recrimination, colorful memos, and noisy meetings.

I wasn't there then and am very conscious of having missed the most important experience in the life of C.S.P.'s community. Those who were present tell me I'm just as lucky, that the experience was excruciating. I'm sure they're right, but beside the point. The point is that people seem to weld much closer together from sharing hardship than from sharing joy. Crises are remembered much longer than celebrations.

I think few of us recognize, or admit, how seductive calamity can be, how long remembered by those who shared it.

San Diego has one of California's two "1906 Clubs" for survivors of the San Francisco earthquake. That seems like an occasion worth sharing with other people who lived through it, even well over a half century later.[8]

John Wood talks of the bittersweet attraction of disasters—of earthquakes, war, and a death in the family. "Who doesn't remember Pearl Harbor as an exciting (though tragic) time?" he asks. "When President Roosevelt died it was a great day. Everyone listened to everyone else—all the women cried and the men became soft, and everyone had plenty of time—no place to rush off to."

By building environments with most hardship eliminated and all risks zoned out, we've forced ourselves and our children far afield in search of shared danger. Some turn to drugs, others to motorcycles, still more to rock climbing. Or various combinations.

A friend of mine, a philosopher, was once on a panel with commercial pilots discussing better procedures for air safety. Finally he raised the question: Do you and your passengers really want more safety? Isn't the risk part of our reason for flying? The howling, the clamoring to shout him down showed how sensitive a nerve the philosopher had struck.

We may never be able to engineer hardship entirely out of our lives, but we have done a pretty good job of eliminating the need to share our trials with too many others.

The opportunity to share risks spontaneously is almost nonexistent. With money, we can buy shared hardship. Outward Bound offers a high-risk disposable community experience to those who can afford the two weeks of survival deprivation.

"When I went up there," said one seventeen-year-old girl of her $450-Outward-Bound experience, "I don't think I'd ever apologized or said I was sorry in my life. I would rather have lost a friendship than admit to being wrong. But somehow, being on that mountain alone taught me how to say, 'I'm sorry.' It doesn't hurt to say it anymore."[9]

Prescott College orients its freshman in an outdoor, shared-danger experience which includes a 150-foot descent of a cliff by rope. Students don't forget the ten days quickly, and it forges a strong common bond on campus.

One way of looking at encounter groups is as induced-crisis. Within hours in a group one can have the fights, anger, tears, tragedy, and confrontation which normally are spread over years in the life of a community. Some of the best encounter groups hover on the verge of disintegration throughout. Encounter is one way we replace the excitement lost when our lives became so safe.

In an interesting blend of encounter and Outward Bound, a marriage counselor at Brigham Young University is sending married couples off for nine days on mountaintops in Utah with only a knife, sleeping bag, change of clothing, and tin can.

"We took this class away from our complex society to force the couples to communicate," explains the counselor.

The experience caused one husband to call their snowy and rainy nine days together "one of the few times in our marriage where Nancy and I were able to share a feeling of accomplishment."

"We stripped away the urban façade and did away with all the distractions," said another participant. "We've been able to concentrate solely on building our marriage—not competing with each other but cooperating."[10]

We've made our communities safe from danger to share. So now we replicate it and charge tuition. I honestly don't know if contrived hardship is better than none at all as a tool for building community. It does seem to work.

Earl Burrows keeps saying he'll take Center members down the Green River on a raft. A consultant on humanizing organizations, Earl says its very important that members have adventures together. An adventure includes stress, and in stressful situations you get to know yourself and see others in brand-new ways.

A raft trip also has the advantage that people can't leave, he points out. You have to learn to live together. You're stuck with each other—for five full days.

A SENSE OF DEVIANCE

Twenty-six miles inland from Comptche is the town of Boonville. Boonville is peculiarly isolated within the Anderson valley, and after the town was founded over a century ago its few hundred residents grew quite clannish. "Outlanders" found Boonvillites "backwoodsy," and made fun of them, called them "squirrel chasers."

Toward the end of the century Boonville residents got in the habit of flaunting their deviance, and to do so invented a language of their own—Boontling.[11]

Boontling is fractured English. Its thousand or so words, with infinite variations, grew directly from local lore. Since the constable wore elevator shoes (owing to a youthful injury), to arrest someone became to "high heel" him. A local guy named B.J. always repeated himself, so repeating anything was known as "beejaying." Baseball was known locally as "buzz chick" because that was the sound of a pitched ball hitting the catcher's mitt. A black man was a "booker tee" after Booker T. Washington. A black woman was a "she booker."

At its peak, Boontling had about five hundred speakers. But any resident of Boonville could understand the language just from associations. No local needed to be told that "madging" meant whoring. A notorious madame in nearby Ukiah was named Madge.

Aside from just being fun, Boontling clearly distinguished "outsiders" from "insiders."

"Boonters," as they called themselves, could talk any old kind of dirty or putdown talk around strangers. When their baseball team played Philo, secret signals could be yelled. Outsiders sometimes would try to catch on and join in the fun, but without success. Boontling was so intimately tied in with the people and culture of its region that no outsider could hope to catch all the nuances. "Barney, for example, as a verb meant to hug and kiss. A local by that name did so often. But "barneys" as a noun meant cowboy boots after another Boonter who wore them.

Boontling is one of the most obvious examples of a creative use of deviance for building community, one which became a self-feeding process. The special language made Boonville residents seem more odd, more deviant to outlanders; the more deviant the Boonters felt, the more they took to Boontling as a defense.

But mostly what Boontling did was confirm members of the community to each other. Even Philo residents who picked up some of the language were never considered "real" Boonters.

A sense of deviance is badly underrated as a tool for building community. Some of our most cohesive communities are based at least partly on their members' sense of being "different"—hill people, religious sects, ethnic groups.

Andrew Greeley says that although tribal separatism perhaps ought not to continue in a rational, industrial world, "One is almost tempted to say that if there are no differences supposedly rooted in common origin by which people can distinguish themselves from others, they will create such differences."[12]

The counter-culture flourished on creative deviance—of appearance, of politics, choice of narcotic, occult practices. One reason that the counter-culture is losing its vigor may be that it's not as deviant as it once was. Once Nixon flashed the peace sign, the end was in sight.

In country and western bars, I used to be impressed with the muted defensiveness of country-music lovers. During years of being scorned as "hillbillies" and "shitkickers," they huddled for warmth in the safety of the bar, and there felt a sense of family. But since Johnny Cash played in the White House, since Bob Dylan went to Nashville and "Hee Haw" topped the ratings, the defensiveness of country-music lovers has declined. Some veterans of the "good old days" say their family feeling has also plummeted.

I think we're just beginning to recognize the value of deviance in fostering a sense of community. Increasing opportunities for joint deviancy are opening all the time. Black, Italian, homosexual, Chicano, ex-mental patient, obese, skinny—liberation movements spring up daily in which almost any one of us might find a home.

Like the Boonters, many such communities look primarily to an "in" language, a specialized vocabulary to signal their deviance. A specialized vocabulary can range from the slang words of a teenage clique through the jargon of professional groups to the elaborate second language of Boontling. But the purpose is always the same: to identify quickly who's in and who's out, and to confirm the speaker's positive sense of deviancy.

There are other symbols of deviance, uniforms for example, or the car you drive. But these can be risky once the oddity wears off. Prescott students used to be able to spot each other by their characteristic Vibram-soled hiking shoes when the college first opened in 1965. But since then "waffle-stompers" have become standard campus footwear, and seeing another Vibram-soled youth may indicate only that he's been reading *Gentleman's Quarterly*.

So with Volkswagens. In the early days, driving a VW meant you had a select family of brothers and sisters around the world. You waved at each other. Now, driving a VW ranks just below a gray-flannel suit in the deviance it buys you.

Twin Oaks, a behaviorist commune in Virginia, has a creative approach to confirming its deviance. At Twin Oaks, all clocks are set an hour ahead of Eastern Standard. That way, when talking about time, commune members always must distinguish between "TO time," and "outside time."[13]

I've been searching for a community of deviance to call my own, but have a problem. My father is a straight WASP with ancestors back to the revolution. My mother is a second-generation Rumanian. One of my grandmothers is Catholic, the other Episcopalian. My father is a Quaker, my mother Jewish. I'm a walking encyclopedia of deviancy, with no oddity in particular.

But at 5′7.62″ I think I've finally found a cause: Heightism—discrimination against short people.

Our grievances are clear. Studies have shown that tall people get hired before, paid more and promoted faster than short people.[14] Nixon was only the second Presidential candidate in this century to beat a taller opponent.[15] And we're still smarting from the heightist debacle of 1860, when big Abe Lincoln smashed the Little Giant, Stephen Douglas.

An ongoing survey of the media shows a blatant bias against short people, with adjectives like "little," "pint-size," "petite," "sawed-off" and "diminutive" being used to describe anyone who isn't tall.

Our very language illustrates the heightist attitudes inherent in

American culture. Contrast, for example, "look up to" with "look down upon."

But we're beginning to get it together. A movement is being born.

This new liberation movement already has a theoretician—Cleveland sociologist Saul Feldman, 5′4″, who is cataloging the various forms height bigotry takes in our society.[16]

Former Assistant Secretary of the Treasury Edwin C. Cohen, 5′5″, suggested while in office that all those under 5′6″ should have to pay only half the taxes of anyone taller to compensate "for the unequities thrust upon the short people of the world."[17]

Our shock troops are the already organized Little People of America—too extreme for some since they all measure under 5′, but useful to the movement as a whole.

The movement has a literature—*The Dwarf* by Par Lagerkvist[18] (winner of the 1951 Nobel Prize)—and a song: "Billy Overcame His Size," by Merle Haggard.

And we have Wendell Wagner, 4′10½″, a student at New College in Sarasota, Florida, who has made the first known demands for courses in short people's history, lowered library shelves, and campus bodyguards to ward off assault by tall people.[19]

We're getting it together, and there will probably be excesses in the early stages. A boycott has been proposed of all movies featuring John Wayne or Vanessa Redgrave. Movement athletes are demanding that one basket on each basketball court be made a hole in the ground.

It's likely that during this militant phase of our struggle, bloc voting for candidates on the basis of their size will be necessary. Thus our ideal President is Shirley Chisholm at 5′. If not her, then George Wallace—the 5′7″ "Fighting Little Judge"—will be second preference. Ideally we will someday have a Chisholm-Wallace ticket to get under.

Annual awards of the movement will go to pioneering figures such as Dick Cavett, Henry Kissinger and Chou En-lai—little men all, who have made it in the face of oppression. Our Hall of Fame includes Pippin the Short, Fiorello La Guardia and Alan Ladd.

A posthumous Franz Fanon Identifying with the Oppressor Award goes to that perennial jack-in-the-box (small on the outside, tall on the inside) J. Edgar Hoover who claimed to be 5′9″ although closer to 5′7″, and reportedly used a high chair to hover over visitors to his office—who sat on a low couch.[20]

If any tall reader thinks the preceding is purely facetious, ask a short person—especially a man.

And if anyone thinks I wouldn't join such a movement—just wait till it gets started.

I feel better already having proposed it.

A sense of deviance is important.

KEEPING THE AIR CLEAR

A couple of Mormon missionaries came by the other day and we talked for awhile. Both were in their late teens, one was from Utah, the other from Idaho.

Their church has a required Monday-night meeting for all Mormon families. Much of this time is taken up with religious instruction but there's also the opportunity to air family members' concerns. The Idahoan told me that his family stuck pretty much to the Bible. But the Utahan said his father would ask what was on people's minds before the end of every meeting and all concerns would get discussed. He said this kept the air clear, and built a very strong "family" feeling.

Basic to any community I want to build is a similar kind of time set aside for airing whatever is on people's minds—confession, arguing, boasting—whatever.

In her study of American utopian communities of the past century, sociologist Rosabeth Moss Kanter found that the most successful "used a variety of group techniques, including confession, self-criticism sessions to solidify the group and deal with deviance and discontent before they became disruptive. The individual could bare his soul to the group, express his weaknesses, failings, doubts, problems, inner secrets. Disagreements between members could be discussed openly. These T-group-like sessions also showed that the content of each person's inner world was important to the community."[21]

The Oneida Community, perhaps the most successful venture of the past century, had regular mutual criticism in which each member sat before the community to hear whatever other members had to say.

Charles Nordhoff, a journalist, visited the Oneida Community in Madison County, New York, during the early 1870s and sat in on one of their mutual-criticism sessions. The subject was a young man named Charles who had volunteered to be criticized. He began the session by confessing intellectual transgressions, lack of faith, doubt in God's existence, and general religious doubts.

The fifteen Oneidans (half women, half under thirty) sat around Charles listening, then started in. They accused the young man of being haughty and supercilious. He wasn't given to consulting others, and had a swelled head from worldly success. His religious faith was definitely in question. Some found him insincere. A case was cited in which he had dealt with another young community member by saying one thing to his face, and another to others.

"Amid all this very plain speaking," wrote Nordhoff in 1875, "Charles sat speechless, looking before him: but as the accusations multiplied, his face grew paler, and drops of perspiration began to stand on his forehead. . . .

"All that I have recited was said by practiced tongues. The people knew very well how to express themselves. There was no vagueness, no uncertainty. Every point was made: every sentence was a hit—a stab I was going to say, but as the sufferer was a volunteer, I suppose this would be too strong a word. I could see, however, that while Charles might be benefited by the 'criticism,' those who spoke of him would perhaps also be the better for their speech; for if there had been bitterness in any of their hearts before, this was likely to be dissipated by the free utterance."[22]

The religious psychologist O. Hobart Mowrer has long contended that the power of the early Christian church was precisely in its practice of what he calls *exomolegesis,* or full and common confession in small groups. Mowrer says this practice had powerful therapeutic effects on top of the religious ones.

He traces the church's spiritual decline from the time when worship groups grew larger, and confession became a private affair. This removed the element of self-disclosure, of making yourself better known to your community, from worship.[23]

What could prove most lasting in encounter groups are those methods which can be grafted onto ongoing communities. Just the realization that problems can be dealt with openly, and hostility worked through, may be enough. Problems discussed openly in a meeting are so much less threatening than those muttered in hallways.

The regularity of such meeting time seems important. It's not enough to deal with tensions only when they're about to explode. By then it may be too late. Having to meet at a specified time to air issues, hostilities, and love is the only way to make sure that happens—and in time.

Our Wednesday meeting at the Center serves this purpose. Sometimes, a couple of times a year, we also find it necessary to get together for a full day, or a weekend, to go deeper with each other. We always find that members have some things buried that they really want to say, about themselves or each other, which can only surface with time.

Rosabeth Kanter adds that one of the most important aspects of mutual criticism—for Oneida as for Synanon—is that it take place in a community context, that "these sessions are composed of people with whom the member lives and works and plays, people whose experience is similar to his and therefore his statements to him are credible."[24]

Most important for me is simply being among people with whom any way I am is acceptable, anything I have to say or feeling I have to share. That's one of the best things I feel among my community of friends here: that I can cry or laugh or get angry or make a fool of myself, and although I may have to take some abuse, I know it's okay and I'm okay with them and they'll be there the next day.

That's a very important thing to know.

RITUAL

Soon after we arrived in San Diego, Jack and Maria Bowen invited us to the christening of their newly born Michael Andrew. We felt ambivalent about going, but tagged along with some friends at the last moment.

The afternoon was informal with good food. The priest was a friend of the Bowens and their community of friends. The ceremony was brief but profound. Andy was introduced to his parents' community, and they introduced themselves to Andy. Water wet his head. It was a moving moment, one which helped us meet the new member of the community, know his parents better, and draw closer to each other.

I never realized that that's what christenings were all about. And since then I've wondered how so many of us have presumed to live for so long without rituals to remind us of our bonds.

The problem is that most rituals we have are historic, rooted in past communities and not speaking to our own. For me, the best ritual is one which relates me to my forebears, is rooted in history—but also grows out of my actual community experience today.

There's a church in town to which we sometimes go, Christ the King. Mostly I go there because their rock band is good, the mass is casual, we can speak personally, sing, dance, hold hands, jump around. The mass at Christ the King is both transcendent worship and community celebration, a truly religious experience.

I'd like to say that this is because their priests have been through encounter groups; because the rock band is young and good; because my kind of people are in the congregation.

But that's not enough. Christ the King *is* a Catholic church, and its mass follows the prescribed basic forms. Its priests are deeply committed members of their church. Modern as it seems, I know that there are centuries of worship built into that ritual, in ways I barely comprehend.

Recently I attended my first seder. Howard put it on with some friends. The parents of one of his friends were there from New York and joined with us. The father sat at the head of the table, and read us every prayer in Hebrew. (His eyesight was failing, so this wasn't easy.) The rest of us took turns reading the translation, as we drank the sweet wine and sampled the bitter herbs.

The father and his daughter would discuss a little, joke a little, argue a little about the meaning of the passage. Though I couldn't take part, it was fascinating to watch. I felt honored to be included.

And, in a strange way, it gave meaning to my own history. In our family, every supper took that form. We'd discuss a little, argue and joke about the issues of the day. They were secular seders, overseen by my Jewish mother. In a dim, confused sort of way, taking part in my first seder reminded me I have a history, a heritage of which I'm barely aware.

Bob Frankel is thick in the middle of a Jewish revival on the east coast. He and thousands of others are trying to revive Judaism's sense of community—inherent in its forms, but somehow lost in the move to the suburbs.

Bob calls their movement "neo-Hasidism" because they seek guidance from the mystical forms of that sect. The Shabbos is their focus. Community members begin this Sabbath celebration with a song of welcome, which they try to sing for an hour or so —together, holding hands, swaying. Later, long periods will sometimes be spent in meditation—two or three hours. A full-course meal may be eaten silently, forcing the diners to look at each other and hear their feelings, rather than talk about them. The group studies the Torah together, and discusses secular readings. Toward the end of Shabbos, on Saturday evening, walks are taken outdoors, nature being a basic focus of Hasidism.

Bob, a bit of an evangelist, says you get "plenty high" on Shabbos. "If you want a tool for community," he tells me, "start with Shabbos."

I've talked of ritual mainly in the context of religion, and don't mean to. Ritual can mean nothing more than sharing a pot of fondue or celebrating a birthday. Ecstatic celebration is an important dimension of ritual. For the past two years I've taken part in a three-week summer encounter institute which peaks in moments of great ecstasy. Reentry into everyday life was especially hard the first year, a little easier the second.

For the longest time I've felt bad after those experiences that I couldn't be that open, that joyous and loving all the time. Now I realize, I think, that no one can. But having the regular opportunity for such experiences in community makes me more open afterward than I'd otherwise be, makes everyday life more bearable and, helps keep my community together.

During last summer's encounter institute, I participated in one group with a Catholic priest. Fresh from the seminary, he was tender and uncertain of his ability to withstand a personal, secular challenge. The priest participated little and finally told us that he doubted our ability to hear his real religious commitment. We asked him to try us, or better yet, to help us develop a ritual based on the feelings which had grown in the group.

He agreed (and just happened to have a portable Mass kit), so we went and bought food. That evening we ate together quietly, then had Don the priest lead us in a Eucharistic service.

The form was definitely Catholic—with a cross, wine in a chalice, and pound cake which we passed around. But the feelings were of *that* group of people, for each other. There were people in the group I had never come to understand and care for—until that moment.

And that to me is what's important about ritual: having times to celebrate what's common. Communities of people need that time as much as they need time to air what divides.

A CULTURE ALL YOUR OWN

While publisher of *Newsday,* Bill Moyers gave a speech about our loss of community, which was excerpted in the paper. In response he got a lovely letter from Jean Ritchie, the Appalachian folk singer who now lives on Long Island.

"My husband, two sons and I live in Port Washington," she wrote him, "a nice enough town, but I know too well the feeling of 'lack of community' of which you spoke." She continued:

I am a former Kentucky mountaineer, and I sing my family songs at colleges around the country, and tell about our life as a family of fourteen, growing up in our little shut-away village of about three hundred people. . . . I have recently been thinking seriously of giving up doing this, since in today's world, what I talk and sing about no longer seems "relevant."

But, people keep asking me to come, and I keep going to them. Sometimes, after my concert, someone will say to me, "There is healing in what you say" or "I feel so refreshed." Sometimes, particularly with young people, fifteen or twenty of them will just come around me, and stand quietly, not saying anything, but they smile and perhaps one or two of them will touch my instruments, ask a question about a song —but mainly they just stand and look. *Much* younger children (fourth grade or so) are more vocal. I get many letters from this age, children whose teachers have read my family story to them in school, and these letters are passionate, filled with longings to "live in a little place, out in the country, be on a farm."

I have been searching for a reasonable reason to keep going. After all, I felt I couldn't just go on remembering the dead past, if that was all that it was, simply for the sake of my own pleasure and nostalgia.

Reading your speech made me realize that it is my lost community and my longing to regain it that I am remembering for others; that is what makes them reach out to try to touch it. If (you think) there is hope that we, even in suburbia, can regain our sense of community, of caring, of knowing each other, then I do have my reason. Thank you.

All best wishes,
Jean Ritchie Pickow

An indigenous culture is a basic tool for any community building itself—a music of its own, an art and theater.

But the problem comes in finding a music, and a whole culture, which speaks of our own community and doesn't have to parasite. Folk music, folk art, folk dancing is always somebody else's. I love Jean Ritchie's music, and the feeling she has for her Kentucky home. And it gives me hope that someday I might have a similar feeling for a place and its people.

Luckier groups of people have an authentic culture to build from—in their history, their ways, their common points of reference.

Urban Mexican-Americans share *corrida* songs describing their life in the barrio.

In New York, Puerto Ricans have a similar barrio music, a little more influenced by rock, but also dealing with life on the street. A member of that community says of one of their singers:

His ties to his past are ever present in his recordings. That is the real reason Joe Bataan is loved.

Joe Bataan has never forgotten his people. He lives in El Barrio, unlike some of the big bandleaders who moved away physically and spiritually . . . . Joe Bataan is tangible, you can see him walking along 106th Street and shopping on Third Avenue with his wife and two children. Andy Gonzales, a Latin bassist who now works with Dizzy Gillespie, once told me, "Whatever happens on the streets you'll hear in Joe Bataan's records." It's true. Bataan's songs talk of cops, riots, unwed mothers, prayers to God, abandoned children, and the names of streets in El Barrio we all know.[25]

Whenever I've asked country and western fans why they like the music, they invariably say it talks to them, describes their lives, is honest and direct.

I've always liked country and western, and find myself listening to it more and more as an antidote to happy buttons. Country music is encounter music, more direct and open than Guy Lombardo's syrup or the esoteric metaphors of contemporary rock. The singers of country music know what soap operaists know—that open sadness is more comforting than a smiling veneer.

But I'm acutely aware that country music isn't *my* music, and that I'm a parasite on its roots. When George Wallace says, "The people who love country and western music will save this country,"[26] he doesn't mean me.

In a larger sense, some rock music, some participatory theater, some TV, some new dances serve communities I belong to more legitimately. But they are communities which meet face-to-face only in passing, if at all.

One larger community I belong to, of humanistic psychology or whatever it's called these days, now has a music which I think is truly *of* that community, the songs of Dory Previn. Her verse therapy sings so honestly, so well of the fears and loneliness and agony we all feel that it makes me more courageous to share, to be open.

"Sacred To Be Alone" is a song she wrote after André Previn left her. It speaks right to me:

> we never stop to wonder
> till a person's gone
> we never yearn to know him
> till he's traveled on
> when someone is around us
> we never stop to ask
> hey what's behind your mirror?
> hey who's beneath your mask?
> we never stop to wonder

till a person's gone
we never yearn to know him
till he's packed and traveled on

Dory Previn's music is very much of a nongeographic community. I hear it and feel close to her and faceless others who have shared similar experiences. Most of us will never meet, but when we do, Dory Previn gives us something in common.

I hope someday to be part of a geographic community with a music of its own, and an art and theater and literature. That may never be, for I may never settle long enough anywhere, or define myself clearly enough, or commit myself deeply enough to a group of people committed to me so that we can begin building a culture reflecting that community.

If I do, I hope that group of people includes artists who can initiate the culture. I'd feel very self-conscious about doing that, myself, and inadequate. But I'd want to help, because having a culture of your own feels so much better than having to borrow someone else's.

OTHER TOOLS

Among tools important for community I've mentioned hangouts, a sense of deviance, air clearing, ritual, and an indigenous culture. These are tools I consider good, or at least not bad.

There are other tools valuable to some communities, but not mine—a deep sense of place, a cause, work to share, legends, heroes.

Then there are tools which can help build community, but aren't ones I care for, such as rigid ideology and authoritarian leadership.

Which is not to underestimate such factors. Studies of utopian ventures in the past and present-day communes usually find that the most enduring are those based on a rigid ideological commitment or a dictatorial leadership.

But that's too high a price for me. Trading my freedom in on community doesn't take account of my need for growing room, for experimenting room, and sheer orneriness. So, like most, I'm reduced to grabbing for community where I can find it.

MY COMMUNITIES

My communities include:

The Keyes community, all people named Keyes but especially those who pronounce it "Kize."

This is a big issue among us, and whenever I meet a fellow right-pronouncing Keyes, I know I've found a brother. I even felt good when I read on page 4 of 79 *Park Avenue* by Harold Robbins about an Assistant District Attorney named Mike Keyes:

> The reporters hit me almost before I set foot on the courthouse steps. . . .
>
> "We hear you're taking over for the D.A., Mr. Keyes. Is that true?"
>
> He wouldn't have gotten an answer even if I had been so minded. I hated people who made it sound like *keys*. The name was Keyes, rhyming with *eyes*. I kept walking.[28]

Wow, to have it right there on page 4 of 79 *Park Avenue* for everyone to see. Harold Robbins knows.

Once in Manitoba, Canada, I stopped at an auto supply house called "Keyes Auto Supply." "How do you pronounce that?" I asked the owner.

"Kize." he replied.

"Why?" I asked.

The man pulled himself straight up and in inimitable British deadpan said "Because that's the way it's pronounced."

There is another low branch of the family who pronounce it "keys." They and a few sellouts from our branch (who have caved in under public pressure)—we tolerate them, but they're not kin.

Muriel once met a college receptionist named Keyes who pronounced it right. They chatted for a few minutes, swapping mispronunciation stories as is our wont when Keyeses meet. Then Muriel asked directions to an anti-Pentagon demonstration. The receptionist's eyes hardened, and as my wife walked off she called after her, "You're not a high Keyes, you're a low Keys."

Saab owners are another community to which we belong. Saabs for years were ugly cars, with two-stroke cornpopper-sounding engines which needed oil mixed with the gas. You had to be odd to own one, and a little defensive. So the community has a solid sense of deviance. Driving a Saab is a cause.

We have heroes: rally drivers Erik Carlsson and Inqvar Lindqvist, who drove Saabs to rally victories in Monte Carlo, Baja, and elsewhere.

Mort Sahl recently broke his back cracking up a Saab sports car, which makes him some kind of martyr, if not a hero of the community.

Though you can buy Saab rally jackets and sweatshirts, the car itself is the real community uniform. There's a Saab parked up the street often, a white one with yellow daisies pasted on. Once I saw the car in La Jolla, and felt instant kinship, though I have yet to see anyone driving it.

Our community has a media, *Saab Soundings*. We have *esprit*, since it's a great product. And hangouts—any Saab garage around the country where fellow owners meet and swap Saab stories.

We left the Saab community once, and bought a Ford. But what do you say to other Ford owners? We did get Saab seat belts installed in the Ford, but it never felt the same.

So we traded for another Saab, and I'm delighted to be back in the community.

Though I haven't felt part of a magazine family since I. F. Stone adjourned his *Weekly*, the *L. L. Bean's Catalog* is a community to which we belong. This worldwide brotherhood is headquartered in Freeport, Maine, where the Bean store is open twenty-four hours a day. The camping/hunting gear company puts out one of the friendliest, most uncluttered and useful catalogs around. Muriel and I love especially their chamois shirts about which the catalog told us: "This is the shirt Mr. Bean used on his fishing and hunting trips. The scarlet is a good fishing shirt as red repels black flies. Also safe for dragging in deer without a coat."

The shirts have a characteristic slanted pocket, which helps in spotting other members of the community. Sam Keen's a member up in Del Mar, and Layne Longfellow over at Prescott.

Layne spent a summer in Alaska and found the Bean community particularly vigorous up there. He hadn't heard of Bean's at the time, but kept hearing from backwoodsmen about this place in Maine that put out a neat catalog from which they ordered most of their gear. When Layne returned, he got a copy and ended up ordering over $300 worth of merchandise. Now he's a proud and evangelistic member of the family.

Collie owners are a community. When I meet another we always have something to talk about—whether or not to shave their coats, how to handle their skittishness, having kids mistake them for Lassie. Lassie, of course, is the community hero. But this is a low-level community for me. There's a collie owners club in town which I've never even contacted.

More important is the community of ex-Antiochians. This one's got everything: a common traumatic/ecstatic experience. A media, *The Antiochian.* Heroes: Peg Bracken, Rod Serling, and the late Robert Manry who sailed the Atlantic alone in a dinghy. A strong sense of deviance is built into every Antioch education. And there are occasional face-to-face gatherings, officially organized alumnae meetings or informal ones like the San Diego Antiochians who meet regularly on the beach during the summer.

There are some communities which I'd like to think I belong to but which don't accept me. I've always thought of myself as an honorary cowboy for example, swaggered sometimes, worshiped Gene Autry and Clint Eastwood, learned how to wrangle horses. Often I wear hightop boots and a cowboy hat.

But mixing uniforms is riskier than metaphors.

Last summer, my long-hair street-people uniform stuck out from beneath my cowboy hat uniform and I succeeded in alienating both communities. I have a vivid memory of running down a street in Pinedale, Wyoming, as a rain started only to hear someone yell, "Better hurry, cowboy, your hair'll get wet."

Finally, there are disposable communities which I enjoy being part of. Music festivals—why not? Some audiences, especially the time I heard Joe Cocker. Maybe basketball crowds again, now that San Diego has a new team.

Weekend encounters have come to seem almost like recreation to me, an emotional respite, a time to try out new ways of being. As such, they're great. Just so long as I don't confuse them with ongoing community.

I'm not sure that I have a real community, a place where I'm known whole. But I'm getting closer to such a community. At the Center I have what feels to me like a village, or extended family, with whom I feel close but not always intimate.

There are elements lacking for me in the Center's community. Our headquarters have white walls and feel like a doctor's office. The place is definitely not a hangout. Though we do care about each other, and share, I'm still struck by the amount of time Center members spend hiding out in their homes. And although we've joined sometimes in semirituals, we've (I've) made no real attempt to build a culture of this community.

Yet the Center is a very important community to me. Its members have taught me a lot about just being human, and listening better. Our ages range from Carl's seventy to Joanne's twenty-three. I like belonging to a group with different generations present. Being regularly around grownups whom I respect gives me models to try on, and makes getting older seem less disastrous. Watching the many families involved, and getting to know their children, has helped give me the courage to consider having my own.

Mostly, though, I know that the Center will probably endure, will almost certainly be around next year as it was last. At the moment that feels very important to me.

My intimate community, my "family," isn't, officially. It's just friends, a dozen or so. We eat together sometimes, share birthdays, go camping, and mumble about living together—"sometime." Some of us have discussed the idea of declaring an "alternative weekend" in the middle of the week which would signal our deviance.

Muriel and I went east for a month after two years in San Diego, and upon our return many people said that they had missed us, that they had noticed when we didn't show up. I think they meant it, and it was great to hear. Also surprising.

In a sense, I've found "community." Not the total, ongoing involvement of yore, but something closer and more committed than I've known before. That's scary to say, because my community could be exploded and scattered to the winds in a year, maybe even by the time this book comes out. But for now, today, I feel in community.

IN CLOSING

As I wrap up three years of work on a book about community, I'm sitting here wondering—What is it that I have to say, in a nutshell? What's the essence, the kernel of what I've learned from studying community, and seeking it?

I began with a fairly conventional perspective on how we became such a lonely people: that mass society dehumanized and cut us off from each other, but that with imagination and new approaches we might defeat these influences and restore our sense of community.

The more I studied the issue, and tried to build a community for myself, the less I found that to be the case. The villain whose trail I kept stalking turned out really to be ourselves—myself; our—my—ambivalence about community; our wish—my wish—not to get too close, thwarting a real hunger to join together.

Something I've realized only slowly is that seeking "community" in the abstract dooms the search. Community is people. I find community only when I find other people. I'm open to a group only when I'm open to its members. When I start looking for some mystical "community" I usually miss the people.

The problem of community, which sociologist Robert Nisbet calls "the single most impressive fact in the twentieth century in western society,"[29] is relatively modern. For most of man's history, group life was a given, and grew naturally out of the ways we were forced to be with each other—to live, work, wash clothes, and die.

This is no longer true. We have less and less necessity to be together, and fewer ways of knowing each other, while our need for community remains constant. So we're forced back on the only immutable reason for joining hands: the human need for company. Without place, without cause, common work or religion, most of us must make that humiliating admission: I can't live alone.

It's a hard confession, and one rarely made right out in the open. I guess that's the main thing I've learned about our quest for community—that the key thing keeping us apart is our fear . . . especially each other. Once the secret's out—that we're all scared —I hope more and more of us can gather to build communities, and begin by discussing our fear.

Once someone, once I, can take the risk, break the ice, and say how I really feel, it's always amazing how many others turn out just to have been waiting their turn. Then the community begins.

But to join that community, each one of us must take the hard, terrifying first step—saying—even to one other person—"I need you."[30]

THE END

Notes

CHAPTER 1: LOSING TOUCH

1. Udall's first comment was in the *New York Times*, January 29, 1971, p. 12, the second in *Newsweek*, February 8, 1971, p. 47.
2. *American Journal of Sociology*, July 1954, pp. 36-45. The comments excerpted appear on p. 38.
3. *Wall Street Journal*, May 27, 1971, p. 1; also, personal interview.
4. *Travels With Charley* (New York: Bantam Books, 1962), p. 174.
5. Words by Arthur Thomas, BMI.
6. *Wall Street Journal*, May 27, 1971, p. 1.
7. *Business Week*, September 26, 1970, p. 46; *Electronics World*, June 1971, p. 31; and *Time*, April 5, 1971, p. 63.
8. *Parade*, November 14, 1971, p. 12 and the *Los Angeles Times*, October 11, 1971, Part III, p. 12.
9. *Los Angeles Times*, November 22, 1971, Part IV, p. 3.
10. Quoted in the *San Diego Evening Tribune*, October 13, 1971, p. B-1.
11. *Statistical Abstracts of the United States* (1970), p. 739 and *Drug Topics*, March 13, 1972, p. 10.
12. *American Druggist*, April 19, 1971, pp. 14-16.

12a. Howard Johnson's advertising campaign is described in *Advertising Age*, October 14, 1968, p. 31.

13. Shakey's ad appeared in *Calendar* (*Los Angeles Times*), February 13, 1972, p. 2.
14. Buick's advertisement appeared in *Newsweek*, Oct. 4, 1971, p. 63.
15. The Sears ad appeared in the *San Diego Union*, June 4, 1972, p. A-9.
16. Art Buchwald's column, *Los Angeles Times*, August 5, 1971, p. II-7.
17. "A Survey of Popular Attitudes Toward Technology" by Irene Taviss, Research Associate, Harvard Program of Technology and Society, p. 3.
18. Harvey Cox, *The Secular City* (New York: Macmillan Co., 1965), p. 48.
19. On the evolution of the jury system see Samuel W. McCart, *Trial by Jury* (New York: Chilton Books, 1964), especially pp. 6-7, and William Rudolph Cornish, *The Jury* (London: Penguin Press, 1968), especially pp. 10-12, 252. The general idea of our growing more diffused communally as we grow more free individually is developed persuasively in Robert Nisbet's *The Quest for Community* (New York: Oxford University Press, 1953).

CHAPTER 2: THE TRADE-INS

1. *Los Angeles Times*, April 17, 1972, Part IV, p. 6.
2. "My Elusive Dreams," by C. Putnam and B. Sherrill, BMI.
3. "Every American Is an Apostle of the Democratic Creed," in Henry Steele Commager, *America in Perspective* (New York: Mentor Books, 1948), p. 90.
4. George W. Pierson, who develops this theme in "The M-Factor in American History," in *The Character of Americans*, edited by Michael McGiffert (Homewood, Ill.: Dorsey Press, 1964), pp. 118-130.
5. Statistics on American mobility are from the U.S. Census Bureau in *Information Please Almanac* (1972), p. 628. The job statistic is cited in the *San Francisco Examiner and Chronicle*, May 30, 1972, p. 32.
6. Jennings writes on mobicentricity in "Mobicentric Man," *Psychology Today*, July 1970, p. 35.
7. The statistic on youth mobility, from the 1970 census, is cited in the *San Diego Union*, February 4, 1971, p. A-7.

8. Ed Kissam, "Nomads," *Clear Creek*, July-August 1972, p. 30.
9. Keith Melville, *Communes in the Counter Culture* (New York: William Morrow & Co., 1972), p. 136. Bennett Berger, a sociologist studying child-rearing in communes, made a similar observation to me in an interview, as has Robert Houriet on p. 168 of *Getting Back Together* (New York: Avon Books, 1971).
10. David French, in "After the Fall," the *New York Times Magazine*, October 3, 1971, p. 20.
11. Wallace Stegner has a good article on social effects of the Interstate System in *Esquire*, April 1972, p. 81, entitled "Last Exit to America."
12. Homerica is the main relocation service and made this claim in the *New York Times Magazine*, August 8, 1971, p. 55.
13. *Los Angeles Times*, March 28, 1971, Section C, p. 2.
14. J. Anthony Lukas describes *Playboy*'s vision on p. 13 of his *New York Times Magazine* article, "The 'Alternative Life-Style' of Playboys and Playmates," June 11, 1972.
15. Toffler, *Future Shock* (New York: Random House, 1970), pp. 66, 73.
16. On Jennings' mobicentricity see *Psychology Today*, July 1970, p. 86.
17. Fuller made the claim in the *Saturday Evening Post*, October 5, 1968, p. 34.
18. Bennis' comments are in "Organic Populism, A Conversation with Warren Bennis and T. George Harris," *Psychology Today*, February 1970, p. 70.
19. Bartell, *Group Sex* (New York: Peter Wyden, 1971), pp. 158-160.
20. "The Secret of Friendship," *National Enquirer*, December 12, 1971, p. 5.
21. Courtney Tall in his paper "Friendships in the Future," quoted in *Future Shock, op. cit.*, p. 94.
22. Jeanne Landrum, "A Therapeutic Community," *Wing Tips*, October 1970, p. 7.
23. George Sargent's observation is from his unpublished paper, "My Inner Journey," for Neil Matheson, United States International University, in partial fulfillment of the requirements for Human Behavior 639, May 1971.
24. "Peanuts" appeared in the *San Diego Union*, November 14, 1971.

25. Didion mentioned this on p. 135 of her essay "On Keeping a Notebook," in *Slouching Towards Bethlehem* (New York: Delta), pp. 131-141.
26. Bennett writes on privacy in "Secrets Are for Sharing," *Psychology Today*, February 1969, p. 31.
27. McLuhan's clearest explanation of this thesis is in his *Playboy* interview, March 1969, pp. 53-74.
28. Burckhardt, *The Civilization of the Renaissance in Italy*, Vol. I (New York: Harper & Row, 1958), p. 143.
29. Hall, *The Hidden Dimension* (Garden City, N. Y.: Anchor Books, 1969), pp. 152, 159.
30. *Los Angeles Times*, September 2, 1971, Part I-B, p. 6.
31. José Yglesias, "Walking My Dog on the West Side," *Esquire*, June 1971, p. 123.
32. Hannay's quote is on pp. 173-174 of his "The American at Home and in His Club," written under the pseudonym George Birmingham, and reprinted in Commager, *op. cit.*
33. Ann Ras, *Los Angeles Times*, September 12, 1971, Section G, p. 3.
34. Armour, "Where Have All the Porches Gone?" *West*, September 19, 1971, p. 39.
35. *Los Angeles Times*, January 24, 1971, Section J, p. 1.
36. Hall, *op. cit.*, pp. 104, 140, 152, 159.
37. Alexander describes the syndrome in his paper on "The City as a Mechanism for Sustaining Human Contact." This paper is quite insightful and has influenced me as much as any single source in writing this book. It is reprinted in *Environment for Man, The Next Fifty Years*, edited by William Ewald, Jr. (Bloomington, Indiana: Indiana University Press, 1967), pp. 60-109, and in *People and Buildings*, edited by Robert Gutman (New York: Basic Books, 1972), pp. 406-434.
38. The Arkansas reader's letter to Abby appeared in the *Los Angeles Times* on March 23, 1972, Part IV, p. 6. I saw the response in the *Nashville Tennessean*, May 28, 1972, p. 9.
39. McKay's comment is quoted in "Thank God for Notre Dame," by Bill Libby, *West*, November 21, 1971, p. 29.
40. The Lutheran survey, conducted by Youth Research Center, Inc. of Minneapolis, is described in the *Los Angeles Times*, July 1, 1971, p. A-14.

41. *Newsday*, December 20, 1969, pp. 10W-12W.
42. The study of Michigan males was made by Ruth Hill Useem, John Useem, and Duane L. Gibson and is reported by them in "The Function of Neighboring for the Middle-Class Male," *Human Organization*, Summer 1960, pp. 68-76.
43. *San Francisco Examiner*, August 20, 1972, p. 1.
44. *Newsweek*, December 20, 1971, p. 30, and the *Los Angeles Times*, December 9, 1971, p. 12, and December 10, 1971, p. 18, where this comment was made.
45. The Von George tragedy is written about, movingly, by Jerry Bledsoe, in "Who Cares What Happened to a Middle-Class Hijacker?" *Esquire*, June 1972, p. 85.
46. The census data on conveniences is reported in the *Los Angeles Times*, May 30, 1971, Section A, p. 7. Information on the appliances industry is from *Business Week*, June 5, 1971, p. 37.
47. The Harvard survey is by Irene Taviss, *op. cit.* The quotation from her is from the *National Enquirer*, July 25, 1971, p. 29.
48. "Is the Kitchen a Thing of the Past?" *House Beautiful*, January 1970, pp. 68-71.
49. *Time*, December 13, 1971, p. 64.

49a. Boorstin, "Television," *Life*, September 10, 1971, p. 36.

50. Bernard's study is summarized in a *London Observer* article reprinted by the *Los Angeles Times*, June 8, 1972, p. 9.
51. *Los Angeles Times*, August 3, 1971, Part IV, p. 3.
52. Dr. Leon P. Ullensvang, "Food Consumption Patterns in the Seventies," *Vital Speeches of the Day*, February 1, 1970, p. 243. The 28% estimate is his.
53. J. Anthony Lukas, "As American as a McDonald's Hamburger on the Fourth of July," *New York Times Magazine*, July 4, 1971, p. 5. See also *New York Times*, June 29, 1969, p. 31, where Mayer's comment appeared.
54. "The Individual and His Eating Patterns from a Sociocultural Frame of Reference," a paper prepared for the Southwest Region School Food Service Seminar, Kansas State University, July 1971, p. 4.
55. *Los Angeles Times*, November 3, 1971, Part IV, p. 1.
56. Dr. Smith's comments appeared in the *National Enquirer*, August 1, 1971, p. 18. His overall views are summarized in the paper "Nutrition and Its Effects on Health," *Proceedings of the 2nd*

Annual Western Environmental Mental Health Conference, April 15-17, 1970, in San Diego.

57. *Life,* September 10, 1971, p. 43.
58. Westman's finding is reported in the *Los Angeles Times,* April 30, 1972, Section G, p. 4. See also Westman's testimony "The Need for Sound Control in the Home" prepared for the U.S. Senate Commerce Committee, June 28, 1971, and his remarks at a New York Press Conference held February 4, 1971, printed as a pamphlet entitled "Auditory Environment in the Home" by Koss Electronics, Inc. Milwaukee, Wisconsin (Westman's statement is on pp. 10-13).
59. The most complete survey of in-home noise to date is "Auditory Environment in the Home," Research Report made by the Environmental Design Department of the University of Wisconsin for Koss Electronics, Inc., Milwaukee, Wisconsin, from which these findings are taken.
60. *Los Angeles Times,* April 30, 1972, Section G, p. 4.
61. The Hoover example is famous in the annals of noise pollution. See, for example, *Time,* May 4, 1970, p. 92; *Business Week,* May 22, 1971, p. 87; and *West* January 23, 1972, p. 10.
62. *Los Angeles Times,* October 5, 1971, Section II, pp. 1, 3.
63. Kenneth Schneider, *Autokind Vs. Mankind* (New York: W.W. Norton, 1971), p. 262.
64. The woman gave her name as "Elaine Sundance," and made these comments in a speech at a weekend symposium, "Communes: Past, Present, Future" given through UCLA Extension, Department of Social Sciences, December 4-5, 1971.
65. "Mobility: From There to Here," No. 5 of "The Markets of Change" Series, *Kaiser News,* 1971, p. 5.
66. Hall, *op. cit.,* p. 177.
67. "twenty-mile zone," appears in *On My Way to Where,* Dory Previn (New York: McCall Publishing Co., 1970-71), pp. 53-56.
68. Seidenbaum's comment appeared in his *Los Angeles Times* column "Antifreeway Frenzy," May 17, 1971, p. II-1.
69. Smith's initial column on the subject appeared in the *Los Angeles Times* November 11, 1971, Part IV, p. 1. His follow-up columns were December 23, 1971, Part IV, p. 1, where the anthropology teacher was quoted, and December 27, 1971, Part IV, p. 1.

70. Hall, *op. cit.*, p. 177.
71. *Time*, May 1, 1972, p. 60.
72. Cronkite, in *The Saturday Evening Post*, September 8, 1968, p. 83.
73. Slater, *The Pursuit of Loneliness* (Boston: Beacon Press, 1970), p. 131. This book is probably the best single work on contemporary community breakdown.
74. The Dallas ordinance is # 12991 amending Chapter 31 of the 1960 Revised Code of Civil and Criminal Ordinances of the City of Dallas, passed July 20, 1970.
75. Beverly Hills' ordinances are cited in the *Wall Street Journal*, September 21, 1971, p. 1, and the *San Diego Evening Tribune*, September 15, 1971, p. X-7.
76. Joan Didion, *Play It as It Lays* (New York: Farrar, Straus, & Giroux, 1970), p. 16.
77. *Time*'s cover story, "Suburbia: A Myth Challenged," March 15, 1971, pp. 14-20.
78. Alexander, "The City as a Mechanism for Sustaining Human Contact," *op. cit.*, pp. 82, 83-84.
79. Fuller's quote is from the *Saturday Evening Post*, "Speaking of Autos," October 5, 1968, p. 34. It is excerpted on p. 31 of *The Great American Toy*, Automobiles in American Culture, by William Pactolus (New York: Herder & Herder, 1970), which is an excellent summation of the car's social impact.

CHAPTER 3: "AND ALL IN THE PRIVACY OF YOUR OWN HOME"

1. *National Enquirer*, May 7, 1972, p. 31, and Louis Botto, "That Family Sure Has Its Share of Problems," *Look*, September 7, 1971, p. 64.
2. Eyewitness News solicited me in the *T.V. Times* (*Los Angeles Times*), February 27, 1972, p. 19, and announced their contest in the *Los Angeles Times*, April 25, 1972, Part IV, p. 14. *Time* wrote up the contest results on June 26, 1972, p. 98.
3. The market research on personalized news was cited in *Look*, September 7, 1971, p. 46.
4. McLuhan, "Sharing the News—Friendly Teamness: Teeming Friendness," a report made for ABC-TV, September 1971.
5. New York's Eyewitness News, advertised in *New York* magazine,

December 14, 1970, pp. 67, 82, December 28, 1970, p. 12, and January 4, 1971, pp. 6, 10.

6. Douglas was offered to me in *Newsweek*, December 6, 1971, p. 123.
7. John Tebbel, "A Campus TV Stare-In," *Signature*, September 1969, pp. 17-21.
8. Wolfe's comment is in Botto, *op. cit.*, p. 64.
9. Friedrich, "Farewell to Peyton Place," *Esquire*, December 1970, pp. 160-168.
10. *Calendar* (*Los Angeles Times*) July 2, 1972, p. 10.
11. The Harris data are from an interview. The television program he took part in was "The Masks We Wear," which appeared on ABC-TV on May 8, 1972. The outside survey was made by Daniel Yankelovich, Inc., and the statistics cited appear on p. 31 of their report entitled "A Study of the Readers of *Psychology Today* and Their Relationships to the Magazine," December, 1970.
12. Welles, "Can Mass Magazines Survive?" *Columbia Journalism Review*, July/August 1971, pp. 7-14.
13. *Los Angeles Times*, April 25, 1971, Section E, p. 6.
14. *Esquire* promotional flyer, "Another Good Match: You & *Esquire*."
15. Hefner's comments were made in an interview with Digby Diehl, *West*, February 27, 1972, p. 23.
16. *Los Angeles Times*, December 29, 1971, p. 2; see also Lukas, "The 'Alternative Life-Style' of Playboys and Playmates," *op. cit.*, p. 13.
17. Michener, in *Esquire*, December, 1971, p. 135.
18. Fessier, "This is the Valley," *West*, November 1, 1970, pp. 22-28; quotation from p. 24.
19. The survey, made by Charles Kadushin, Julie Hover, and Monique Tichy, was reported in the *Public Opinion Quarterly*, Spring 1971, and excerpted in promotional copy sent out by *The New York Review*. The quotation is from an accompanying letter signed by A. Whitney Ellsworth, Publisher. The 40 percent figure was referred to in a "Notice to Subscribers" which appeared on p. 42 of the *Review* for October 7, 1971.
20. Lukas, "The 'Alternative Life-Style' of Playboys and Playmates," *op. cit.*, pp. 13, 74. See also the summary of Playboy's annual meeting in the *Los Angeles Times*, November 22, 1972, p. III-12.

21. The *Physicians Management*, *Innovation*, and *db* programs are described in their announcements to readers, reprinted by Tele-Sessions, Inc., New York. The *Physicians Management* quotation is from such an announcement. The Friedman comment was quoted in *Innovation*'s announcement.
22. TeleSessions' advertisement ran in *New York*, November 23, 1970, pp. 64-65 and December 7, 1970, pp. 20-21 and elsewhere. The $500,000 claim is made in a TeleSessions' publicity sheet entitled "What Are TeleSessions?" Descriptions of their approach are made in other publicity sheets. The observation about ease in chairing dialed meetings was made by Allyn Brodsky, TeleSession Operations Manager in a telephone interview, and is expanded by their Research Director, George Silverman in TeleSessions' publication *On the Line*, November 16, 1970.
23. On "phone phreaking" see Ron Rosenbaum's excellent article, "Secrets of the Little Blue Box," *Esquire*, October 1971, p. 117.
24. *National Enquirer*, September 5, 1971, p. 4.
25. *Los Angeles Times*, May 16, 1971, Section C, p. 1.
26. Ann Landers' column, *Newsday*, February 4, 1970, p. 7-A.
27. *San Diego Union*, August 8, 1970, p. B-5.
28. *National Enquirer*, June 20, 1971.
29. Julie Baumgold, "Radio-Therapy: Surrogate Father at Night," in *New York*, April 3, 1972, pp. 33-36.
30. *San Francisco Chronicle*, August 14, 1972, p. 18.
31. Margaret McEachern, "The Town Meeting is Not Dead—It's Alive and Well on Radio," *Today's Health*, July 1970, pp. 32-33, 70.
32. *Los Angeles Times*, February 6, 1972, p. J-11.
33. Sam Bloomberg, "Suicide Anonymous," *Proceedings of the Fourth International Conference for Suicide Prevention*, International Association for Suicide Prevention (Norman L. Farberow, editor), p. 111.
34. The Hotline founder's comment is on p. 2 of the *Proceedings, Second International Hotline Conference*, May 25-28, 1971, Pacific Grove, California. The quotation from the psychologist, Gerald Bissiri is on p. 298 of *Seventeen*, August 1970, in "Take Your Troubles to the Hotline."
35. The report of the conference is from an interview with Carl

Rogers as well as the *Proceedings, op. cit.* Succeeding quotations are from the *Proceedings* except for the final anecdote, which was recalled by Dr. Rogers.

36. The report on MINERVA is from a telephone interview with Richard Remp of the Center for Policy Research Staff, and from Center reports entitled, "Minerva: A Study in Participatory Technology," Working Paper I, February 1972; "Technology to Facilitate Citizen Participation in Government," Working Paper II, February 1972; and "Public Television Channels in New York City: The First Six Months," Working Paper IV, February 1972.
37. On cable television see Ralph Lee Smith, "The Wired Nation," *Nation,* May 18, 1970, pp. 582-606, considered the best of a considerable amount of press coverage. A recent Stanford Research Institute report on trends in cable television, including most of the predictions mentioned, was reported by the *Los Angeles Times,* January 2, 1972, Section B, p. 1.
38. The Alternate Media quotation is from MINERVA, Working Paper IV, *op. cit.,* p. 16. Community Cablevisions Manager was quoted on p. 23 of *Calendar*'s "Cable Television: Splice of American Life," by Joseph Bell (*Los Angeles Times*), June 4, 1972, p. 1, which is also a good summary of cable's current status. An excellent survey of this field, not widely available, is *Cable Television: The Evolution of a Revolution* by Peter Robinson, unpublished thesis, Trinity College (Connecticut) April, 1972.
39. *San Francisco Chronicle,* July 8, 1972, p. 15.
40. Joe McGinnis, *The Selling of the President 1968* (New York: Trident Press, 1969).
41. McLuhan's analysis of 1968 was made in his *Playboy* interview, *op. cit.,* pp. 61-62.
42. McGinnis, " 'Real' Candidates Would Put Voters to Sleep," *Dayton Daily News,* December 28, 1969, p. 1-B.
43. Cavett's first quote is from *Newsweek,* April 26, 1971, p. 60. The second is from *Time,* June 7, 1971, p. 85; and the third from "Does Dick Cavett Have It?" by Betty Baer, *Look,* July 15, 1969, p. 64. The fourth is from *Calendar* (*Los Angeles Times*), March 7, 1971, p. 61.
44. Chris Welles, "The Sociology of Dumb," *Esquire,* May 1971, p. 104.

CHAPTER 4: THE NATIONAL HOME TOWN

1. Vaughn, "Growth and Future of Franchising," Farnsworth Publishing Co., 1969, p. 6. On franchising generally, see Robert Emmons, *The American Franchise Revolution,* (Newport Beach, California: Burton House, 1970) and Harry Kursh, *The Franchise Boom* (Englewood Cliffs, New Jersey: Prentice-Hall, Inc., 1968).
2. On Southland see "The Convenience Store Study," *Progressive Grocer,* September 1971, especially pp. 5-6, and "Bantam Franchise Boom—Why?" in *Chain Store Age,* July 1969, p. 19. Also see the Annual Reports from the Southland Corporation for 1970 and 1971 and their "The Southland Corporation: The Successful Introduction of Convenience Into Retail Food Selling" (mimeo). The "Store Agreement" between Southland and franchisees (revised, February 1972) reads: "(c) OWNERS shall not add any improvements or fixtures to the leased premises or make any changes in the leased premises or the leased equipment without prior written consent of 7-ELEVEN, which changes, if any, shall belong to 7-ELEVEN."
3. *New York Times,* November 28, 1971, p. 60. This article, "Garish Strips Stir Hostility, Coast to Coast," by Douglas E. Kneeland, is a good summary of the controversy surrounding franchise architecture.
4. McDonald's is famous for its millimeter-perfect consistency, which has been noted in the *San Francisco Examiner and Chronicle,* August 27, 1972, p. 7; *Newsweek,* September 25, 1972, p. 78; and Lukas, "As American as a McDonald's Hamburger on the Fourth of July," *op. cit.*, p. 5. Turner's quotation is from Lukas, p. 25, as is the data on condiments.
5. Vaughn's comment was in a letter to me dated December 27, 1971.
6. Cited by Hall, *op. cit.*, p. 105.
7. On Holiday Inn generally see *Time*'s cover story, "Rapid Rise of the Host with the Most," June 12, 1972, pp. 77-82; "Kemmons Wilson: The Inn-Side Story" by Frederic A. Birmingham in the *Saturday Evening Post,* Winter 1971, pp. 66-71; and "The Holiday Inn Story" by Kemmons Wilson, Holiday Inn. Inc. Memphis, Tennessee, July 1971.

8. Cited by Rosenbaum, *op. cit.*, p. 224.
9. Perrot's comments are in "The 'Miracle' of Memphis," March-April 1971 (mimeo.), translated from the French publication *Prestige de l'Hotellerie de la Restauration et du Tourisme*, Mars–Avril 1971 "Le 'Miracle' de Memphis."
10. Wilson, "The Holiday Inn Story," *op. cit.*, p. 12.
11. James Naughton wrote of Muskie in Room 520 in "The Taste of Defeat," *The New York Times Magazine*, p. 85. I saw Muskie conceding at an Inn podium on NBC-TV, April 5, 1972.
12. Bremer was mentioned in the *New York Daily News*, May 17, 1972, p. 3. McGovern's Holiday Inn vigil is described in *Life*, November 17, 1972, pp. 10-12.
13. Silva Mind Control's ad appeared in the *San Francisco Chronicle*, August 10, 1972, p. 13.
14. On Weight Watchers, see Louis Botto, *Look*, "High Priestess of the Weight Watchers," May 27, 1969, p. 82; Jean Pascoe, "What Makes Weight Watchers Lose Weight," *Woman's Day*, August 1968, p. 8; *Time*, February 21, 1972, p. 71; and Jean Nidetch, *Weight Watchers*, as told to Joan Rattner Hellman (New York: Signet Books, 1970).
15. George McDonald, "The Business of Caring" *Franchising Today*, February 1971, p. 12.
16. The data on Oakland's Institute of Human Abilities is from "Sgt. Bilko Meets the New Culture, The First Church of Christ, Realtor" by Robin Green, *Rolling Stone*, December 9, 1971, p. 40. This is one in the series of excellent social reports done by *Rolling Stone*.
17. Kissam, *op. cit.*, p. 30.
18. Charles Berner, founder of Los Angeles' Institute of Ability, as reported by Sara Davidson in "The Rush for Instant Salvation," *Harper's*, July 1971, pp. 40-54.
19. McLain's findings were written up as "The Pursuit of a Water Experience in Urban Environments. . . ." (unpublished, undated).
20. *Los Angeles Times*, December 11, 1970, Part IV, p. 4.
21. On laundromats generally, see the *Los Angeles Times*, December 11, 1970. Muhich's comments are from p. 4 of the *Los Angeles Times* article and an interview.
22. The Boonville trial is cited in *Time*, January 24, 1972, p. 42, as is Nader's Raider on p. 15 of the July 31, 1972, issue.

23. Margo's column was reprinted by *NALCC News* ("The Voice of the Coin-Op Laundry-Drycleaning Industry"), March 1971, p. 4.
24. *Esquire*, March 1971, p. 107.
25. The TraveLodge commercials were broadcast throughout the Democratic National Convention, July 10-13, 1972, on the CBS Radio Network.
26. "Trust Abby," is advised by *The Jersey Journal*, May 24, 1972, p. 32.
27. The poll on trust was done by Oliver Quayle for *Harper's* which reported it on pp. 39-40 of their July 1972 issue.
28. About the Nuers, see Rober Redfield, *The Little Community* (Chicago: University of Chicago Press, 1960), p. 118.
29. The policemen were community relations specialists being trained in a program at San Diego State College during May 1971.
30. Rosenbaum, *op. cit.*, p. 224.

CHAPTER 5: HANDI-DISPOZ COMMUNITY

1. Student-adult groups are described by William Schutz in *Joy* (New York: Grove Press, 1967), pp. 190-209.
2. Brown's experience was reported by him in "Saving Face," *Psychology Today*, May 1971, pp. 55-86. Aronson's views are in "Who Likes Whom and Why," *Psychology Today*, August 1970, pp. 48-74.
3. Bartell, *op. cit.*, p. 122.
4. The Southern California surveyor of swinging is Charles Varni, who did his master's thesis at San Diego State College on local swinging, and made this comment in "A Participant Observer Study of Spouse Swapping," a paper presented at the Pacific Sociological Association Meetings, Honolulu (1971), p. 11.
5. Both quotes are from Nena and George O'Neill, "Patterns in Group Sexual Activity," *Journal of Sex Research*, May 1970, pp. 101-112.
6. Symonds, "Pilot Study of the Peripheral Behavior of Sexual Mate Swappers," an unpublished Master's thesis for University of California/Riverside, June 1968, and "Sexual Mate Swapping and the Swingers," a paper presented to the Mid-winter Symposium/Workshop of the California State Marriage Counseling Association in San Diego on February 13, 1971, and published in *The*

Marriage Counseling Quarterly, Spring, 1971. Her comment was in a letter to me dated April 25, 1971.

7. Quoted by Edward M. Brecher in *The Sex Researchers* (Boston: Little Brown & Co., 1969), pp. 263-64. On the Smiths' work, see also "Co-Marital Sex: The Incorporation of Extra-Marital Sex into the Marriage Relationship" a paper presented at a symposium of the American Psychopathological Association on "Critical Issues in Contemporary Sexual Behavior" in New York, February 1971, and "Co-Marital Sex and the Sexual Freedom Movement," a paper presented at the 12th Annual Conference of the Society for the Scientific Study of Sex on November 1, 1969, in New York City, reprinted in the *Journal of Sex Research*, May 1970.
8. O'Neill, *op. cit.*, p. 111.
9. Grold, quoted in *Los Angeles Times*, May 18, 1971, Part II, p. 1.
10. *Good Times*, March 19, 1971, p. 7.
11. The co-ed's comment to Bernard is quoted on pp. 78-79 of her "Sex as a Regenerative Force" in *The New Sexuality*, edited by Herbert Otto (Palo Alto, Calif.: Science and Behavior Books, 1971), pp. 69-93.
12. Quoted by Fred Hechinger in the *New York Times*, June 2, 1969, p. 44.
13. Speech at the "Communes: Past, Present, Future" symposium, *op. cit.*
14. Bennis, "Beyond Bureaucracy," *The Temporary Society*, by Bennis and Philip Slater (New York: Harper & Row, 1968), p. 73.
15. Farson, "How Could Anything That Feels So Bad Be So Good?" in *Saturday Review*, September 6, 1969, p. 20. Since making this comment, Farson has revised his views somewhat, wondering whether he didn't jump the gun, and underestimate the durability of existing institutions.
16. Houriet, *Getting Back Together*, *op. cit.*, p. 162.
17. On serial marriage see Betty Rollin, "The American Way of Marriage: ReMarriage," *Look*, September 21, 1971, pp. 62-68. These statistics are given by a Census Bureau official, and cited on page 62.
18. Quoted in John Groutt, "The Communal Movement as a Deviant Subculture," an unpublished paper written at Temple University, June 4, 1970.
19. On waiting lines see the *New York Times*, April 25, 1970, p. 31,

and *Newsday*, May 23, 1972, p. 3A-7A, from which these quotes are excerpted. An interesting study of overnight queues as social systems is Leon Mann, "Queue Culture: The Waiting Line as a Social System," *American Journal of Sociology*, November 1969, pp. 340-354.

20. Trillin, "A Nation of Shopkeepers Loses Three of Them through Contact with a Nation of Violence," *Atlantic*, January 1971, p. 74.
21. Blair Sobol, writing in the *Village Voice*, July 15, 1971, p. 18.
22. Janice Mitchell and Rodger Schmitt were mentioned in the *Los Angeles Times*, June 7, 1971, Part III, p. 2, and the divorce case appeared in the same paper, October 19, 1971, p. 2.
23. Berger, "Audiences, Art and Power," *Trans-Action*, May 1971, p. 28.
24. *Newsweek*, August 7, 1972, p. 54.
25. William Penn Mott, Jr., "Outlook for Our Recreational Environment," *Proceedings of the 2nd Annual Southwestern Environmental Mental Health Conference, op. cit.*, p. 19.
26. On trends in camping see the *Wall Street Journal*, June 7, 1972, p. 1; the *San Francisco Chronicle*, August 2, 1971, p. 1; *Time*, August 2, 1971, p. 46, and August 28, 1972, p. 55; and *Life*, "Hotels with No Rooms Are Booming," by John Neary, September 29, 1972, p. 53.
27. The Starcraft ad appeared in *Popular Science*, May, 1971, p. 45.
28. Powers' experiences were described in "Just Add Smoke and Stir," *WEST*, August 1, 1971, pp. 26-31.
29. Roger Starr, *Urban Choices: The City and Its Critics* (Baltimore: Penguin Books, 1966), p. 43.
30. Slater has written about temporary systems in *The Pursuit of Loneliness, op. cit.*, and in his sections of *The Temporary Society, op. cit.* The quotation is from his paper in that book, "Some Consequences of Temporary Systems," pp. 77-96, and appears on p. 136 fn.
31. The hitcher, Randy Brook, is quoted in *Life*, August 27, 1971, p. 36.
32. On United Airlines, see and hear all their ads. The information on Southwest Airlines is from the *Saturday Review*, December 4, 1971, p. 72.
33. The social evolution of 747s has been described to me by various

people related to the airline industry, and was written about in the *Los Angeles Times*, December 30, 1971, p. 1.

34. *Los Angeles Times*, December 30, 1971, p. 12.
35. Ken Sobol, "Suburb in the Sky," *Village Voice*, July 22, 1971, p. 5.
36. United announced their new approach in mid-June releases, written up in the *San Francisco Examiner*, July 14, 1972, p. 43, and the *San Francisco Chronicle*, July 18, 1972, p. 14, and in a series of subsequent ads booming their "Air Show," "Whole Sky Catalog," and "Great Wide Way to New York."
37. On the CAB, see the *Los Angeles Times*, June 2, 1972, Section III, p. 15.

CHAPTER 6: SERVE THE COMMUNITY, BE THE COMMUNITY

1. On shopping centers see C. T. Jonassen, *The Shopping Center vs. Downtown*, Bureau of Business Research, Ohio State University, 1955; Gordon H. Stedman, "The Rise of Shopping Centers," *Journal of Retailing*, Spring, 1955, pp. 11-26; Jack Morris, "Shopping Centers: Main Street Moves to the Mall," *Management Review*, May 1969, pp. 48-51, condensed from the *Wall Street Journal*, February 20, 1969; "Downtown in the Cornfields," *Sales Management*, November 1, 1970, pp. 34-36; the *New York Times*, March 7, 1971, Section 3, p. 1; reports on shopping centers in the *Architectural Record* for April 1968, October 1969, and March 1970; and the Annual Shopping Center Report of *Chain Store Age*.
2. Leyton's observations (*passim*) were made in an interview with the author.
3. The figures on mall covering are from "Enclosing the Open Mall," *Chain Store Age*, September 1968, pp. E27-E38; "Debartolo Leads in New Space," *Chain Store Age*, May 1972, p. E44-45. The Knoxville item is from *Chain Store Age*, May 1972, p. E16.
4. The Pittsburgh mall director is quoted in the *Wall Street Journal*, December 2, 1970, p. 1, where the description of the Plymouth Meeting Center also appears. Verley's observations are in *Chain Store Age*, October 1968, p. E 19.

5. *Management Review*, May 1969, p. 50.
6. The report on the Powell decision is from the *San Francisco Examiner and Chronicle*, July 16, 1972, Section A, p. 18. It is also covered in *Time*, July 10, 1972, p. 37, and *Civil Liberties*, October 1972, p. 4. Earlier decisions are reviewed by Morris O. Forkosch in "Picketing in Shopping Centers," *Labor Law Journal*, February 1970, which originally appeared in the Fall 1969 *Washington and Lee Law Review*. The Mosk decision was reported on pp. 1, 3, 5 of the *Metropolitan News* (Los Angeles) for December 22, 1970.
7. *Los Angeles Times*, June 11, 1972, p. L-1 and September 17, 1972, p. K-1.
8. The Detroit center is Northland, whose flag is mentioned in Spencer MacCallum's *The Art of Community*, Menlo Park, California: Institute for Humane Studies, Inc., 1970, p. 37. The Florida center is Jacksonville's Regency Square Shopping Center described in *Stores*, June 1968, p. 16.
9. Fessier, "LA: In Search of the City; Part Six, Topanga Plaza: Our Town, 1971," *WEST*, February 14, 1971, pp. 15, 17, 20.
10. On the Davis trial, see the *Los Angeles Times* coverage for June 5, 6, and 11, 1972, and *Newsweek*'s summary, June 19, 1972, p. 30.
11. On Manson, see *Time*, April 12, 1971, p. 42 (where the forty-eight-year-old juror is quoted on p. 42), and *Life*, "The Manson Jury: End of the Long Ordeal," by Barry Farrell, April 16, 1971, pp. 44-48.
12. Alioto's jurors were mentioned in the *Los Angeles Times*, June 11, 1972, p. A-6.
13. The Panther 21 developments were covered in "One Year Later: The Radicalization of the Panther 13 Jury" by Catherine Breslin, *New York*, May 29, 1972, pp. 53-63. (The 21 had become 13 by the time of their trial.) The quotation appeared originally in the *New York Times* and was reported in Breslin's piece.
14. *Los Angeles Times*, April 22, 1971, Part IV, p. 12.
15. Linda Pembrook, "You the Jury," *New York*, July 12, 1971, pp. 64-65.
16. Bennett Berger cites the study of dance-band performers, done by Howard Becker, on p. 29 of "Audiences, Art and Power," *op. cit.*

17. Klein, *Community Dynamics and Mental Health* (New York: John Wiley, 1968), p. 19.
18. Nidetch, *Weight Watchers, op. cit.*, pp. 64, 67, 73, 83-85; Pascoe, *op. cit.*, p. 92.
19. Stunkard, in a letter to me dated October 25, 1971. He reported his work in "A Study of a Self-Help Group for Obesity," *Proceedings of the 8th International Congress on Nutrition*, Prague, August 28-September 5, 1969, pp. 223-225.
20. Quoted in a *Los Angeles Times* article June 20, 1972, Part IV, p. 1, which covered the growth of Families Anonymous.
21. The 1962 survey is cited by Edward Sagarin in *Odd Man In* (Chicago: Quadrangle Books, 1969), p. 57.
22. *Time*, May 22, 1972, p. 103.
23. Hurvitz's comments are from his paper "Peer Self-Help Psychotherapy Groups and Their Implications for Psychotherapy," *Psychotherapy: Theory, Research and Practice*, Spring 1970, pp. 41-49; quotations from pp. 44, 47.
24. Mead, "We Are All Third Generation," in McGiffert, *op. cit.*, p. 135.
25. *Encyclopedia of Associations*, National Organizations of the United States, (7th edn.; Detroit: Gale Research 1972).
26. Mhyra S. Minnis, "The Patterns of Women's Organizations," in Marvin Sussman, editor, *Community Structure and Analysis* (New York: Thomas Crowell Co., 1959), p. 277.
27. DeTocqueville, *Democracy in America*, as quoted in McGiffert, *op. cit.*, pp. 45-46.
28. Will Rogers, as quoted by Arthur M. Schlesinger, "What Then Is the American, This New Man?" in McGiffert, *op. cit.*, p. 116.
29. *New York Post*, March 21, 1969, p. 32.
30. Quoted in an ad for a Dale Carnegie course, which appeared in *Time*, March 6, 1972, p. 6.
31. *San Diego Evening Tribune*, March 8, 1972, p. A-25.
32. The NYU psychologist is Daniel Malamud. His program is described in "The Second-Chance Family: A New Medium for Self-Directed Personal Growth" by Malamud in *COMmunication* (newsletter of "Well-Being," San Anselmo, California) February 1972, pp. 21-24.
33. *San Francisco Chronicle*, August 8, 1972, p. 12; *Los Angeles*

Times, August 23, 1970, p. 22; and *Newsweek,* October 16, 1972, p. 35.

34. Paley's comments are from an interview. See also Jerry Bowles, "If Cartier, Tiffany, Porthault, Harry Winston, Bonwit Teller, Charles Jourdan and Bergdorf Goodman Can't Make the Rich Happy, Who Can?" *Esquire,* September 1972, pp. 119-20.
35. Sagarin, *Odd Man In* (*op. cit.,*) p. 29. He mentions the Alcoholics Anonymous/Schizophrenics Anonymous member on p. 48.
36. On Bobby Fischer, see *Time,* July 31, 1972, pp. 32-7; *Newsweek,* July 31, 1972, pp. 42-6; the *San Francisco Chronicle,* August 11, 1972, p. 7 and August 17, 1972, p. 2; and *Life,* August 11, 1972, pp. 41-44, from which the friend's quote is excerpted.
37. For Burger's summary of his case see "Agapurgy: Affection As A Service Ready for Anglo-American Industrialization," Institute of Electrical and Electronics Engineers, *Transactions on Systems Science and Cybernetics,* Vol. SSC-5, No. 1, January 1969, pp. 97-98. *Science Digest* covered Burger and love machinery generally in "My Machine Loves Me," by Barbara Ford, September 1970, pp. 43-55.
38. The finding of the Michigan economist, Eva Mueller, was cited in *Science Digest,* September 1970, pp. 46-7.
39. Quoted by Hunter Thompson, *Hell's Angels* (New York: Ballantine Books, 1967), p. 119.
40. Burger, IEEE *Transactions,* January 1969, p. 98.
41. Reported by the Associated Press in the *Los Angeles Times,* February 2, 1972, p. B-5 and the *San Diego Union,* March 12, 1972, p. A-22.
42. Burger, *op. cit.,* p. 98.
43. *Newsweek,* June 5, 1972, p. 59.
44. The study of Stanford psychologist, Robert Hess, was covered by the *San Diego Evening Tribune,* November 15, 1971, p. D-5, and *Behavior Today,* June 7, 1971, p. 3, from which this quotation is taken.
45. The Atlanta and Cincinatti medical clinics were reported by the *National Enquirer,* October 24, 1971, p. 24, from which the quotations are taken.
46. *National Enquirer,* December 13, 1970, p. 1, and subsequent issues. A word on the *Enquirer.* This used to be a sex-and-gore

tabloid, but in recent years has turned respectable in order to get on grocery-store shelves. With at least 2.6 million readers (outsold on newstands only by *TV Guide*), it's a fascinating index of current concerns, of which loneliness is the most apparent. Although they have a bad habit of lifting material published elsewhere without attribution, the *Enquirer's* accuracy seems dependable. (The chief staff writer says they bend over backwards to check facts because of their sordid past.) For more on the *Enquirer*, see *Editor and Publisher*, August 23, 1969; *Newsweek*, September 8, 1969, p. 79; *Wall Street Journal*, April 12, 1971, p. 1.; *Los Angeles Times*, May 6, 1972, p. 1; and *Time*, February 21, 1972, p. 64.

47. *Los Angeles Times*, June 8, 1971, p. 3. For a description of the work of this remarkable woman, see Malcolm Muggeridge, *Something Beautiful for God* (New York: Harper & Row, 1971).
48. Quoted in Frances C. Jeffers, "You and the Aging in Your Community," *Gerontologist*, Spring, 1970, p. 59.
49. The St. Petersburg Sociologist, John Bauldree, is covered in the *National Enquirer*, May 2, 1971, p. 25.
50. *New York* reported their readers' affluence on July 12, 1971, p. 4, and ran the articles on butchers, "Butchers Prime and Choice" by Elin Schoen, April 26, 1971, p. 73-77; on telephone counseling, "Spring Is the Time for the Big City Blues" by Jane O'Reilly, April 24, 1972, pp. 66-81; on window-peeking, "Here's Looking at You: Voyeurism in New York" by Dorothy Kalins, March 3, 1969, pp. 34-40.
51. The Marin County volunteer worker, Margery Sell, is quoted in *COMmunication*, April 1, 1972, p. 16.

CHAPTER 7: KNOWN AT LAST!

1. *Los Angeles Times*, February 8, 1972, p. 5; *Time*, February 21, 1972, p. 44.
2. *Los Angeles Times*, March 28, 1971, Section B, p. 1.
3. *Time*, March 15, 1971, p. 42.
4. *Los Angeles Times*, February 26, 1971, Part IV, p. 1.
5. Simmel's views on community are summarized and analyzed by Robert Nisbet, *The Sociological Tradition*, (New York: Basic Books, 1966). The quotations appeared on pp. 103 and 105.

Pp. 47-106 of this book are a good summary and analysis of "community" in sociological thought.

6. Quoted by Brock Brower, "Don't Get Agnew Wrong," *Life,* May 8, 1970, p. 66B.
7. Jourard, *The Transparent Self* (Princeton: Van Nostrand Company, 1964), p. 41.
8. Lennon does this especially on his album, "Plastic Ono Band" (Apple Records), which was recorded soon after he completed Primal Therapy.
9. Baez was quoted to this effect in "Where the Kissing Never Stops" in Joan Didion, *Slouching Toward Bethlehem, op. cit.*, p. 47.
10. *New York Daily Column,* July 30, 1969, p. 11.
11. McIlwain, "A Farewell to Alcohol," *Atlantic,* January 1972, pp. 29-35.
12. Mikva made his comment while still a Congressman, in a book review of *O Congress* by Donald Riegle, which appeared in the *San Francisco Examiner and Chronicle,* August 13, 1972, p. B-3. He was subsequently defeated in the 1972 election.
13. "Only Me and My Hairdresser Know" by Arthur Thomas, BMI.
14. *Rolling Stone,* November 12, 1970, p. 18.
15. Jourard, *Self-Disclosure: An Experimental Analysis of the Transparent Self* (New York: John Wiley & Sons, 1971), p. v; Jourard, *The Transparent Self, op. cit.*, p. 24.
16. *Newsweek,* July 31, 1972, p. 74. See also, *Newsweek,* August 30, 1971, p. 84 and September 6, 1971, p. 76, where he first wrote of his illness.
17. "Scribe," in a letter to Abby, *Los Angeles Times,* January 31, 1971, Section D, p. 6.
18. *Los Angeles Times,* November 8, 1971, p. 7. Excerpts from tapes Helton made before dying ran in *WEST,* January 16, 1972, pp. 8-13.
19. Village Park makes this claim on television commercials. "The Villages" made their pitch in the *San Francisco Chronicle,* September 9, 1972, p. 15. Hometown Markets' ad appeared in the *San Diego Union,* July 23, 1970, p. D-10. Carnation's 1880s ice cream is described on their milk cartons. Village Park's kitchen ad was in the *San Diego Union,* November 28, 1971, p. F-4.
20. Muskie made this comment on television several times during the 1972 primaries.

21. The evolution of the Santa Cruz bus line is described in the *San Francisco Chronicle*, July 17, 1972, p. 15.
22. Hawthorne, *The Blithedale Romance* (New York: W.W. Norton, 1958), p. 85.
23. Houriet, *Getting Back Together*, *op. cit.*, p. 22.
24. Lawrence Bloomberg, Paula Bloomberg, and Richard Louis Miller, "The Intensive Group as a Founding Experience," *Journal of Humanistic Psychology*, Spring 1969, p. 99.
25. Matthew Davis, "Confessions of a Community Dropout," *The Modern Utopian*, November-December/January-February 1969, back cover.
26. Krippner, in a telephone interview. See also his paper, with Don Fersh, "Spontaneous Paranormal Experience among Members of Intentional Communities," (mimeo.), of which a shorter version appeared in the *Journal of Psychedelic Drugs*, September 1970.
27. Hillery, "Selected Issues in Community Theory," a paper presented before the annual meeting of the Society for the Study of Social Problems, Washington, D.C., August 30, 1972, and published in *Rural Sociology*, December, 1972, pp. 534-552. Hillery's "Definition of Community: Areas of Agreement," which appeared in *Rural Sociology*, June 1955, pp. 111-23, remains the definitive work on this topic.
28. Sundance, speech at the "Communes, Past, Present, Future" symposium, *op. cit.*
29. See "Death of the Hired Man" in *The Road Not Taken: An Introduction to Robert Frost*, Louis Untermeyer, ed. (New York: Holt, Rinehart & Winston, 1951).
30. Coulson, *A Sense of Community*: *That Education Might Be Personal* (Columbus, Ohio: Charles E. Merrill, in press). Bill McGaw is a friend, who gave me his definition of community in a conversation. The girl's quotation is from "Report of the March Conference," *COMmunication*, April 1972, p. 17.
31. Krippner, in a telephone interview.
32. The Open Ender's comment was Quoted by John Hilary Barth, "Two and A Half Years in Open End—A Personal Experience," *COMmunication*, February 1972, p. 12.
33. For descriptions of the nonresidential communities mentioned, and others, see *COMmunication*, especially the May 1972 issue.

CHAPTER 8: BLOCKS IN BUILDING COMMUNITY

1. Lee Coleman, "What Is American?" in McGiffert, *op. cit.*, p. 26.
2. White, *One Man's Meat* (New York: Harper & Brothers, Publishers, 1944), p. 277.
3. Barclay, "The Ecology of Man," a paper presented to the Chicago Medical Society Postgraduate Education Course on Internal Medicine, Chicago, Ill., November, 1970.
4. See Calhoun, "A Glance into the Garden," *Three Papers on Ecology*, Mills College Assembly Series, 1965-1966, Mills College, Oakland, Calif., pp. 19-36; "Space and the Strategy of Life," *Ekistics*, June 1970, pp. 425-437.

4a. Kleeman, "How to Establish Office Distance," *Contract*, August 1971 pp. 80-83.

5. Anthony Jay, *The Corporation Man* (New York: Random House, 1971), excerpted in *New York*, September 20, 1971, pp. 29-35. The comments quoted appeared on pp. 33-4.
6. Calhoun, "Space and the Strategy of Life," *op. cit.*, pp. 425-26.
7. Park, *Race and Culture* (Glencoe, Ill.: The Free Press, 1950), p. 22.
8. Dubos, *So Human an Animal* (New York: Charles Scribner's Sons, 1969), p. 154.
9. "How to Live in the City and Stay Sane," *Mademoiselle*, April 1970, pp. 250-251.
10. Sundance speech, *op. cit.*
11. Matthews, *Neighbor and Kin, Life in a Tennessee Ridge Community* (Nashville: Vanderbilt University Press, 1965), p. 17.
12. On the Leadership Dynamics Institute, see the *San Francisco Chronicle*, August 25, 1972, p. 1, and August 26, 1972, p. 1. The news report was in *Newsweek*, August 21, 1972, p. 68.
13. Nearly two decades after it was written, Whyte's *The Organization Man* (Garden City, N.Y.: Doubleday, 1957) remains among our most insightful social commentaries. The quotation is from pp. 399-400.
14. Fall 1869 *Whole Earth Catalog* (Portola Institute/Random House), p. 81.
15. Rogers' comment was made in a conversation with me.
16. Houriet, *op. cit.*, pp. 381-388.

17. Sennet, *The Uses of Disorder* (New York: Alfred A. Knopf, 1970), p. 135. Sennet's book is an interesting defense of cities as the best setting for rediscovering authentic community.
18. Eugene Litwak and Phillip Fellin, "The Neighborhood in Urban American Society," *Social Work*, July 1968, p. 75. See also Litwak and Ivan Szelenyi, "Primary Group Structures and Their Functions: Kin, Neighbor and Friends," *American Sociological Review*, August 1969, pp. 465-81.
19. Cox, *The Secular City*, *op. cit.*, p. 52.

CHAPTER 9: TOOLS

1. Sundance speech, *op. cit.*, which I'm quoting a lot, but so be it. She had a lot of good things to say.
2. Greeley, *Why Can't They Be More Like Us?* (New York: Institute of Human Relations Press, Pamphlet 12, 1969), p. 18.
3. Bryant's case is made in his paper "Sawdust in Their Shoes: The Carnival as a Neglected Complex Organization and Work Culture," portions of which were read to the 33rd Annual Meeting of the Southern Sociological Society, Atlanta, Georgia, April 11, 1970. The quotation is from an interview with Bryant which appeared in the *Louisville-Courier-Journal*, March 8, 1971, p. A-16.
4. Slater, "Must Marriage Cheat Today's Young Women?" *Redbook*, February 1971, p. 164.
5. Hamill, "A Hangout Is a Place . . .," *Mademoiselle*, November 1969, p. 51.
6. On the Puerto Rican clubs of New York, see the *New York Times*, March 23, 1970, p. 43.
7. Matthews, *Neighbor and Kin*, *op. cit.*, p. 48.
8. *San Diego Union*, April 18, 1971, p. B-3.
9. On Outward Bound see the *Los Angeles Times*, September 24, 1971, Part I, p. 1, from which this quotation is taken.
10. *Washington Post*, June 28, 1971, p. B-12.
11. On Boontling, see Charles C. Adams, *Boontling: An American Lingo* (Austin: University of Texas Press, 1971).
12. Greeley, *Why Can't They Be More Like Us? op. cit.*, p.21.
13. Groutt, *op. cit.*, pp. 30-31, and Houriet, *op. cit.*, p. 292.
14. Studies of heightism include "Buying Brains by the Inch," by Leland P. Deck, *The Journal of College and University Personnel*

Association, May, 1968, pp. 33-37; and "Physical Recruiting," by David L. Kurtz, *Personal Journal*, December, 1969, pp. 981-983.

15. The fact that taller Presidential candidates tend to get elected has been pointed out often in the press, most recently in *Parade*, October 8, 1972, p. 6, citing the research of Dr. Saul Feldman (see below).
16. Feldman reported his findings in "The Presentation of Shortness in Everyday Life—Height and Heightism in American Society: Toward a Sociology of Stature," the revision of a paper presented before the 1971 meetings, American Sociological Association, Denver, Colorado. Feldman's ASA speech received extensive press coverage.
17. Cohen made this proposal in "Remarks Before the Federal Tax Institute of New England," Boston, Massachusetts, April 29, 1972.
18. Par Lagerkvist, *The Dwarf* (New York: Kill & Wang, 1945).
19. Wagner's pioneering efforts were picked up by the Associated Press and reported widely. I learned of him from the Los Angeles *Times*, November 28, 1971, p. F-12.
20. Hoover's predilection was mentioned in *Newsweek*, May 10, 1971, p. 32.
21. Kanter, "Commitment and Social Organization: A Study of Commitment Mechanisms in Utopian Communities," *American Sociological Review*, August 1968, pp. 499-517; and "Communes," *Psychology Today*, July 1970, pp. 53-78, in which the quotation appears on p. 55. She has since expanded her work in *Commitment and Community* (Cambridge, Mass.: Harvard University Press, 1972).
22. Nordhoff, *The Communistic Societies of the United States* (New York: Schocken Books, 1875, 1970), pp. 290-93.
23. Mowrer elaborates this thesis in *The New Group Therapy* (Princeton: D. Van Nostrand Co., 1964), pp. 17-20; and in "Belated 'Clinical' Recognition of the Pathogenic Secret" (mimeo.), Spring 1970, pp. 4-16. See also his interview in the *Champaign-Urbana News-Gazette*, June 19, 1966, p. 2.
24. Kanter, "Are Utopian Communities An Answer to Urban Problems?" unpublished paper, November 1968, p. 7.
25. Felipe Luciano, "The Songs of Joe B," *New York*, October 25, 1971, pp. 49-55.
26. Wallace, as quoted in the *Los Angeles Times* April 1, 1972, p. 3.

27. Scared to Be Alone," in *On My Way to Where, op. cit.*, pp. 106-107. Also see the record by the same name.
28. Robbins, 79 *Park Avenue* (New York: Pocket Books, 1956), p. 4.
29. Nisbet, *The Quest for Community, op. cit.*, p. vii.
30. My friend Howard Saunders once designed a calendar-poster entitled: "The shortest distance between two points is a straight line. A straight line like, 'I need you.' " Below that he wrote: "A straight line like, 'You really hurt me.' A straight line like, 'I haven't been honest with you.' A straight line like, 'I love you.' Sometimes these words seem so basic that we take them for granted. But think about the things that you wanted to say that were left unsaid. To a parent who is gone. To a lover who walked away. To a child who ran away. Our hope for this new year is to leave as little unsaid as we possibly can. And maybe if the words we say can influence the words we write, then the printed word can begin to shorten the distance between the points." The ending of my book is obviously stolen from Howard. He's a good person to steal an ending from.

73 74 75 76 77 10 9 8 7 6 5 4 3 2 1